THE DAWN OF LITERATURE

ROCK OF BEHISTUN

THE DAWN
OF LITERATURE

BY

CARL HOLLIDAY

PROFESSOR OF ENGLISH IN THE
SAN JOSE (CALIFORNIA) STATE COLLEGE

THOMAS Y. CROWELL COMPANY
PUBLISHERS   ::   ::   NEW YORK

PREFACE

The study of classic letters is customarily focussed almost exclusively upon Greek, Roman, and perhaps Hebrew. How rich the fields which lie beyond, few realize.

In "The Dawn of Literature" we tread many unfamiliar paths—but all the more alluring because of both strangeness and beauty. There were rich treasures of song and story when Greece was but a barbaric waste, and Rome lay centuries ahead. A thousand years before the Greeks and the Romans had composed their *Iliad* and their *Æneid,* the Egyptians, the Hindus, the Babylonians, the Persians, the Chinese, and the Hebrews had written lofty poetry, enchanting fiction, and profound philosophy.

The humanness of these writings of four or five thousand years ago may come as a surprise to the Western reader. Here are the same emotions, the same thoughts, the same struggles with the problems of life and death as we of to-day experience. Here are the same efforts to capture and explain the meaning of human existence. The reading of these authors of a civilization ancient before Athens or Rome was founded compels us to realize how little, if at all, human nature changes throughout the ages.

Not all of the writings here noted, however, belong to "The Dawn." In some lands of the Orient, such as India, Persia, and China, there has been a continuing

fruitage, and it has seemed best to include literature
of a more recent date as well. While emphasis has
been placed upon earliest sources, this book is really a
survey of Oriental Literature from ancient to modern
times.

Not the least difficulty in this survey has been that
of documentation. Where writings have persisted for
centuries, reappearing in different dress, it has been a
constant problem to decide (1) what was the first
source in English, and (2) what version was best for
the present-day reader. In many instances, for present purposes, the author has made his own versions, or
slightly adapted existing ones—as the footnotes show.
A very full Bibliography at the end will further orien-
tate (surely a correct word in this connection!) the
reader.

C. H.

San Jose, California
July 1, 1931.

CONTENTS

LIST OF ILLUSTRATIONS

I

THE DAWN IN EGYPT

WHERE now the Sphinx gazes out across the desolate sand and the Great Pyramid looks down upon a far-reaching desert, there once arose the hum of the myriad voices of citizens of a vast and mighty empire. Proud cities vied with one another in riches and pomp; great temples dedicated to now-forgotten gods sent up the smoke of the burnt offering; palaces of magnitude dominated the land. In far-flung wheat fields, in exquisite gardens, in huge quarries, labored millions of slaves gained through the conquest of other nations. On the broad surface of the Nile floated the merchant ships of all civilized peoples.

This was Egypt, long monarch of the Ancient World—Egypt the seemingly unconquerable, gorgeous, rich beyond compare, mysterious, learned in arts and trades and sciences, religion and magic.

We moderns can only conjecture as to the age of that civilization which for so many centuries was the envy and the fear of the races of other days. It was venerable seven thousand years ago. It was of such antiquity that its architecture and art had reached a stage astounding to the explorer, the archæologist of our times. Who to-day can explain the Sphinx of Gizeh, or the Pyramid of Cheops? Yet these two examples—among the many results of untold centuries of civilization—were looking down upon the Valley of the Nile four thousand years before the Christian era.

The Egyptians were a race of permanent builders. Their very dead were preserved to outlast the ages, and their tombs and monuments were erected to rival the mountains in endurance. To such a people both life and death were serious matters, and, like all energetic and ambitious nations, they viewed oblivion as the worst of all fates.

It was but natural, then, that the Egyptians should be zealous recorders of their own deeds and accomplishments. Their tombs, their pyramids, their palaces, their temples became vast storehouses of history and legend. They wrote in stone that all the ages might know of the pride and glory that was theirs. And to-day even the fragments excite the wonder of scholars that any one nation could have told so much about itself, or could have had so much to tell.

But the centuries came and went, and that magnificent civilization, as all other civilizations seem destined to do, passed away. The gray sand heaped itself over fields and cities and palaces, alien tongues spoke a jargon where a precise and cultured language had once been heard, and the mouths of prophets and poets, priests and historians, conquerors and rulers, were stopped with dust. Even the very symbols in which they had engraved their deeds and thoughts lost all meaning, and men in later generations gazed upon gigantic records that were simply baffling, mysterious puzzles.

Then suddenly, after the silence of centuries, the key was found that unlocked this greatest of national libraries. In 1799 some common soldiers of Napoleon's

THE ROSETTA STONE

army, working along the banks of the Nile, dragged forth from the mud a fragment of stone, a tablet containing three parallel columns of writing. One was in the familiar Greek; the other two were in the symbols seen on obelisk, pyramid, and the ruins of temples. The Rosetta Stone had opened up to modern man a whole unexplored continent of civilization and literature.

Through the indefatigable labors of a French scholar, Champollion, the writings on that stone were at length deciphered. The words were nothing extraordinary in themselves—simply certain rules or orders written in Greek, in ancient hieroglyphics, and in a more modern form of Egyptian characters known as demotic; but the deeper meaning of the accomplishment was, and is, that the symbols were revealed by means of the ingenuity of scholarship, and that their interpretation meant the unlocking of the records of four thousand years of a nation's existence. Egypt was no longer the dark mystery that it had been throughout the centuries.

Even, however, when the words of the ancient records on many a tomb and pyramid had been spelled out, the meaning was often far from clear. Here was a people whose genius was so alien to us moderns, a people whose views of life and its purposes and ideals were so different from ours, that great sections of the story they have left were incomprehensible. Added to all this was a profuse use of symbolism that further obscured the meaning.

We can now, however, grasp the chief principles of the Egyptian philosophy of life. It is repeated too often on those monuments to be overlooked. Threefold are the principles: this life is brief; the real life is after death; man's duty is to make ready here for that real life beyond. Whatever the Egyptian did, whether it was the conquering of another nation or the preparation of his father's body for the tomb, these basic thoughts seem never to have been absent. There is, therefore, in Egyptian Literature a certain deep seriousness amounting almost to somberness and gloom, a certain heaviness of tone and style, a certain practical turn, scarcely paralleled in the writings of any other people.

While the earliest Egyptian inscriptions are from six thousand to seven thousand years old, the nation's record does not begin to be fairly continuous until about 3700 B.C. Naturally among a people with so lengthy an existence the form of writing gradually changed. The first portions were in what we call hieroglyphics, which is a form of picture-writing. Then, perhaps a thousand or fifteen hundred years later originated the hieratic, an easier version of the glyphics, a sort of glorified shorthand, as it were, for commercial and other common transactions of daily life, and more easily adapted for writing upon papyrus. Then came that modification of both characters and language, known as demotic, a type of speech for market and street. Finally, about 200 A.D., the Egyptian tongue had become so permeated with Greek, Arabic, and other foreign terms that the language of the Nile Valley was no longer pure Egyptian, but Coptic.

What are the records, legends, stories, poems, or histories told in lasting stone or on equally lasting mummy case through all those thousands of years?

There were bombastic annals and legends of the tremendous exploits of conquerors; the glorified accounts of the reigns of innumerable Pharaohs—the foes overcome, the territory annexed, the cities founded, the temples, pyramids, statues and obelisks erected. There remain to-day the hymns to the gods—pathetic petitions and prayers; for what nation has ever known just how to plead with or praise the Supreme Being? There were religious formulas and teachings, often so buried in symbolism as to be practically unintelligible to our era. There were rituals for government and temple ceremonies, and especially rituals for the dead. There were short tales, often spoiled in their ending by the introduction of magic, but nevertheless revealing much concerning the life in palace and in street. And here and there in the later days were snatches of poetry of love and grief, convincing evidence that throughout the ages the human heart has changed but little. Throughout this writing, no matter what the type, the religious note was ever present. It is said of Coleridge that he was "enamored of God"; the same may be said of the ancient Egyptians. Their deities were ever present; their gods were a part of the State; the lowliest act of daily life was carried out with a consideration of the Rulers of Heaven and Hell.

The original deity—the Primeval God—seems to have been a personification of all the elements and laws of Nature—not at all a crude or puny idea of the Maker of the Universe. But at an early date these Egyptians began to reveal a most human weakness for glorifying and deifying special attributes of the One God. Thus a personified function of the Creator, an attribute known as Ammon-Ra, typified by the sun, became ruler of the kingdom above the horizon, or the Heaven. Osiris, typified by the sun under the horizon, became ruler of the kingdom below, or the Realm of Death. And such qualities of the Divine Being as strength, wisdom, and justice were represented by various animals glorified and sanctified, such as the bull, the crocodile, and the cat. Intensely and for thousands of years these people of the Nile meditated upon this baffling, tantalizing question of the Great Principle. The result is a vast store of mysterious theology, rituals, and prayers.

In the Egyptian, then, we have the longest stretch of literary endeavor ever presented by any nation, ancient or modern. Reaching—with some gaps, it is true— back to at least 6000 B.C. and almost continuously from 3700 B.C. to 200 B.C., it is a remarkable revelation of the intellectual vitality of a people. It reveals a splendor, an almost ruthless national vigor, a certain solidness and earnest thoughtfulness scarcely paralleled, if indeed approached, in the annals of any other nation, and it excites to-day our wonder if not our admiration.

The World's Oldest Book

It is from the banks of the Nile that we have the oldest book in the world. In the papyrus roll known as the Prisse Manuscript and preserved now in the Bibliothèque Nationale at Paris is this most ancient of man's extant efforts to express himself in literature. Its name is *The Precepts of Ptah-Hotep,* and though it speaks from the first dawn of literature it speaks well, even nobly, with seriousness and dignity. Discovered by Prisse at Thebes, this priceless bit of frayed papyrus is of about 2500 B.C.; but this, in turn, is a copy of a far older book written by a governor, Ptah-Hotep, son of Assa, who became King of Egypt in 3850 B.C. Thus a voice speaks to us from nearly six thousand years of time.

Is it crude, naïve, uncultivated—this voice of sixty centuries agone? By no means. Here we find a tone, a style, a viewpoint toward life indicating that it was intended for a cultured reading class long accustomed to just such books of instruction or advice. And the book and its author are so human! Ancient Ptah-Hotep might have been the corner-grocery philosopher of one's childhood town. His reflections on life and living have indeed something of the homely shrewdness of *Poor Richard's Almanac,* but the style has a far higher dignity—a dignity approaching now and then the tone of the Proverbs of the Bible. Surely Ptah-Hotep has a right to speak with deep seriousness and authority; for does he not declare in the book itself that he is one hundred and ten years of age at the time he is writing it? He who has lived a century—whether now or six thousand years ago—warrants a careful hearing.

The author of *Ecclesiastes* might well have written some of these opening sentences.

A man waxeth old, his strength decayeth, he getteth in years, his youth fadeth away. Day by day the heart of an old man fainteth and is troubled. His eyes see not, his ears hear not, his power is lessened and abated. Behold, his mouth speaketh not as of yore, his mind is feeble and remembereth not the deeds of yesterday. Yea, his whole body is afflicted, good is to him evil, his tongue savoreth no longer. Alas, the old age of a man is full of misery, his nostrils drink not the breath of heaven, his lungs wax feeble, he delighteth neither to stand nor to be seated.

And what are his counsels to the young man of that long-forgotten day? Apparently the aged deemed the same advice necessary for youth as our young people are proffered to-day:

Be not puffed up with thine own knowledge, but honor the truly wise. Nor shalt thou fail to honor even the simple.

The portals to knowledge are closed to no man. But whoever enters therein, even though he should strive for perfection, shall indeed never gain it.

The words of wisdom are hidden, yea, even as the emerald and the adamant, for which the slave digs, are hidden in stony earth.

Give way to that man who falls upon you, if his strength be greater than thine. Be not aroused to anger nor lay thy hands upon him. For thus shalt thou escape calamity. Such a one is froward, and it shall not be to thy advantage to contend against him. Therefore when he rageth against thee, struggle not with him. Thus in the end thou shalt prevail against him.

If any man rail at thee and insult thee, answer him not. Instead, be like one who cannot be moved. Even thus shalt thou conquer him. For all who behold shall declare that he who, in spite of provocation, holdeth his tongue, is mightier than he who provoketh. So shalt thou be respected by those who have wisdom.

If, by command of one having authority over thee, thou must do evil, the gods will not condemn thee for it.

No man may know the day of adversity, when it is to come, nor the day of prosperity, when it shall lighten him; for the high purposes of Fate are hidden from all.

He that abuseth his servant shall surely be brought low; for the gods who bestowed power upon him shall snatch it away, and great shall be that man's fall.

If thou be wise, keep watch over thy household. Grant honor to thy wife and love her exceedingly. Feed her stomach and clothe her back, for this is the duty of a husband.

Give her ointments and cosmetics in abundance; fail not to caress her every day; permit all the longings of her heart to be fulfilled. For, verily, the man who is loving to his wife and honoreth her likewise honoreth himself.

Lay not violent hands upon her; let not cruelty toward her enter thy heart; but speak gently and thus win her over. Thus shalt thou keep her love from straying to another. Converse with her, give her all thy love, and she will respect thee. Open thine arms to her and she will surely come unto thee.

Verily, a good son is a gift of the gods. Such a son doth more than is demanded of him and seeketh to please the soul of his father, and striveth to increase his strength through righteousness.

Thus shall health be to thy body, and in all things shall thy master be pleased with thee. Thy days shall be many under the sun, and the strength of years shall be thine.[1]

In this day, when psychologists, judges, and thinking men in general are seeking to discover the cause of the failure of marriage and the source of the divorce mills, what woman will not agree with old Ptah-Hotep as to the means of averting domestic catastrophe? And is there not in those sayings of long ago some advice that might well be applied to the present-day problem of employer and laborer? Well might this old Governor of the Nile Valley declare: "Wisdom has uplifted me to a high place, and multiplied my

---

[1] Version by the author. See also Howard Osgood's translation of French version by Philippe Virey, *Records of the Past*, Washington, Records of the Past Exploration Society, 1902, Vol. I, p. 306. For full translations see B. G. Gunn: *Instruction of Ptah-hotep*, London, J. Murray, 1908; Norman Davies: *Mastaba of Ptahhetep*, London, Egypt Exploration Fund, 1900; *Egyptian Literature*, N. Y., Colonial Press, 1901.

years, to live long in the earth, even five-score and ten years. And this have I found: that the best favor of a king is given to him who laboreth all his days and findeth honor with all men."

This, then, is the first of the volumes to come down to us from the literary dawn of mankind. Is it not surprisingly mature? Is it not intimately comprehensible to us of these modern days? Does it not sound the tone of wisdom—that calm wisdom which only long, long racial experience can grant?

The Book of the Dead

Ptah-Hotep told the Egyptians how to live; who told them how to die?

In the Royal Museum at Berlin repose the remains of a book the most widely read, doubtless, by the ancient people of the Nile, and certainly the one most frequently used in that mysterious empire of the dawn of civilization. To its native readers it was known as the *Going Out by Day*, but to us moderns it is more familiar under the somber title of *The Book of the Dead*. Appropriate indeed is this latter name. For here that vanished nation found its guide for the dark and feared journey to the Other World, and here we too may discover the same wonder and fear concerning that journey which all must make.

Thousands of years ago no Egyptian could hope for happiness after death without some knowledge of this *Book of the Dead*. Without its precepts and formulas and charted ways, the bewildered soul might wander long before reaching the Judgment Seat of God, and, if by chance he found the road that led to that throne, what could he, ignorant of the required phrases presented in this volume, say before the Supreme Judge? Therefore, let the living and the dead beware of ignorance of this grim, celestial guide-book. Selections from it were painted upon the mummy-cases; chapters from it were often enclosed with the corpse; sentences from it were engraved upon the walls of the tomb; the living, if they were wise, painfully learned large portions of it word by word.

As it is to most of us, so to the early Egyptian, dying was a most serious business—something to be attended to thoroughly with conformity to long established ritual and custom. The body must be so preserved as to last indefinitely; the tomb must be of the most permanent character; in the case of the powerful and rich the structure for the final rest must be vast, stupendous. To persons of real vitality the thought of oblivion is abhorrent; to many millions of our own day the idea of a Hereafter of Torture is preferable to the idea of a Hereafter of Nothingness. To those energetic, conquering people of the Nile, life after death was similar to the existence here on earth, something with action in it, desires, pleasures, even physical wants. Therefore, the custom of placing with the mortal remains such articles as represented foods, animals, arms, even toys of this present life. Will not such things, reasoned your Ancient Egyptian, be of comfort, even necessary, to the dead in that strange journey to the Realm Beyond?

This ancient race had reached, thousands of years ago, some definite conclusions as to the mortal and the immortal elements of man. There was the soul. of course, known as *ba;* there was the body, the expressing and expressive instrument of *ba;* but there was also an intellectual part called *chu;* and a personality or personal genius, or astral body, known as *ka,* which remained or dwelt in the tomb where the earthly body lay. Woe to him who opened and disturbed the final home of the corpse; for what might not that outraged personality, that unseen presence, *ka,* do if it escaped from the tomb to sweep over the land?

But *ba,* the soul, and *chu,* the intellect, must go along the bewildering path out to the Next World; well for them if they knew the charts, if they were aware of certain precise procedures and ceremonies, if they could recite certain precious phrases. If, said the Egyptian, if I possess the symbols, the keys to the situations as they arise out there, then it will be well with my soul; if not—annihilation.

With such a glimpse into the inner thoughts of those ancients, perhaps we moderns can begin to realize the overwhelming importance of this precise, stilted, monotonous *Book of the Dead.* To-day the volume, gathered from this tomb and that, from this mummy and that, consists of one hundred and sixty-six chapters. We must not assume, however, that any one time or any one section of Ancient Egypt possessed all these chapters. One city may have known intimately a certain set of sections from the book; another metropolis may have found its consolation and guidance in other chapters or even in other versions. The mere composing or writing of this sublimated guide-book covered a period greater, probably, than the life-span of any two modern nations combined. One at least of the chapters is believed to have been first written as early as 4266 B.C.; certainly a large number of sections were inscribed before 3000 B.C.; others came many centuries later.

Far in the West is the Amenti, the Paradise. There are rivers to cross, mountains to climb, deserts to traverse, monsters to overcome, before the harassed soul may reach the Celestial Land. Every such emergency is foreseen and provided for in this powerful helper, the *Book of the Dead*. Prayers there are, phrases for opening stubborn gates, charms against evil spirits, and —thanks to whatever gods may be—a marvelous ritual, precise, accurate, reliable, highly effective, to be recited by the soul in its own defense before the Judgment Bar. At that Bar sits Osiris, Ruler of the Realm of the Dead. Surely he will heed those who know the exact words of the mystic rituals.

But the record of one's life must agree with the formal declaration one makes before that Seat. If the soul could prove its worth it received again all its human faculties, and with them an eternity of pleasant activity. If, however, all the bad deeds, weighed in the scales that forever wavered before the Throne of Osiris, overbalanced the good deeds by as much as a feather weight, woe to that soul. An ever-hungry beast, eternally standing in waiting by the scales, devoured both *ba* and *chu* of the desolate wanderer from the earth.

How pathetic has ever been man's endeavor to express himself to God! Perhaps those writers of the dawn of literature did wisely to throw aside all flowery phraseology, all rhetorical subterfuges, and, like Job of old, speak up with sturdy spirit and declare their own justification. Would not the mighty Osiris himself secretly admire the steadfast words of this "declaration of innocence" recited from the *Book of the Dead* by the righteous soul?

Ye Masters of Truth. I bring you the truth.
I have not secretly wronged my fellowmen.
I have not oppressed those in sorrow.
I have not falsified.
I have not caused the laborer to do more than his just work.
I have not been an idler.
I have not been a drunkard.
I have not been immoral.
I have not defamed the servant to his master.
I have not been the cause of hunger.
I have not made any to sorrow.
I have not committed murder.
I have not cheated.
I have not used the sacred bread of the altar.
I have not defrauded any when weighing.
I have not withheld milk from the mouths of babes.
I have not slandered any men.
I have not snared birds sacred to the gods.
I have not stopped the waters for irrigation.
I have not stolen the meat-offering of the gods.
I have not failed to make due offerings to the gods.
I have not failed to give food to the hungry, drink to the thirsty, clothes to the naked.
I am innocent! I am pure![2]

There are a myriad books that tell us how to live, but what nation ever told so precisely, so completely just how to die and how to enter the portals of Heaven? In the *Book of the Dead* we find revealed

[2] Abbreviated version by the author. For complete translations, with highly figurative titles of the gods, see E. A. Wallis Budge: *Book of the Dead,* Chicago, Open Court Pub. Co., 1901, p. 366; *ibid.,* London, Longmans & Co., 1899; *ibid., Egyptian Literature,* N. Y., Colonial Press, 1901, p. 104.

the soul of a nation building permanently, not only for this world but for the next.

So ever-present was the thought of the final day of each mortal, and the long, long journey he must take that, according to the Greek historian Herodotus, at banquets given by wealthy Egyptians, "just as the company is about to rise from the table a small coffin is borne around containing a perfect representation of a dead body. As it is exhibited, the bearer exclaims, 'Behold this figure! After death you shall resemble it. Drink and be happy!' "

There is in the British Museum a papyrus of about 1500 B.C. containing just such a banquet dirge of about 2500 B.C., often called the *Festal Dirge of Antef.* This King Antef, or Entuf, belonged to that eleventh dynasty of Egypt ruling at Thebes between 2533 and 2466 B.C. Whether he himself wrote it or whether one of his court poets composed it in his honor or memory is not certain, but certain it is that it echoes the same somber thought that is found painted on mummy and engraved on sepulcher of the ancient dead.

O Mortal Man, though thou attain all wisdom and power, though thy fame be magnified, whether thou be here in poverty or amidst riches, yet one end cometh to all men, that is, Death.

Behold what is fortune or fate? The house of a man passeth into nothingness, and what may be the thoughts and the deeds of one who is dead no man hath yet returned to tell us.

Therefore, let all the desires of thy heart be fulfilled. Be happy. Anoint thy body with rich ointment; array thyself in fine linen and adorn thyself with precious ornaments. Enjoy whatever the gods have granted thee.

For does not the hour come to every mortal when he shall never again hear the voices of men? Yea, he who is dead heareth no more the lament of the mourner; no tears bring back the dead to life.

Eat, then, and drink, and take thy joy. For when thou goest down into the grave thy goods go not with thee. He that goeth down to death cometh again no more for ever.[3]

Once more the tone of fatalism, the cry of the preacher of *Ecclesiastes:* Vanity of Vanities, all is vanity! Only an old, old civilization could have brought to any people so deep a conviction of the futility of attempting to solve the mystery of life and death.

TALES OF THE MAGICIANS

We must not conclude, however, that these people of the Nile thought only of death and the after life. They were indeed human, and to them, as to us, music and song and story had their subtle charm. From the richly carved and painted chambers behind the massive columns of palaces and temples floated the pensive melodies of songs now silent; harmonies from strange, long forgotten string and wind instruments filled the evening air; reciters in mansion and on street corner told tales of other days that even then were ancient beyond the memory of man.

What were these stories that skilled narrators related to royal audiences or to weary laborers in the twilight hours of five thousand years ago? Are they beyond our comprehension, or do they reveal the same

[3] Excerpts by the author, based on full translation by C. C. Goodwin in *Transactions* of Society of Biblical Archæology, London, Vol. III, part 1. Translations may also be found in Adolf Erman: *Literature of Ancient Egypt*. London, Methuen & Co., 1927, and *Egyptian Literature*, N. Y., Colonial Press, 1901.

passions, the same temptations, the same bitter or sweet endings that we find in the latest fiction of our day?

There is in the Berlin Museum a manuscript, written probably in 2800 B.C. and now known as the Westcar Papyrus. In it we discover a collection of stories of far greater antiquity, the so-called *Tales of the Magicians*. By means of these narratives, told supposedly by his sons to the mighty King Khufu, or Cheops, builder of the Great Pyramid, we can gain some idea of the plots that the people delighted to hear.

Like all other nations, the Egyptians were lovers of tales; they were indeed just as "fiction mad" as our inveterate novel readers of to-day. Possibly it would not be strictly accurate to call those ancient bits of narrative by the name of short stories; for they lack the technique and qualities in general that have made the modern short story an almost mechanical master-piece. But these tales are not only interesting, but positively surprising in their display of fantastic imagination, while their hints as to the life and customs compel us to see how little, after all, human nature changes.

Let us picture the scene as the reciter, bowing before the mighty Pharaoh, begins one of the age-old, ever popular Tales of the Magicians. It is dusk, and up from the Nile lowlands comes the murmur of the resting city—snatches of song, minor melodies from harp and flute, the laughter of children, the swish of the oars as the pleasure boats sweep along the river, the chanted prayer of the priests in the vast temple. Through the darkening air of the palace clouds of incense float. There is a faint rustle of heavy curtains along the walls as the breeze from the Nile comes through the long series of massive columns. The golden lamps of oil have not yet been lighted; his Awful Majesty, Rameses, prefers it so.

Perhaps there are a few solemn chords from the harp—the somber prelude to the tale. Then the reciter speaks the customary formal opening words that preface any narrative of this type:

Once, when King Khufu lived and ruled over all this Empire, he said unto his Chief Officer, his Chancellor, "Call before me now my sons and my wise men." And the sons and the wise men stood before him. Then said he to them, "Know ye of any man who might tell to me the stories of the deeds of the magicians of old?"

Then the noble son, Khafre, stood before the King and declared, "I can tell, O Majesty, a tale of the days of thy forefather Nebka, the Blessed—a tale of what came to pass when he entered the temple of Ptah Ankhtaui."

The King nods his willingness to hear the story; in the gloom the vaguely outlined figures of the royal companions may be seen leaning forward, listening intently, and the skilled story teller proceeds:

His majesty was walking to the temple of Ptah, and went to the house of the chief reciter, Uba-aner, with his courtiers. Now, when the wife of Uba-aner saw a certain page who stood behind the king her heart longed for him. And she sent her servant to him with a present of a chest of garments.

Then he returned with the servant. Now, there was a lodge in the garden of Uba-aner, and one day the page said to the wife of Uba-aner, "There is a lodge in the garden; let us take our pleasure in it." Then the wife sent to the steward who had charge of the garden, and commanded, "Have the lodge that is in the garden made ready." And she and the page went there and remained and drank until the sun went down. And the page came forth in the evening to bathe in the lake.

Then the steward declared, "I must go and tell Uba-aner about this affair. Now, when that day was past and another day had come, then went the steward to Uba-aner and told him of all these happenings.

Then commanded Uba-aner, "Bring me my casket of ebony and electrum." So they brought it, and he fashioned a crocodile of wax, seven fingers long, and he enchanted it, and said, "When the page comes out and bathes in my lake, seize him." And he gave the crocodile to the steward and said to him, "When the page goes down to the pool, as he is daily wont to do, then throw in this crocodile after him." And the steward went forth bearing the crocodile.

Again the wife of Uba-aner sent to the steward who had charge of the garden, and directed, "Let the lodge that is in the garden be made ready, for I am coming to rest there." And the lodge was made ready with all good things, and there she came and made merry in it with the page. And in the evening the page came forth to bathe, as was his custom. Then the steward cast the wax crocodile into the water after him. And, behold, it became a great crocodile, seven cubits in length! And it seized upon that page.

And Uba-aner abode seven days more with the King of Upper and Lower Egypt, Nebka, the Blessed, while the page was stifled in the crocodile. And then, after the seven days were passed, the King of Upper and Lower Egypt, Nebka, the Blessed, set forth, and Uba-aner went before him.

And Uba-aner said to his majesty, "Will your majesty come and see a wonder that has come to pass in your days unto a certain page?" And the King went with him. And Uba-aner called to the crocodile and said, "Bring forth the page." And the crocodile came forth from the lake with the page. Uba-aner said to the King, "Behold, whatever I command this crocodile to do, he will do it." And his majesty said, "I pray you send back this crocodile." And Uba-aner stooped and took up the crocodile, and it became in his hand a crocodile of wax. And then Uba-aner told the King that which had passed in his house between the page and the wife. Then the King commanded the crocodile, "Take to thee thy prey." And the crocodile plunged into the lake with his prey, and no man knew whither he went.

And his majesty, the King of Upper and Lower Egypt, Nebka, the Blessed, commanded, and they brought forth the wife of Uba-aner to the north side of the harem, and burnt her with fire, and cast her ashes into the river.

This is the wonder that came to pass in the days of thy fore-father, the King of Upper and Lower Egypt, Nebka, the Blessed, of the acts of the chief reciter, Uba-aner.[4]

As the story began, so must it end with an almost fixed formula. What shall the Ruler of Upper and Lower Egypt do for such an interesting story teller? For thousands of years reciters repeated the same closing lines—as a hint, no doubt, as to how the listeners should recompense the man who could thus weave a tale:

His Majesty, the King of Upper and Lower Egypt, Khufu, then said, "Let there be presented to the King Nebka, the Blessed, a thousand loaves, a hundred draughts of beer, an ox, two jars of incense; and let there be presented a loaf, a jar of beer, a jar of incense, and a piece of meat to the chief reciter, Uba-aner; for I have seen the token of his learning." And they did all things as his majesty commanded.

The Song for Neferhotep

A great pride must have risen in the bosom of Kings and High Priests as they looked from their lofty tem-

[4] Version by the author, based on translation by W. M. Flinders Petrie in *Egyptian Tales*, London, Methuen & Co., 1895. Other specimens may be found in Gaston Maspero: *Popular Stories of Ancient Egypt*, New York, G. P. Putnam's Sons, 1915.

ples far up and down the Nile Valley and beheld the wide fields of wheat, the walled cities, the stupendous pyramids. It was a justifiable pride; for what is more inspiring than the vision of a mighty nation industrious, productive, highly civilized, living peacefully under law and order?

But man goes to his long home, and for him these things are no more. Well for him indeed if he can leave behind some memories, some monument proving that he once lived, reminding posterity that he too had his part in this vast development of a people. Thus the Egyptians of the better class must have reflected, and they transformed their reflections into deeds and mighty memorials.

For example, there was that priest of the seventeenth century, B.C., Neferhotep of Thebes. He is portrayed on the walls of his tomb sitting with his wife, his son, and his daughter while his harper chants in his honor a song that after more than thirty-five centuries is still existing. We know not what weird chords that harper composed to accompany the memorial lyric, but throughout the stanzas runs the minor tone of an old, old thought: "Man that is born of woman vanisheth when his race is run."

We may not quote the entire poem, but somehow certain lines sound astonishingly like some of the prayers and chants we supposedly sophisticated mortals of modern days utter. Have we not heard the priests in our own holy temples appeal to God in such words as

Holy Father, grant that the day return with thy blessing.
The fragrant odors of our oils on thy altar rise to thee.
Accept the flowers that we offer thee to-day.

Behold, thy sister dwelleth in thee as in a temple.
Place these, our lotus flowers in her arms and in her bosom.
For she sitteth beside thee—at thy right hand.
May our harp and our song be pleasing unto thee;
May it drive away all gloom.
Be content, then, even unto the day when all of us, as pilgrims,
    enter Amanti,
Welcomed by him who has gone before us.

O Father, vouchsafe that the day come quickly.
He whom we adored was pure of heart and just of deed.
Even as the life of all passeth away, so passed he.
Lo, he once was, and now is not. Nor doth any know his
    dwelling place.
So hath it ever been, even since Ra went forth; so shall it
    forever be.
Scarcely are the eyes of man opened when they are quickly
    closed again.
His soul taketh of the mystic waters, and with all who are gone
He drinketh of the sacred River of Life.[5]

And have we not been told that good deeds are the
only consoling memory in the hour of death?

When the harvest faileth, forget not the poor who cry unto
    thee;
For then shall thy name be remembered for ever,
And worshipping throngs shall come to the feast of thy sacri-
    fice;
And in thine honor shall the priests, adorned with panther
    skins, pour out the sacred wine,
And offer cakes, and chant before thy sanctuaries.
In that hour when before Ra, great Sun-God, thy servants
    shall stand,

[5] Author's version, based on the German translation by Ludwig
Stern in *Zeitschrift für Ägyptische Sprache,* 1873, p. 58.

Shu shall bring forth the rewarding harvest in its season,
And all glory shall crown thee.
But upon the wicked destruction shall surely fall.[6]

How universal this thought of the change we call
death! From these lines of an ancient poet of the Nile
to the *Thanatopsis* of William Cullen Bryant—how
the theme persists in repeating itself over and over.

Brethren, the hour of your departure shall surely come; there-
fore let your hearts gain understanding.
For where ye go, ye shall not return henceforth forever.
Verily the righteous shall prosper, but the wicked shall perish.
Be ye, therefore, upright; for the upright shall be blest.
But whether a man be brave or afraid, or gifted with friends
or forsaken,
None may escape the grave; none shall overcome Death.
Grant us, then, of thy riches, and be thou remembered forever
of Isis.[7]

PENTAUR'S ODE TO RAMESES II

Perhaps to his subjects Rameses, the Pharaoh,
seemed the most fortunate of men. For could he not
raise unto himself such temples and monuments and
tombs and pyramids that mortals ten thousand years
later would be compelled to remember that he once
was among the mighty living? Might he not hire
poets to compose heroic lines about his deeds, and
might he not pay sculptors to carve those lines in far-
seen letters upon temples and monuments and upon
the very mountains themselves?

There was Rameses II, possibly the greatest of the
Pharaohs—a valiant warrior, a conqueror of many
nations, the ruler to be forever famous or infamous as

[6] *Ibid.*   [7] *Ibid.*

the Pharaoh of the Oppression of the Israelites, an energetic, ever ambitious monarch, a liberal patron of arts and science and literature. Well he knew his ability and his right to endless fame—and he possessed an overwhelming ambition to have all the future know it. Wisely he attended to the business himself, and trusted not to a fickle posterity. What heroic images of himself he had carved! What massive temples in honor of himself! What bellicose accounts in lasting rock of himself and his exploits!

He even seized upon the unfinished memorials of his predecessors and completed the monuments and their descriptions—with some slight changes in the wording—to fit the story to Rameses II. The obelisk, for instance, now in Central Park, New York, was originally designed by and for one of his forefathers; but this Rameses II, alias Ses, alias Sestesu, alias Sethoris, alias Sesostris, et cetera, appropriated the partly-carved shaft for himself, and covered it with the records of his own life. We moderns almost glory in his vast, his god-like egotism!

Of all the deeds of his sixty-seven years of kingship —and those deeds were innumerable—he apparently found most pride in a certain campaign against the Hittites in Northern Syria. There, at Kadish, on the Orontes, the very god of all Egypt had come down and stood by his side in the war-chariot, and the dismay and the slaughter of the Hittites on that memorable day had been of epic proportions.

Such a triumph must be commemorated in song and story. It is so ordered. In 1326 B.C., two years after the battle, the court poet, Pentaur, had completed the ode of heroism, and Rameses II saw to it that it was

carved upon the walls of all the chief temples. And
it was an illustrated poem too. Huge sculptures added
what the poet's imagination might have failed to
vision.

Hear the story itself, you mortals of this embar-
rassed, self-deprecating day, and wonder at the mighty
publicity of the ages when advertising was really in
its zenith:

The King of the vile Hittites mustered many warriors. His
chariots were as the sand of the sea, and three men of war
stood in each car; and all the strength of his army was arrayed, footmen and horsemen. They stood, but durst not
advance against Pharaoh the King.

But the King of the Hittites prepared an ambush to the
northwest of Kadesh; and the chief part of his army was concealed there. But others went forth from the south of Kadesh
and fell upon the center of Pharaoh's army, and, taking them
unawares, overthrew them, even the legion of Pra-Makhu.

.   .   .   .

Then arose Pharaoh, in strength like unto his divine father
Mentu, and took weapons in his hand, and put on his armor,
like unto Baal.

And he took his horses, called "The Victory of Thebes,"
which were from the royal stables of Miamun;

And Pharaoh smote the horses, and they charged into the
center of the host of the Hittites, and there was none with the
King.

And the King looked, and lo! the enemy surrounded him,
two thousand and five hundred of their best warriors in their
chariots, three men in each chariot; and they came behind the
King and upon each side of him.

.   .   .   .

And Pharaoh said, "O Father Ammon, where art thou?
Shall a father forget his son? Behold, thou knowest my ways.

I have not erred from the judgments of thy mouth; the vows that I vowed unto thee have I kept. Shall the King who rules in Egypt bow beneath the yoke of the stranger?

"Verily Ammon should prevail over the herders of cattle, and should stand above him who knoweth not God.

"Have I not sacrificed unto thee of my substance, even ten thousand oxen, and burnt woods of sweet savor upon thy altars, and withheld naught that thy heart craved?

"Put thou, therefore, to shame him that disobeyeth thee, and give honor to him that lifteth up his hands unto thee.

"Behold, my heart has ever inclined itself unto thee; I have done thy will, and called upon thy name.

"And now, behold! I stand alone in the midst of a multitude, which are as the sands of the sea in number, and my men and my chariots were afraid and have deserted me, not giving ear unto my voice when I, the King, cried unto them for aid.

"But the strength of Ammon is greater than the strength of a myriad of fighting-men and ten thousand chariots; yea, than ten thousand brothers and sons gathered together in one place to help me.

"Behold, Ammon is the Lord, and beside him all men are as nothing!

"That which hath come to me is according to thy word.

"Behold, I will obey thy word, and alone I will uplift my voice unto thee, even from the ends of the earth,

"Saying, 'Help me, O Father Ammon, against mine enemy, the Hittite!' "

.   .   .   .

I shouted for joy, for from behind, his voice came unto me, saying,

"Lo, I have hastened unto thee, Rameses Miamun!

"Lo, I stand beside thee! Lo, it is I, even thy father, Ra, the mighty sun-god!

"Lo, my hand shall fight for thee, and my arm be strong to aid thee!

"And my power shall prevail against the myriads who come against thee.

"For I am the God of victory, and the heart of a brave man is pleasing unto me.

"And in thee have I found a righteous spirit, and my soul rejoices in thy might and thy valor."

Now, when this came to pass, behold, my heart was changed within me, and I became like unto Mentu, the God of Battles.

My left hand shook the spear, and my right hand held the sword, even as Baal, before them that saw me.

And I charged into the midst of them, two thousand and five hundred chariots with horses, and the hoofs of my horses trampled upon them.

None raised his hand against me, for their hearts failed them, and with fear were their limbs loosened, and the spear and the dart they dared not wield against me.

And I cast them down into the water, as falls the crocodile from the bank, so fell they. Yea, one by one they fell upon their faces, and at my pleasure I smote them.

．　　　．　　　．　　　．　　　．　　　．

I smote them. There was none to escape me.

Then I lifted up my voice, and shouted to my men of war and my charioteers,

"Ho, my warriors, my charioteers, take courage, and fear not; for lo, I was alone, yet Ammon was my helper, and his power is even now with me!"

Then Pharaoh made haste and fell upon the hosts of the Hittites,

Yea, six times he charged upon them, like Baal in his wrath,

And he smote them and slew them, and made no end of slaying, and none escaped him.[8]

[8] Adapted from the translation by Dr. H. K. Brugsch: *History of Egypt,* London, J. Murray, 1881, Vol. II, p. 56. The first, though less accurate, translation was in French, by Vicomte de Rougé, in *Seance des Cinq Académies,* August, 1856.

Is it any wonder that this monarch had erected at Tanis a gigantic image of himself, the greatest colossus yet attempted—ninety-two feet in height, with a pedestal almost as tall? Such a hero should, for the sake of eugenics, be the father of a mighty race; he almost was, for he had one hundred and nineteen children. It was with almost equal pride that he could boast that he built and stocked the largest library in the history of the East, and gave it the appropriate name of "the Dispensary of the Soul."

Thus ages ago man longed for immortal fame—and got it. For as long as mortals shall study the records of the past, so long shall Rameses II and Pentaur, his poet, stand forth in bold relief among those who gloried in gaining glory among men.

The Tale of Two Brothers

Once upon a time there were two brothers; Anpu was the name of the elder, and Bata was the name of the younger. Anpu had a house and a wife. But his little brother was to him as a son; he made for him his clothes; he followed his oxen to the fields; he did the ploughing; he harvested the grain; he did for him all the matters that were in the field. The younger brother grew to be an excellent worker; there was not his equal in the whole land; the spirit of a god was in him.

Thus begins what was in all probability the most famous and most popular story told to pharaohs, priests, and people of the Nile, the *Tale of Two Brothers*. To-day it may be seen in the D'Orbinery Papyrus in the British Museum; but the faded document found there is but an enlarged version of a far more ancient narrative—a version prepared by the scholar and author, Anena, for the entertainment of Prince Seti II, about 1300 B.C.

It starts off as though it were going to be a re-telling or first telling of the Biblical tale of Joseph, but soon it turns aside into an oft-repeated narrative of magic so beloved by those early Egyptians. It has, however, that idea of love turned to hate and its resulting revenge found in many a romance of more modern times.

Bata daily followed the plow or drove the cattle forth to the meadows, and every evening he returned to place before his brother the products of the field, and then went to the stable to lay him down with the beasts, whom he understood so well that he knew their very language. Thus the years passed, and he waxed into glowing, strong manhood.

Then came the temptation. Returning hastily from the fields one day to obtain some seed, he was accosted by Anpu's wife, who had noted with longing eyes the growing strength and power of the young man. "Come stay with me, and it shall be well with thee!" she exclaimed. Well he understood her meaning. Then Bata became like a panther of the South with fury at the evil speech, and in his wrath he cried, "What is this wickedness that thou hast said to me? Say it not to me again! For I will not tell it to any man; for I will not let it be uttered by the mouth of any man!"

But she feared him and his secret, and that evening when her husband returned she was stretched upon her bed, moaning that Bata had assaulted her and beaten her. Great was Anpu's anger; hidden behind the door of the stable, he awaited his brother's coming with the cattle.

But each of the loving animals, as it entered the shelter, said quietly, "Behold, thy elder brother standing before thee with his knife to slay thee. Flee from him." And he looked beneath the door and saw the feet of his brother, and he fled. Hotly pursued, he cried unto the god, Ra Harakhti. And the god heard, and lo, suddenly there was a great water between Bata and Anpu, and the water was full of crocodiles!

Then the younger brother told the elder the truth of it all, and Bata, in his disgust and shame, took out his knife and cut from his own body so much flesh that he fell down in a swoon. From the other bank Anpu wept and cursed his own folly, and longed in vain to succor his younger brother.

Then, awakening from his swoon, Bata said sorrowfully to Anpu, "I am going to the valley of the acacia. And this is what shall come to pass; I shall draw out my soul and shall put it upon the top of the flowers of the acacia, and when the acacia is cut down and it falls to the ground and thou comest to seek for it, if thou searchest for seven years let not thy heart be wearied. For thou wilt find it, and thou must put it in a cup of cold water, and expect that I shall live again, that I may make answer to what has been done wrong. And thou shalt know that things are happening to me when one shall give thee a cup of beer in thy hand, and it shall be troubled. Stay not then, for verily it shall come to pass with thee."

And Bata went into the valley of the acacia. But the elder brother returned to his home, slew the un-

faithful wife, threw her body to the dogs, and mourned
many a day for his lost brother.

Bata in the delectable valley spent his days hunting
the wild creatures, but each evening he came back to
sleep under the acacia that bore upon its flower his
soul. Then the Nine Gods, observing his loneliness,
made unto him a beautiful woman. "The essence of
every god was in her," but the Seven Fates, coming to
look upon her, cried out with one voice, "She shall die
a sharp death."

Many a day Bata and she lived in felicity, but the
sea, longing for her, gained a lock of her perfumed
hair and carried it to the land of Pharaoh. And
Pharaoh sent forth men to capture her, and with them
a woman with such jewels and ornaments as tempt
women, and the wife of Bata returned with the messengers to the King.

And she in her passion for Pharaoh bade him send
men again to cut down the acacia on the flower of
which lay the soul of Bata. It was done, and instantly
her husband fell down dead. And the woman thought
to dwell long in safety and joy with Pharaoh.

But then came Anpu to the house of the younger
brother and saw him lying lifeless on a mat. Forth
went Anpu to seek the soul of the dead man under
the acacia tree, but for three years he sought in vain,
and at length declared, "On the morrow I shall return
to Egypt." But on the morrow he discovered the soul
in the form of a seed, and cast it into a cup of water.
And Bata shuddered in all his limbs, and opened his
eyes and gazed longingly at his brother. Then Anpu
gave him the cup to drink, and, behold, the soul en-

tered the body, and the younger brother stood upright and strong.

Then Bata declared that he must turn into a great bull, "bearing every good mark," and that Anpu must lead him to court of Pharaoh. "Thus when the sun arises I shall be in the place where my wife is, and I shall make answer to her." So it was done, and Pharaoh, seeing the huge and perfect animal, was delighted with it, and paid a great price for it.

And the bull, passing near the woman, said, "Behold, I am alive again." And she asked, "Who art thou?" "I am Bata," declared the bull. "Behold, I am alive again." Then the wife, having delighted Pharaoh, demanded a reward of him, and he, with an oath to the gods, exclaimed that she should have whatever she asked for. "Let me eat, I pray thee, of the liver of the bull."

With sorrow the King fulfilled his promise. And thus Bata was again slaughtered for the sake of an evil woman. But as he was being carried on the shoulders of men, in his death agony he shook his head, and two drops of his blood fell upon the great portals of Pharaoh's temple. And, behold, in the morning the two drops had become tall trees!

And the woman came to see the marvel, but one of the trees spoke to her, "O thou deceitful one, I am Bata! I still live, though I have been sorely mistreated." Then did she contrive to please Pharaoh once more, and again he swore that she might have whatever she desired. "Let, then, these two trees be cut down," she demanded, "and let them be cut into strong planks." And Pharaoh granted her request. But even as they were cut down, a chip from one of

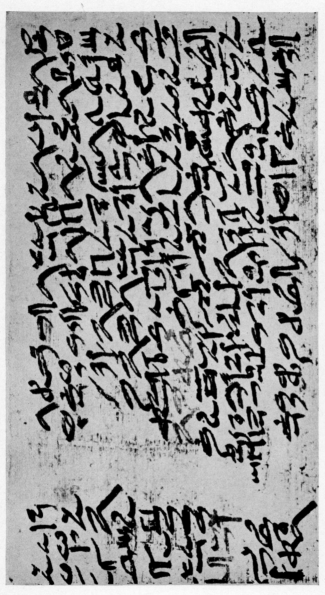

DETAIL OF PAPYRUS ROLL, "THE SHIPWRECKED SAILOR"

Collection of the Imperial Palace, St. Petersburg

the trees flew forth into the mouth of the woman, and before she was aware she had swallowed the bit of wood. And, wonder of wonders, the woman found herself with child, and in the course of days gave birth to a son!

Then the boy, conceived of the bit of wood, was looked upon as the royal son of Pharaoh, and in after years became King of All Egypt. Then he gathered the nobles and the powerful of the land about him, and caused the faithless wife to be brought forth, and he revealed himself to the people and judged her, and slew her. And, remembering the sorrow of Anpu, he sent for the elder brother and made him a prince in Egypt, and when, after thirty years, Bata was gathered unto the gods, Anpu, his brother, reigned in his stead.[9]

This, then was the tale told in the twilight along the Nile, before the door of many a hut and in the palace of Rameses and under the lofty roofs of the temples of the priests. How often, as the rays of the setting sun shone across the glittering river, the dark-eyed Egyptians must have listened and seen, as in a trance, the old days when the gods rewarded Bata the faithful and punished her, the unfaithful wife.

THE SHIPWRECKED SAILOR

Certainly one of the oldest tales known among the peoples of the ancient Egyptian empire was *The Ship-wrecked Sailor*. The manuscript, now in that Russian city of many names, formerly called St. Petersburg, is of about 2500 B.C., but the story presented in the papyrus is doubtless a copy of a far earlier narrative.

[9] See for complete story, W. M. Flinders Petrie: *Egyptian Tales,* London, Methuen & Co., 1895, Second Series, p. 36.

Strange indeed that a bit of fiction could possess such vitality as to survive nearly five thousand years—especially such a simple and somewhat crude tale as this.

Of the large crew of a shipwrecked vessel one lone survivor reaches the Island of Plenty, where he lives amidst the material abundance of a Robinson Crusoe land. He has, however, as a companion a talking serpent—who talks profusely. The serpent prophesies that the sailor will return after four months to his homeland, and within that period he is indeed rescued and appears with gifts of spices, perfumes and other precious things, before Pharaoh, to whom he tells his tale.

Apparently to the Egyptian the old, old tale was entrancing; to us it seems to be hardly worthy of the name. But there can be no disputing about individual tastes—especially when one group of the individuals have been in their tombs four or five thousand years.

THE EXILE OF SANEHAT

Did these early people of the ancient Nile know homesickness, the love of fatherland, and the stirrings of patriotism, as we of to-day? Let the less than three hundred and fifty lines of the old story of the Exile of Sanehat—so old that it was common property of Egyptian reciters twenty-three hundred years before the Christian era—answer the question. Here in a bit of autobiography we hear the call of the fatherland coming to a man after half a lifetime of prosperity and honors in a far country. And how gladly he hearkens to that call of the home of his early days!

As a general, while leading his king's army in a

victorious campaign, he hears that the old monarch has passed away and that a new and perhaps unfriendly one has succeeded. His must be flight—flight to the distant kingdom of Palestine. Vividly indeed he tells of the toil, the privations of that strenuous journey. But his fame has preceded him. Instead of receiving the humiliation of an exile, he has high honors bestowed upon him; he becomes the chief general of the army of these kindly foreigners; he is given a wife from the royal household; many children and great riches are his.

Then, after long, happy years, comes a message from the monarch of Egypt. The document is presented in the midst of the story in full, official language; it offers him forgiveness, safety, and honors among his own countrymen. And what a tremendously high-sounding, majestic tone to the opening phrases of that kingly mandate—all the glory that is of Egypt in a few mighty words! "The Horus, Life of Births, Lord of the Crowns, Life of Births, King of Upper and Lower Egypt, Kheper-Ka-Ra, Son of the Sun, Usertesen, Ever Living Unto Eternity, Royal Command for the Attendant, Sanehat."

And what of the command?

Leave all the riches that thou hast and that are with thee, altogether. When thou shalt come into Egypt behold the palace, and when thou shalt enter the palace, bow thy face to the ground before the Great House; thou shalt be chief among the companions. And behold day by day thou growest old; thy vigor is lost, and thou thinkest on the day of burial. Thou shalt see thyself come to the blessed state, they shall give thee the bandages from the hand of Tait, the night of applying the oil of embalming. They shall follow thy funeral, and visit the tomb on the day of burial, which shall be in a gilded case, the head painted with blue, a canopy of cypress wood above thee, and oxen shall draw thee, the singers going before thee, and they shall dance the funeral dance. The weepers crouching at the door of thy tomb shall cry aloud the prayers for offerings; they shall slay victims for thee at the door of thy pit; and thy pyramid shall be carved in white stone, in the company of royal children. Thus thou shalt not die in a strange land, nor be buried by Amu; thou shalt not be laid in a sheep-skin when thou art buried; all people shall beat the earth, and lament on thy body when thou goest to the tomb.[10]

"Thou shalt not die in a strange land." Thus in old age Sanehat hears the appealing call of the land of his birth, and returns to his native cities and fields. "When this order came to me I was in the midst of my tribe. When it was read to me I threw me on the dust; I threw dust in my hair; I went around my tent rejoicing and saying, 'How may it be that such a thing is done to the servant who with a rebellious heart has fled to strange lands? Now, with an excellent deliverance, and mercy delivering me from death, thou shalt cause me to end my days in the palace.'" And he left behind him the wealth, the wife, the children of the strange land. Great was the reward:

Years were removed from my limbs; I was shaved, and polled my locks of hair; the foulness was cast to the desert with the garments of Nemau-shau. I clothed me in fine linen, and anointed myself with the fine oil of Egypt; I laid me on a bed. I gave up the sand to those who lie on it; the oil of the wood to him who would anoint himself therewith. There was given to me the mansion of a lord of serfs, which had

[10] Adapted from Petrie's "Egyptian Tales." Excellent version by C. C. Goodwin, *Frazier's Magazine,* London, 1865.

belonged to a royal friend. There many excellent things were in its buildings; all its wood was renewed. There were brought to me portions from the palace thrice and four times each day; besides the gifts of the royal children, always, without ceasing. There was built for me a pyramid of stone among the pyramids. The overseer of the architects measured its ground; the chief treasurer wrote it; the sacred masons cut the well; the chief of the laborers on the tombs brought the bricks; all things used to make strong a building were there used. There were given to me peasants; there was made for me a garden, and fields were in it, as is done for the chief royal friend. My statue was inlaid with gold, its girdle of pale gold; his majesty caused it to be made. Such honor is not done to a man of low degree.[11]

THE STORY OF SETNA

The audiences of the story-tellers of this early kingdom were for thousands of years exceedingly fond of tales of magic. And, as we began with a story of black art, so let us close the account of the fiction of the Nile with a curious narrative of the same use of magic lore. Let it be the *Story of Setna,* probably written down as late as 400 B.C., but dealing with monarchs and royal folk of the fourteenth century before the Christian era.

Setna, son of Rameses II, lover of old books and student of occult sciences, was told of a manuscript which Throth, god of science and magic, had written. It was now in the tomb of Na-nefer-Ka-ptah, only son of an early Pharaoh. The scholar risked the curse of the gods to enter the tomb to obtain this book, and there he met the ghosts of Na-nefer-Ka-ptah and his wife and his son. The spirit of the wife, Ahura, after

[11] *Ibid.*

endeavoring vainly to persuade him not to take the sacred roll, finally proposed a game of skill to settle the question, and she won the game. But Setna, by means of outside help, carried off the manuscript nevertheless.

Who, though, can gain victory over destiny? Na-nefer-Ka-ptah, through the instrumentality of the very same magic with which the book deals, causes Setna to fall into strange hallucinations, and the student's heart is broken by his imaginary spirit of corruption. And thus Fate persuades him, in his misery, to return the written work of a god to its resting place. And Na-nefer-Ka-ptah seizes upon the opportunity to compel the repentant young man to promise to transfer to this tomb near Memphis the bodies of Ahura and their son from their distant burial place, to rest beside the husband and father.[12]

Thus thousands of years ago under the shadow of the pyramids these children of the Nile heard their romances of travel and war and broken love and mysterious doings. These—the dark inhabitants of that great valley—had their dreams and told them, just as you and I of to-day.

Love Lyrics and Hymns

Did the usual companion of story—poetry—find its place in the hearts of those people? Assuredly; we have seen that they were intensely human. They had their lyrics of love, their hymns and chants, their rhythmic prayers to the Ruler of Earth and Heaven. We have noted some specimens of their poetic appeals

[12] The story of Setna may be found in full in F. L. Griffith's *Stories of the High Priest of Memphis*, Oxford, Clarendon Press, 1900.

to the gods, but it may come as a pleasant surprise to know that where now the desolate sand shifts about the stolid countenance of the Sphinx, men and women once sang of love as passionately and as artistically as a Burns or a Moore of our own era.

> Beloved, it is only thy breath
> That keepeth my heart from death.
> Since I it is that found thee,
> May Amen grant thee to me
> Through time and eternity.[13]

And is there not tenderness—and subtlety—in these lines of a lovelorn Egyptian of thirty-five or forty centuries ago?

> I lay me down upon my bed;
> I am sick in heart and head.
> Soon the neighbors will come in
> To visit me—kith and kin—
> But she, my sweetheart, comes also—
> The doctors she will laugh at so.
> For she alone knows what is wrong;
> 'Tis she alone can make me strong.[14]

But the noblest, the most majestic poetry of Egypt, as we have stated earlier in this chapter, is found in those dignified, almost massive hymns to the gods or to their earthly representatives, the Pharaohs. Of all these sacred productions certainly one of the most spiritual and most significant in its grasp of the idea of God is the *Hymn to Usertesan III,* a chant ad-

[13] Author's version.
[14] Author's version. Various other specimens of love poetry may be found in Maspero's translations in *Etudes Egyptiennes,* Paris, Vol. I. Translations by C. C. Goodwin in *Transactions of Society of Biblical Archæology,* London, Vol. IV.

dressed to the son of a monarch whose tomb and
pyramid were being erected five thousand years ago
near where the papyrus of the poem was discovered a
few years ago.

Is there not the high dignity of genuine poetry—the
high dignity that we feel in a Homer and a Milton—
in such phrases as these?

Twice joyous are the gods; thou hast made firm their worship!
Twice joyous are thy children; thou hast made their homeland!
Twice joyous are thy fathers; thou hast added to their wealth!
Twice joyous is Egypt in thy strength; thou hast maintained
    her power!
Twice mighty is the monarch of his fortress, more than a
    million warriors!
(As for others who rule, they are but servants.)
Twice mighty is the monarch of his fortress; he is as a strong
    dyke,
Restraining the river in a great flood!
Twice mighty is the monarch of his fortress; he is like a rock,
Turning back the winds of the storm!

.   .   .   .   .   .

He hath come; he hath crushed the nations;
He hath struck down the people who realized not his might.
He hath come; he hath made safe his far stretches;
He hath brought back the stolen captive.
He hath come; he hath gained security for our declining days.
He hath come; we feed our babes in peace;
We bury our old under his blessed protection.[15]

Or consider, as another example, the hymn of King
Akhenaten to his one god, the Sun—an anthem composed about 1450 B.C. This same king renounced
all the hoary religious traditions of his native land,

[15] Author's version.

denied the innumerable deities that the ages had created for his people, and declared the worship of the One God, symbolized by the radiant Sun. The Egyptian world, however, was not ready for so advanced an ideal in religion, and after the good king's death the orthodox priesthood, suppressed during his reign, burst forth with all the passion of bigotry, destroyed his monuments and temples, and rooted out every vestige of his highly spiritual faith and creed. But in spite of their fanatical efforts King Akhenaten's enthusiastic chant in praise of the Sun has survived the wreckage of time, and brings down through the ages that same love of the glorious sunshine that we of to-day feel.

Glorious is thy splendor rising o'er the far horizon,
O vibrant, vital Aten! Thou art the source of all life.
When thou appearest over the eastern heavens,
Oh, thou floodest all the earth with thy beauty!
How radiant, how mighty, when high above,
Thou embracest the lands of all thy creation!
Thou art the Sun! Thou glowest o'er all in thine universal
    love.
Far distant, yet the world receives thee.
Though thou art in the heavens, yet the day follows in thy path.
The great ships glide up and down the rivers;
All highways fly open at thy coming.
The very fishes in the streams leap upward toward thee;
Thou gleamest down upon the mighty seas.

.   .   .   .

Oh, thou dwellest in my soul, O Sun!
There is one only that knoweth thee—
Thy Son, the only Son of Ra.
Thou makest Him wise in thy ways;
Thou grantest Him thy strength.

All things of this world are in thy hand;
They are as thou hast created them.
When thou risest, all live;
When thou goest down, all is death.[16]

It is this very same spirit of thanksgiving and enthusiasm for the Creator of Nature and the beauties
of this universe that inspired some unknown poet of
seventeen centuries before the Christian era to sing to
mighty Amen Ra, God of Thebes, such vibrant lines
as—

All hail, mighty Ra, Lord of Truth!
Thy sanctuary is hidden, thou god of gods.
Thou art compassionate when men pray unto thee;
Thou hearest the lament of the down-trodden;
The oppressed thou deliverest from the proud oppressor;
Thou heedest the call of the lowly, the miserable.
O God of wisdom, there is savor in thee!
The Nile riseth at thy command,
Thou Lord of love! thou Lord of affection!
Thou art the maker of the light of day.
The gods are jubilant in thee;
With leaping hearts they joy in thy glory.
Thy beauty is in the skies of the South;
Thy softness is in the skies of the North.
Thy loveliness causeth men's limbs to tremble,
Their hands to fall, their hearts to wonder.
The soul grows faint at the vision of thee.
All creatures cry, Hail to thee!
All nations cry, Praise to thee!
From the highest heavens, from the breadths of the world,
From the depths of the sea, Hail to thee! [17]

[16] Author's version.
[17] Author's version.   Excellent translations of hymns to Amen,
by C. C. Goodwin, may be found in *Transactions of the Society of
Biblical Archæology*, 1873, p. 353.

"Each in his own tongue"; throughout all time each
nation has endeavored to express its longings, its hopes,
its ideals of the Supreme Being, the mystery of whose
existence has never been and never will be solved.   And
of all such national expressions and outpourings to the
Deity, surely those of Egypt rank high.

Songs to the Dead

On the walls of those massive homes of the dead—
tombs and pyramids—there is frequently found the
image of a harper playing before the mummy of the
dweller in the darksome home.   And beside that pic-
tured musician may be seen in hieroglyphics the song
of praise or consolation which he is supposed to be
chanting to the dead.

How often indeed it is lyrical admonition to the
living also to enjoy life while life remains, for there
can be no returning to know its pleasures again.   We
have heard earlier the dirge of or to Antef, with its
reiterated advice: "Follow thy heart so long as thou
existest; enjoy thyself beyond measure; follow thy
desire and thy happiness while thou art on earth. With
radiant face make a good day, and rest not on it."

Of a similar tone is the song in the tomb of Osirian,
father of a High Priest famous in the ancient realm
of the Nile.   Live fully, oh wise ones of this earth; for

> Men have passed since the birth of time,
> And the young have taken their place.
> Ra has come forth morn after morn,
> And has sunk in the Mount of the West;
> And men have begotten, and women given birth,
> And all have breathed the incense of morn;
> And all who shall come after, yes, all,
> Shall live in our stead.

Joyous, then, O Father, be thy days.
Rejoice thy nostrils, then, with perfumes;
Adorn thee with garlands of lotus,
Yea, garlands for the breast of her,
Thy love, who dwells in thy heart.
Let music and song resound before thee;
Drive sorrow away, and live thou in joy.[18]

As the centuries passed away, and conquest after conquest swept over that vast valley, a tone of pessimism seemed to invade the soul of the poet of the tomb, and the dreary darkness of the mysterious land of death evidently cast its shadow over the living. Hear, for example, this lament from the dead wife of Pasherenptah, a priest in the days of the later Ptolemies in the first century before the Christian era. As the unknown poet speaks for her, we hear no more the typical Egyptian sturdy philosophy of the living concerning the dead, but a pagan somberness more akin to the attitude of the later Greeks, who were now ruling the kingdom of the Pharaohs.

Over all this world
Amenti doth swirl
    Darkness and sorrow;
Here where the dead so cold
Each his own place must hold,
Wrapped in sleep's endless fold,
    Knowing no morrow.

You, in the sun's warm light,
Where the waters run so bright,
    Drink, but never I.
For you the streams do flow;
I such joys may not know,

[18] Author's version.

Nor whence I came, where I go,
Blind, unthinking, lie.

Here Death alone doth rule;
Throughout this realm cruel
None may gainsay him.
Hated, but obeyed by all,
His laws on all do fall;
None here in prayer doth call—
Prayer may not stay him.[19]

Four thousand years of living had at length destroyed the philosophy of death which the race had evolved for itself. The mystery of it all, the thought of departing forever from the radiant sunlight of this earthly existence, the vagueness, the uncertainty of the hereafter had finally brought to this weary nation a pessimism, a dread, that no display of magnificent tombs and huge pyramids could dissipate.

EGYPTIAN COUNSELS

The long ages of existence, if they could not relieve the sting of death, could at least teach men how to conduct in safety their earthly affairs. Many indeed are the sage pieces of advice discovered in the monuments of the dead and on the manuscripts of the living.

For instance, there was a good and merciful king who reigned some twenty-five centuries before the Christian era, one named Amenemhat, who had devoted all his physical and mental powers to the safety and the uplifting of his people. And what had been his rewards? Attempts within his very household to assassinate him! Humiliated, discouraged, he decided

[19] Author's version.

to make his son king, and for that boy, Usertesen I, he wrote a book of guidance, so that the young monarch might be spared some of the errors and resulting shame that had come to the royal father.   And thus it came about that the *Teachings of Amenemhat* was a work of such good sense and wisdom, albeit somewhat bitter, that the schoolboys of many succeeding generations had it placed before them as a text for their reading and writing exercises.

What is the gist of his counsel gained through harsh experience?   It is simply this: beware of too much friendship; guard against undue familiarity; expect little gratitude; be your own guide and ruler.

Let every man be on guard as to his associates; for it is true that men turn in reverence toward him who arouseth some fear in them.   Be not, therefore, too open with any one.   Pour not forth thine heart to any man as a brother.   Place no man before another as thy chosen friend.   Permit no casual, familiar callers who hinder thy work.

When thou liest down with any human being, keep thy inner soul to thyself.   For the friends in whom you have confided fade away in the hour of stress.   I have given to a beggar, and I thereby caused an orphan to exist.   Behold, I gave authority to a man of no standing, and it was this eater of my bounty that created rebellion.   I lifted a man with my hand, and he forthwith filled the land with terror.   I clothed my favorites with my finest linen, and they became spies upon me. Yea, they who were perfumed with my frankincense laughed me to scorn even as they anointed themselves.[20]

We have opened this account of Literature in Egypt with the *Book of Precepts* by Ptah-Hotep; and we

[20] Author's version.   A full translation of the *Instruction of Amenemhe'et* may be found in B. Gunn: *Instruction of Ptah-hotep*, London, J. Murray, 1912.

close it with another book of proverbs which had accumulated through thousands of years of experience. The *Maxims* of Any are of a far later date than the *Precepts,* but contain, nevertheless, much the same quaint principles of wisdom.

Keep aloof from the strange woman who is not recognized in her own city. Know her not; yea, let thine eyes not be upon her when she cometh and goeth. For such a woman is like unto the waters of a deep whirlpool, the dark depths of which are not known. Such a woman, when her husband is afar, sendeth secret messages to thee daily. When there is none to behold, she then ariseth and spreadeth her snare. It is a sin, yea, death to heed her. He, then, who is indeed wise will draw afar from such an one and while he is yet young take unto himself a wife.

Drink not much beer. That which cometh forth from thy mouth is forever spoken. Thou stumblest, fallest, breakest thy legs, but no man cometh to extend a helping hand to thee. Thy companions drink on, or they arise and shout, "Put this drunken one out!" And when any man cometh to visit thee or to ask thy advice, lo, he seeth thee lying in the dirt like a helpless child.[21]

Moderation, diligence, cleanness of mind and soul and body—we see the same elements of wise living taught ages ago as to-day in the pulpits of the modern world.

We have taken but a glimpse at the vast store of Egyptian written records in prose and poetry. It is sufficient, however, to reveal that here was a nation which, in spite of an antiquity almost beyond our comprehension, was thinking deeply and feeling keenly the

[21] Author's version. A full translation may be found in Adolf Erman: *Literature of the Ancient Egyptians,* New York, Dutton & Co., 1927.

same problems of life and death as our own. Then, as now, the writer was a man of power, one who could sway the multitude through his imagination and insight. Surely the learned in lore and experience shall lead the ignorant, even though they realize it not, and, as an Egyptian sage declared, "the unlearned whose name no man knoweth is like unto a heavy-laden ass driven by a scribe."

II

THE DAWN IN BABYLON AND ASSYRIA

"BABYLON has fallen! Babylon has fallen!" When that cry swept over the lands consternation struck the nations. It was unbelievable, beyond comprehension. Babylon the magnificent, the admiration and terror of the world of her day—mistress of untold riches, queen of riotous sin, harlot of unabashed licentiousness, audacious in her prodigality, her triumphs, her wickedness, her splendor—Babylon had gone the way of all flesh! She had dazzled the world for centuries. She had risen to such heights of culture and civilization, she had sunk to such depths of drunken debauchery as man had never before conceived. But the hand had written upon the walls of her royal temples and palaces—and she expired amidst the ashes of her desolation. And to-day explorers from lands that were a wilderness when she was in her glory dig deep beneath the sand that covers her ruins, and marvel that such an empire could have passed into nothingness.

Possibly civilization is the most self-destructive invention of mankind. Time after time it rises to a mighty height, only to disintegrate and decay by means of the very wealth and luxury and corresponding physical and moral weakness which it itself has produced. Just as Egypt, Greece, Rome and a score of others were at length destroyed by greed and its consequent imperialism, riches and its consequent sloth—so passed Babylon.

But how vital, how magnificent was that Babylonian national life while it lasted! As to its age we can only surmise. Ancient as Egyptian culture may have been, assuredly it had a close rival in that civilization comprising Babylon and Assyria.

Certainly in Babylonia, the most fertile section of Mesopotamia, "land between the rivers," the Tigris and the Euphrates, a high state of intellectual and manual activity existed at least four thousand years ago, and further explorations may reveal an even earlier period of cultural existence. To the North, in those early days, lived the Akkadians; to the South dwelt the Sumerians. Both belonged to the Turanian branch of man, the name "Turan" signifying "land of darkness"—a root word which to this day survives in the word "Turk."

At length Semitic invaders overran the Babylonian territory and mingled their blood with that of the Sumerians. Among such invading hosts were the Elamites and the Chaldeans, while from the Northeast came the Cosseans, who in the fifteenth century B.C. swept down upon Babylonia and for more than five centuries ruled much of the vast plain. We know, by means of the tablets dug from the mounds which once were prosperous cities, that about 1200 B.C. Assyria gained power over the valley of Mesopotamia and accepted as her own the customs and the literature of her Southern neighbor, Babylonia.

Thus time after time there came into the nation fresh infusions of blood—strong, vigorous blood, a strain that could counteract for a considerable period the devastating influence of too much wealth and luxury and ease. With these invaders must have come new ideas, new knowledge of other lands, new methods of trade and science and art. It is well, perhaps, for a people to be shaken now and then by misfortunes and catastrophes—to be shaken out of the rut. It may be that through its sorrows and bitter struggles and revolutions Babylonian and Assyrian civilization obtained and retained for centuries a vitality which otherwise might have been short-lived.

It was a full-flowered civilization that the cracked, jagged, and broken tablets of thirty and forty centuries ago reveal to us. There were palaces, temples, city walls, and viaducts that were nothing short of architectural triumphs. There were immense libraries and advanced methods of circulating books throughout the empire. There were vast canal systems for irrigation and commerce—waterways that served as courses for what was probably the first parcel-post system in the history of man. There were researches in the sciences so advanced that the movements of stars and constellations were explained, accurate calendars devised, and the laws of Nature so comprehended and used that the outside world looked upon many Babylonian practices as nothing short of magic.

Above all else in importance, this early and highly original nation had invented an alphabet which for many a century was not equaled in simplicity and practicalness. Composed of arrow-shaped figures (cuneiform) representing single sounds and syllables or entire ideas, it was, as an effective medium of communication, far in advance of the hieroglyphics of the Egyptians. And how strangely indeed has the modern world come into possession of the meaning of these cuneiforms imprinted upon burnt brick and baked tablets of some four thousand years ago! A German scholar, Grotefend, after long puzzling over the characters, discovered in 1802 that many of the inscriptions opened with the same three words, two of which never changed, but one of which varied slightly. He "guessed" that the varying word might be a king's name, and he "guessed" Darius. Another bold "guess" —that the two unchanging words meant "King of Kings." His intellectual leap was correct; his suppositions proved to be realities; the alphabet was solved.

It is a stirring record that this alphabet engraved upon baked clay opens to us. We hear of the splendid reign of King Sargon I, who ruled the land from his throne at Akkad at least thirty-eight hundred years before the Christian era. Twelve hundred years later Assyria had been settled by colonists from Babylon. Three centuries passed, and then we read of the fall of Babylonia before the Elamites, probably in the twenty-third century, and learn that even in that dim, distant day Babylon, the capital, was a great and marvelous city. Some fifty years later, about 2245 B.C., an energetic ruler, Asshur, founded a rival city, Nineveh—the rich, powerful, and sinful city so bitterly described and denounced in Old Testament lore.

Another leap of seven centuries, and the wild, virile Cosseans disrupted and transformed this ancient civilization of Mesopotamia, and then, about 1200 B.C. the miracle city, Babylon, fell into the hands of the Assyrians. But it was not to be so easily conquered and held. From 1300 B.C. until 690 B.C.—more than six hundred years—the terrors of war swept back and forth over that metropolis and the territory it was

BAKED CLAY CYLINDER INSCRIBED WITH THE ANNALS OF
ASSURBANIPAL, KING OF ASSYRIA
British Museum

supposed to govern. Then came the mighty conqueror, Sennacherib, who leveled its walls to the earth, tore its temples brick from brick, and with flame and pillage destroyed its ancient glory.

But Babylon was to arise with a new and vaster magnificence; for under Nabopolassar and Nebuchadnezzar it was rebuilt and fortified and embellished with temples, mansions, monuments, and statues until it stood the wonder—and the despair—of the ancient world.

THE TIAMAT LEGEND

The real treasures of Babylonian and Assyrian Literature belong to the wonderful seventh century during and after the days of Nebuchadnezzar. The height of the literary Golden Age is under the reign of Sardanapalus or Assurbanipal (668-608), a man who genuinely loved reading and was evidently a born antiquarian. He it was who gathered in his great library at Nineveh the vast collection of ancient documents and copies of the books of all known nations and had them transcribed and translated. How high sounding are the phrases on his book-stamp—the token of ownership attached to every tablet and manuscript in his collection!

The Palace of Assurbanipal, King of Regions, King of Multitudes, King of Assyria, to Whom the God Nebo and the Goddess Tasmeti have granted attentive Ears and Open Eyes to Discover the Writings of the Scribes of My Kingdom, Whom the Kings My Predecessors have Employed. In My Respect for Nebo, the God of Intelligence, I have Collected These Tablets: I have had Them Copied: I have Marked Them with My Name: And I have Deposited Them in My Palace.

Undoubtedly hundreds or even thousands of the leading scholars of the ancient world were on his payroll, and through their zealous efforts there was assembled in his library the richest essence of all the worth-while writings of the races that had lived before his time or even then living.

What is this literature that readers of ancient Babylon perused? First, there are all the usual writings that accompany the power and the glory of an early Asiatic monarch—orders and rules and decrees, state documents, chronologies of historical occurrences preserved in order that posterity might read of the strength, the triumph, the magnificence of King This or That. There are, likewise, poetic chants and prayers, hymns of supplication or praise to gods whose temples have moldered into dust these three thousand years. There are even more ancient poems—cosmogonic verses that endeavor to explain the origins of things. There are descriptions of battles and victories of emperors and the bitter vengeance they wreaked upon their enemies. And, perhaps most interesting of all, there are tales from a mythology so antique that the romantic stories about the Greek and Roman gods seem but of tender years in comparison.

That these people of Mesopotamia were a thoroughly wide-awake commercial nation is proved by the enormous number of contracts, business letters, bills, and receipts, and the frequent excerpts from commercial law found among the wreckage of the cities. Especially was there a heavy exchange of letters during the fifteenth and sixteenth centuries B.C. between Assyria and Egypt, and the fact that nearly all of such communications were written in cuneiforms instead of hieroglyphics or Egyptian hieratic gives a strong hint as to the growing importance of the Babylonian folk and their commercial power.

Such clay documents are undoubtedly of value to students of the material civilization of ancient races, but there is a higher civilization—the culture of the soul—with which literature deals, and to this spiritual expression of the Babylonian soul we shall confine ourselves.

Of the Assyrian cosmogonic legends or the lengthy poems explaining the beginnings of earth and of heaven and of all that dwell therein, certainly the group dealing with Tiamat, the Female Principle of the Universe, is one of the most impressive. There is something titanic about this Mother of all things, this Arch-Rebel against her mighty sons, the gods. She is fit, through her primitive vigor and stupendous valor, to be the Mother of Celestial Monarchs. In the beginning—so this legend of the Mesopotamian plains declares—two vast, vague forms, Tiamat, the female, and Apsu, the male, mingled their essence and thus created the gods. "Before the heavens and the earth were named, when the ocean, first parent of both, (met with) the Abyss Tiamat, the mother of both, the waters of these two mingled. Then, when no fields existed to till, no dry lands anywhere, before the gods had produced these, then were created the gods." But even the gods come and go, live, flourish, and pass out, like earthly dynasties. Who those first Rulers of the Universe were, created by Tiamat and Apsu, who can tell? There were successions of cloudy, nebulous deities long before the better known gods of Babylonia, Anu and Ea, came to reign over the inhabitants of that land.

Thus out of Chaos the Mother Tiamat brought order and separate beings and things, just as in the first chapters of Genesis we discover God making the heavens and the earth from cloudy disorder. And, just as the same first book of the Bible tells of the establishing of a Garden of Eden, so another cosmogonic poem of Babylon relates how the Powers on High devised a land of beauty. Discord, however, entered the Realm of the Gods, just as in the ancient Hebrew legend the angels rebelled against the Most High. But in the Assyrian epic it is the supreme Creator herself who rebels against her apparently over-ambitious and high-handed offspring. It is the eternally recurring story of the struggle between the old and the new—with its pathetic extinction of the old.

Tiamat rises against her children and attempts to hurl them from the celestial thrones. The terrifying message speeds throughout the Kingdom of the Mighty. Who shall arise and go against her who would destroy the very Rulers of the Universe? Even Auer and Ea, chief of all the deities, are filled with consternation by her threats and by the monsters and horrible fiends she marshals for her army. The angry gods gather, planning bitterly, "restless by night and by day." Tiamat, Mother and Creator of them all, assembles the hideous helpers of her own gods— vipers, wild dogs, beings that are half-men, half-scorpions. She chooses Kingu chief of her army. The crisis of the universe is at hand! Who shall lead the ranks of the modern and righteous monarchs of heaven and earth? At length Anshar invites all the gods to a feast and conference. Marduk, the God of Babylon, dares to lead the army of law and order, and

Anshar sends forth this message from the valorous chief: "If I succeed and thus save your lives, you must declare me supreme god of gods. . . . Whatever I do shall be unalterable, my words never be reversed or denied."

With this message before them the assembled gods partake of the feast. "The sweet wine enters their souls." They, in their exalted state of mind, promise to Marduk all that he demands:

> The words of thy mouth shall be unresisted,
> No god shall enter upon thy realm.
>
> . . . .
>
> Thine it shall be to create and to destroy.

They placed before him a magic garment; it came and went as he commanded. It should be a protection to him in battle and a bewilderment to her, Tiamat, implacable foe to the gods. Then Marduk, the fearless, seized his vast bow, his arrows, his mighty spear. Lightning flashed about him. Four poisonous horses he harnessed to his chariot; he grasped the thunderbolt; he went against Tiamat with a net. He went with piercing eyes steadfastly fixed upon the raging Mother. Kingu, her general, lost all thought; he stood powerless. But Tiamat stood unaffrighted.

> She cried wildly, she quivered with rage. . . .
> They rushed to battle—Tiamat and Marduk. . . .
> Over her he cast the net.

In her frenzy she shrieked, but into her widespread mouth he thrust the evil winds until her body was swollen unto bursting. With gasping jaws she then stood speechless. Then ran Marduk his great spear

through her body. He cut out her heart. Her gods
fled, terror-stricken. But his net captured them all;
"they filled the world with their cries; they knew their
doom." He thrust them all conquered into prison.
Then he returned to the corpse of Tiamat, bade the
North Wind take her blood and hide it in one of the
secret places of the Universe. Then with his wondrous keen sword Marduk cut her body into two parts.
Of the upper half he made the vaulted heaven, and
in it built a star-adorned palace for Anu, Bel, and the
many other gods. And in the vaulted dome he fixed
the stars in their places; he established the months and
the year. To the sun-god he gave control of the lofty
realm in the day; to the moon-god he gave control in
the night. . . .

Here the story on the tablets breaks off. The
ravages of war, the destruction of cities, the devasta-
tion of time have torn from us the remainder of this
titanic epic of the gods of Ancient Babylon. Some day,
perhaps, our explorers will discover the records which
tell the remainder of this gigantic vision of the age-
long effort of the Female Principle to conquer the universe of gods and men.

In it all is there not something reminiscent of that
momentous battle of Greek mythology when the
younger generation of the Celestial Rulers rose against
the Titans and brought about a new dynasty in the
annals of Heaven? Such a poem as this of Tiamat is
the fruit of long evolution. It is not the sudden work
of one man; but stratum upon stratum, it has been
built up. And over into other national lores has gone
this legend of the misty Mesopotamian empire. Surely
Tiamat is the Tekom of Genesis, the primeval chaos

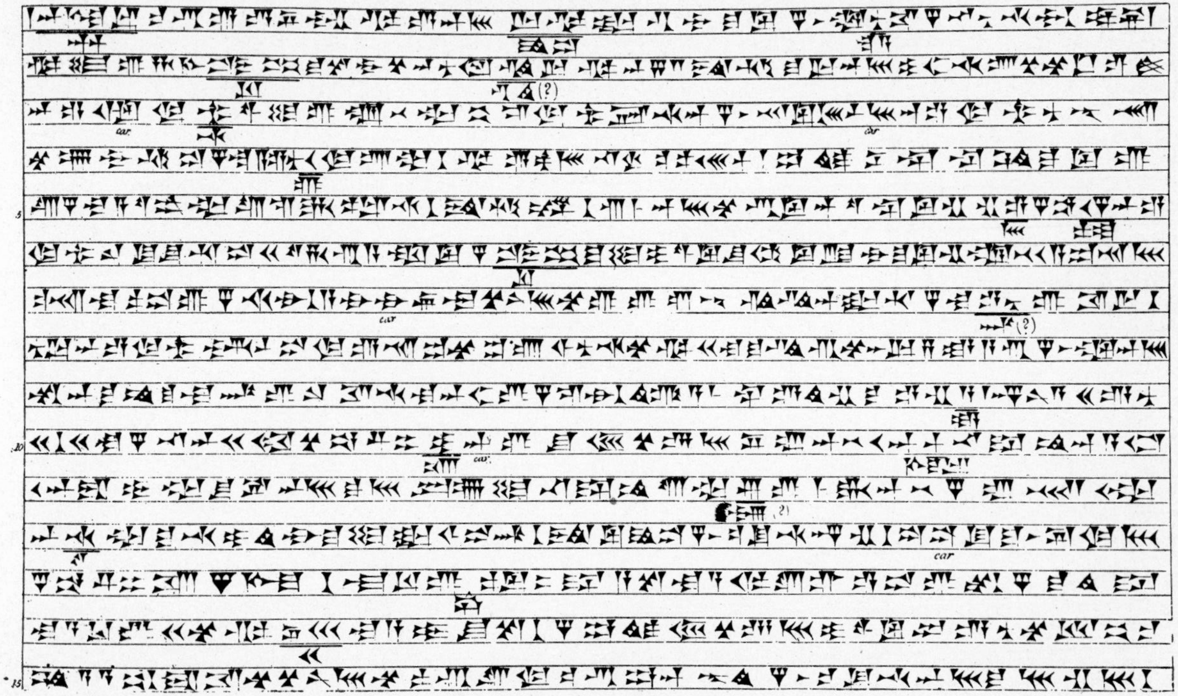

ANNALS OF SARDANAPALUS, ABOUT B.C. 880

British Museum

or abyss, while her struggle with Marduk is but a fore-runner of the venerable legend of Michael and the Dragon.[1]

THE IZDUBAR EPIC

Even more closely related, in one respect, to the lore of the Old Testament is that Babylonian story of time immemorial, the Izdubar or Gilgamesh Epic; for in this wild Mesopotamian tale of war and love and jealousy and far wanderings is found the original of the Biblical legend of the Flood.

This Izdubar poem, discovered by George Smith in 1872, is inscribed upon twelve tablets, each relating a separate episode or chapter or canto. Thus the first tablet reveals the hero delivering the nation from the Elamites, about 2000 B.C. The next four sections are fragmentary, but evidently are intended to tell of his slaughter of the Elamite leaders. In the sixth tablet comes the fierce passion of Ishtar, the Babylonian goddess of love, for the hero, Izdubar. She shame-lessly offers herself to him, but he, mindful of the mys-terious fate that had befallen so many of her previous lovers, rejects her. She, however, is the daughter of the mighty god Anu, and to him she hastens, begging vengeance. That all-powerful father sends against Gilgamesh or Izdubar a mighty bull, but the beast falls before the strength of the hero. Then Ishtar, in her mad jealousy, heaps a curse upon him, but the curse is returned upon her. Vengeance must be hers. Down to the nether world she goes to seek further means of punishment.

---

[1] For specimens from fragments containing the Tiamat Legend, see George Smith's *Chaldean Account of Genesis,* New York, Scribner, Armstrong & Co., 1876, p. 99.

It is a vague, unhappy sort of place—this realm of
the dead—not a kingdom of dire torture akin to the
orthodox Hell, but, rather, the indefinite, wearisome,
monotonous Sheol of the ancient Hebrews. "In that
abode of darkness and famine earth is their food, clay
their nourishment. No light is seen there; all dwell in
darkness. There ghosts, like birds, flutter their wings.
The dust lies undisturbed on the door and the pillars
of the gates."

> There live the rulers and unconquerable ones,
> The poets, the mighty ones,
> And monsters of the deep.

To this gloomy realm came Ishtar. To the keeper
of the gates she cried, "O Keeper! Open thy gates!
Open thy gates, I say, that I may enter. If thou
openest not thy gates, I will assault the doors; I will
break down the gates; I will attack the entrance; I
will split open the portals. I will raise the dead to be
devourers of the living. The dead shall prey upon
the living."

But the porter said to the mighty Ishtar, "Stay,
lady. Shake not the door. I will go and tell this to
the Queen Nin-ki-gal." And the gate-keeper went to
the Queen and declared, "Thy sister Ishtar blasphemes
thee with great curses."

"Ah," cried Nin-ki-gal, "I will cure her rage! I
will repay these curses to her! Light up consuming
fires. Let her groan with the husbands who deserted
their wives. Let her groan with the wives who departed from their husbands' side. Let her groan with
the youths who have led dishonorable lives. Go,

The Dawn in Babylon and Assyria 61

Porter, open the gate to her, but strip her as others are stripped on such occasions."

Then opened the keeper the gates. "Enter, Lady. It is permitted. The Sovereign of Hades will come to meet thee." And Ishtar passed the first gate, but she was detained and the great crown taken from her head. "Keeper," she exclaimed, "take not the great crown from me!" "Enter, Lady," was the reply of the gate-keeper; "for the Queen of this land demands her jewels."

Thus through entrance after entrance she passed, each time leaving behind her some ornament or garment, until past the seventh and last gate she went, naked, to stand before her ireful sister. Then came bitter words and looks of hatred, and at length the command that she, Ishtar, the Babylonian Goddess of Love, should be put to the torture.

But without the Goddess of Love how could the world survive? For what is life without love? The earth began to wilt and fade; all living creatures began to approach the end of existence. Then the sun and the moon drew nigh to the God-King, Hea, and weeping declared, "Ishtar has descended beneath the earth and has not risen again, and since she has departed the bull has not sought the cow, nor the male of any animal the female. The master has ceased to command and the slave to obey. Peace has gone from the world; confusion reigns."

Then Hea, the crafty god, devised a phantom in the image of a man and said to it, "Go, Phantom, save her. The seven gates of Hades will open for thee, and Nin-ki-gal will come to meet thee. Then awe her with the names of the great gods. Then prepare thy frauds. Bring forth fishes from empty vessels. So astounded will Nin-ki-gal be over these things that she will restore Ishtar her garments. Go, Phantom, and save her. The vast assembly of the people shall crown thee for it."

And thus the Goddess of Love was freed from the darkness of the underworld, and happiness and order prevailed once more in the universe.

So throughout the remaining tablets, mere shattered fragments miraculously saved during the thousands of years of war and wreckage, this hoary tale of gods and god-like heroes weaves its way. At length Izdubar, desperately ill and longing for a remedy, seeks among the fellowship of the immortals his ancestor, old Hasisadra, the Noah of Babylonian legend. And from this patriarch the young hero hears the story of the Universal Flood—the first account of it in the annals of man.

Shamas, the Sun-God, decreed a mighty flood and spoke thus to the pious Hasisadra, "In the night I will cause it to rain from the heavens. Enter, therefore, into thy ship and make fast the door." And the man went into his ship, and for sealing it he gave to Buzur-Sadirabi, the boatman, the palace with all its goods. Then began the raging of the storm "from the horizon of heaven extending far and wide. Vul in the midst of it thundered, and Nebo and Saru went in front; the throne-bearers went over mountains and plains; the destroyer Nergal overturned; Ninip went in front and cast down; the spirits carried destruction, and in their glory they swept the earth. The flood of Vul reached to the heavens. The glorious earth was

turned to a waste. Brother no longer saw his brother;
it spared no people."

Then even the gods in Heaven were filled with fear
and ascended to the highest realm of Anu. "There
the gods were crowded in droves, prostrate like dogs."
And Ishtar uttered these words, "All were turned to
corruption, and I long ago prophesied evil in the
presence of the gods. I declared that the people whom
I, the mother, have begotten, now like the young of
the fishes fill the sea." Then the gods, grieving for
the dead, wept with her; the gods, seated in their
places, covered their lips in sorrow for the approaching
evil.

For six days the deluge, the wind, the storm overwhelmed all. But on the seventh day the turmoil
ceased, and the flood, which had destroyed like an
earthquake, was calmed. The god caused the sea to
dry and the hurricane and the waters ended. And
then Hasisadra saw the sea tossing and all of mankind
on it turning to corruption. "The corpses floated like
reeds." He opened a window, and looked forth. "I
sat down and wept; the tears flowed over my face."

At length, however, the land began to rise from the
ocean. And the ship came to the mountain of Nizir
and was not able to pass over it. Six days there was
nothing to be seen but Nizir and the water. Then,
declared Hasisadra, "On the seventh day I sent forth
a dove, and it left. The dove returned; for it found
no resting place. I sent forth a swallow, and it too
returned. I sent forth a raven. And the raven went
and saw the corpses on the water and did eat. It wandered away and did not return."

Then he sent forth the animals "to the four winds."

"And I poured out a libation, I built an altar on the peak of the mountain. I took seven jugs of wine, and at the bottom of them I placed reeds, pines and spices. The gods collected at that burning; the gods gathered like flies over the sacrifice."

This, then, is the legend which the Hebrews obtained from the Babylonians, possibly as early as 1600 B.C.—a legend which was further impressed upon them during their exile "by the waters of Babylon" in the sixth century B.C. Strange, is it not, that this bit of folklore, possibly brought to the Babylonians by invading tribes of centuries long before the first coming of the Hebrews, should have persisted throughout more than thirty-five hundred years and should have become an accepted part in a book considered sacred by nearly half of the inhabitants of the globe? [2]

FOLK TALES

Such stories as the ones just related are "in the grand style," epical, cosmic. Were there no tales of a humbler type, shorter, simpler, that might be told about the evening fire? Assuredly. Judging by the specimens discovered among the shattered stone and clay tablets of the ruined cities of the Mesopotamian plains and valleys, there were innumerable briefer narratives to please the simple-minded laborers and peasants.

There was, for instance, the story of the hostility

[2] For full account of Izdubar Legend see George Smith: *Chaldean Account of Genesis*, New York, Scribner, Armstrong & Co., 1876, and the same author's *Assyrian Discoveries*, Scribner, Armstrong & Co., 1875. The above account of the flood is based on George Smith's translation in *Publications of the Society of Biblical Archæology*, December, 1872, London, Vol. II. C. J. Ball's translation of Paul Haupt's German translation may be found in *Records of the Past*, London, S. Bagster & Sons, 1874, Vol. I.

BABYLONIAN CLAY TABLETS
Metropolitan Museum of Art

between the eagle and the serpent, who complained to the sun that the eagle had devoured all the young of the snake. The sun advised the serpent to seek to ensnare the robber bird by means of a dead ox as bait, but the wise old eagle escaped through his sagacity. And there is another legend concerning the eagle and an ambitious mortal, Etana, who aspired to visit the high heavens. Clutched in the talons of the eagle, the man rose through the celestial zones until, in the words of the eagle, the ocean seemed but a gardener's ditch and the land like to the bed of a tiny yard. They ascended even to Anu's realm, and then on toward the far kingdom of Ishtar. "Two hours more the eagle bore him higher, and said, 'My friend, see the land, how it lies.'" But the mortal heart of Etana began to lose its courage, and in fright he begged the eagle to fly no farther. And at that moment, when the heart of the one failed, so failed the heart of the other; the strength of the bird suddenly passed, and Etana, possibly the first "bird man" or aviator mentioned in human annals, crashed with the eagle to the earth.

Whether the narrative is a bit of allegory dealing with man's vaulting ambition, or whether it is intended to impress the thought that when human courage fails all else fails, we shall never know. The legend remains after all the centuries as a curious invention of the dreams of early mankind.

Then, there was that ancient story—probably of the sixteenth century B.C.—of Adapa and the South Wind. Doubtless for hundreds of years toilers in the streets of Babylon and Nineveh and in the far-stretched fields of Babylonia and Assyria told and retold this venerable

bit of fiction.   Adapa, out fishing one day, was playfully
overwhelmed by the South Wind and was "ducked."
In a sudden rage he broke the wings of the Wind.
But the world began to wither because of the failure
of the balmy South Wind to blow, and the High God,
Anu, summoned Adapa to appear before the heavenly
throne and answer for himself.   But the wise one, Ea,
instructed Adapa as to what he should do and as to
how he should act when he appeared in the celestial
realm.   He should be dressed in mourning garments,
and he should reject all food and drink.   And thus
Adapa enters, "armored in cunning," before the mighty
Anu.   The excuses presented by the youth appease the
God, but the host regrets that the earthly one has refused food and drink in the heavens; for in so doing
he has rejected immortal life.

> Anu looked at him with mournful eyes—
> "Why, O Adapa, hast thou now
> Refused to eat and drink?
> Now canst thou not live forever!"

It is a tale somewhat akin to the Eden story of
Genesis.   For in both a mortal loses immortality by
disobeying a ruling dealing with food.   It may well
be that the Hebrews, through their close relationship
with the Babylonians through many centuries, accepted
and transformed many a legend or idea for the earlier
chapters of the Old Testament.[3]

Vainglorious Boastings

Of course, from among these peoples of the Babylonian or Assyrian empires we hear coming down the
ages the same heroically boastful tones of sovereignty

[3] For other specimens, see Smith's *Chaldean Account of Genesis.*

as have echoed through thousands of years of national
life in other great realms of the East. The announce-
ments of a monarch of the Mesopotamian government
of three or four thousand years ago possess all the
vast, portentous dignity that we have learned to
expect from Oriental potentates. Hear, for example,
these lines from an inscription dealing with King
Sennacherib:

> Sennacherib, the Great, the Mighty One,
> King of Assyria, Monarch of the World,
> And Ruler of the Four Zones.
> Wise Shepherd of the Flocks,
> Beloved of the great gods,
> Lover of the right and Defender of justice,
> Strength to the weak, granter of aid,
> Perfect as hero, steadfast as warrior,
> The chief of kings.
> Conqueror of rebels, slayer of foes.

Then follows, with unabashed boastfulness, an account of his conquests—how the rebellious princes fled
to the hills at his coming, how he destroyed their captured leaders, and how he bound their corpses to poles
about the cities.

And Hezekiah of Judah, who had not bowed before me, his
strong cities—forty-six of them—and innumerable smaller
towns I besieged and tore down, and two hundred thousand,
one hundred and fifty men and women, young and old, I took
as spoil. And as for Hezekiah, I shut him up in his own city,
Jerusalem; his own walls I fortified against him. Hezekiah
was overcome with fear of my glittering power. All the
Arabians and other strong warriors whom he had brought into
his city for its defense bowed in fear. And then I brought

with me to Nineveh, my own city, thirty talents of gold, eight hundred talents of silver, couches of ivory, ivory thrones, precious gems, the women of his own palace. Then sent he messengers to offer me tribute and to pay me homage.

And what have the oppressed, the victims of this all-powerful Sennacherib to say of him and his victories? Read it in the Second Book of Kings of the Old Testament of the Jews of that day:

Now in the fourteenth year of King Hezekiah did Sennacherib, King of Assyria, come up against all the fenced cities of Judah, and took them. . . . And the King of Assyria appointed unto Hezekiah, King of Judah, three hundred talents of silver and thirty talents of gold. And Hezekiah gave him all the silver that was found in the house of the Lord and in the treasures of the King's house.

And Rabshakeh (of Assyria) said unto them: ". . . . Hath any of the gods of the nations delivered at all his land out of the hand of the King of Assyria? Who are they among all the gods of the countries that have delivered their country out of mine hand, that the Lord should deliver Jerusalem out of mine hand?

And Isaiah said unto them, "Thus shall ye say to your master, Thus saith the Lord, 'Be not afraid of the words which thou hast heard, with which the servants of the King of Assyria have blasphemed me. Behold, I will send a blast upon him, and he shall hear a rumor, and shall return to his own land; and I will cause him to fall by the sword in his own land.' "

And it came to pass that night that the angel of the Lord went out and smote the camp of the Assyrians an hundred fourscore and five thousand; and when they arose early in the morning, behold they were all dead corpses. . . . And it came to pass, as Sennacherib was worshiping in the house of his god, that his sons smote him with the sword, and they escaped into the land of Armenia. And Esarhaddon, his son, reigned in his stead.[4]

This, then, was the vainglorious monarch of Babylonia and Assyria who strove to oppress the Hebrews and vanquish the Hebrew God of those tumultuous days in the dim dawn of civilization. "Vanity, vanity, saith the preacher, all is vanity!"

BABYLONIAN CHANTS AND PRAYERS

Far more human, far more touching, far more pathetic and dramatic are the chants and prayers that winged their way heavenward from the powerful but often unhappy people of the Mesopotamian empire. To-day we find on the scarred faces of the ancient tablets the same heart-felt plaints as might come from the tortured soul of some repentant transgressor of the twentieth century. Here was a genuine religious consciousness—a high development of the religious spirit, such as the average modern might consider as belonging only to our own era. It is the old, old cry of contrition for mistakes and blunders and sins of the flesh.

Frequently composed with the same parallelism of structure as is found in the Biblical Psalms, these hymns and supplications of the ancient enemies of the Hebrews speak with not only a sincerity but an art and dignity befitting the theme. Frequently the composition is in the form of an anthem, or musical dialogue, the repentant one calling upon the gods for forgiveness, and the priest replying. Through the great halls

[4] For Assyrian account of Hezekiah see George Smith: *Assyrian Discoveries.*

of the lofty temples of worship echoed the sorrow-laden voice of the sinner:

> Full of sin, I cry to thee.
> Thou dost accept; hear the earnest prayer of a sinner!
> Whomever thou lookest upon liveth.

Then the deep tones of the priest roll solemnly forth among the vast pillars, calling upon the Most High to hear the plea of the sorrowing one:

> He calleth unto thee.
> Turn thy face to give, grant him thy hand!

Once more the praying mortal cries to his Deity:

> Look down in pity upon me!
> Oh, accept my sorrow!
> For there is no other God to guide me.
> Behold, like the dove, I am filled with sighing!
> Oh, Divine One, let thy face he softened,
> Let thy kindness beam upon me!

Hear once more the priest and the suppliant in a penitential psalm. First the cry of the sinner:

Besides thee there is no god who guideth aright.
Look with true favor upon me and accept my supplication.
Declare "how long" (I am to wait) and let thy liver be pacified.
When, O my mistress, will thy face be turned?
Like the doves do I moan, in sighs do I abound!

Then the priest adds his plea to the Power Above:

With woe and grief, full of sighs, is his soul;
Tears doth he weep, laments doth he pour forth.

. . . .

Because of his face, which he doth not raise on account of tears,
doth he raise lamentations to thee.

Because of his feet, on which fetters are laid, doth he raise
lamentations to thee.

Because of his hands, which are exhausted through weakness,
doth he raise lamentations to thee.

Because of his heart, which like a flute pipes forth in cries, doth
he raise lamentations to thee.

Then the suppliant in deepest remorse:

O mistress, in the anguish of my heart have I raised cries of
anguish to thee; declare forgiveness!

O mistress, to thy servant declare respite! May thy heart be
at rest.

Unto thy servant who hath experienced sorrow, grant mercy.[5]

Or, perhaps, we enter the great temple just as the
full-voiced priests are chanting an ancient hymn to the
mighty goddess, Ishtar. Is it so different from the song
of praise that resounds in our own cathedrals every
Sunday?

A light of heaven, which like fire rises resplendent over the
earth, art thou,

Goddess, when thou appearest on the earth;

Glorious like the earth art thou!

As for thee, the path of justice bring thee gracious blessing.

When thou enterest the house of man—

A jackal, who goes on the hunt for a lamb, art thou,

A lion, who roams about in the field, art thou.

Welcome, maid, beauty of heaven.

Maid Ishtar, beauty of heaven!

Adorned with splendid decorations, beauty of heaven,

Sister of the Sun-god, beauty of heaven.[6]

[5] Translation by R. F. Harper: *Assyrian and Babylonian Literature,*
New York, D. Appleton & Co., 1901, p. 433.
[6] *Ibid.,* p. 429.

There is no lack of the "agony of tears" in these petitions of three or four thousand years ago—no lack of even that bewilderment which sometimes confuses the stumbling prayer of modern man as he seeks to discover how to express himself to the Infinite One.

> The sin which I have done, I know not.
>   The God angry with me—
>   The Goddess angry with me—
>   May they be appeased!
>
> O Lord, how many are my trespasses!
>   How great my sins!
>
> I have searched for help,
>   But there was none to take mine hand.
> I wept,
>   But there was none came to me.
>
> Sorrowful I lay me down upon the earth;
>   I look not up.
> O God, gaze down upon me,
>   And hearken to my prayer! [7]

Through bitter experience those praying souls of long ago had learned what many a seeker for help has since learned—how feeble a reed is man, how fickle our hopes in mortal stability and the changeable efforts of men:

> What do they know, men of any degree?
> Nothing they know.
> They know nothing, even though they do good or evil.
> Then, God, cast not from thee thy servant.
> O Lord, forgive my sins, though they be seven times seven!

Have the revolutions of the hands of the clock of Time greatly transformed the heart and soul of man?

[7] Author's version.

In the cries of these aching hearts of the long ages past do we not hear the voice of our brother? Have the marvels of science, the inventions of modern times made us, in our innermost spirit, strangers to those dark people who gathered in the streets of Babylon and Nineveh? Surely we may say with that Babylonian proverb: "The life of yesterday goes on every day." [8]

[8] For specimens of Babylonian liturgies see *Records of the Past,* Washington, Records of the Past Exploration Society, 1912, Vol. 10. For Babylonian divinations, *ibid.,* Vol. 12.

III

THE DAWN IN INDIA

DOWN through the highlands and jungles of India some thirty-five or forty centuries ago, came a race of people who called themselves Aryans. What their original source was we do not know, but we do know that they appeared in the north-western part of India and that they had, in all probability, moved over from the eastern portion of Persia, long known as Aria.

They were a proud people—proud of their blood, proud of their differences from the Sudras and other dark tribes that they found already inhabiting the Indian valleys, and proud of their occupation as tillers of the soil. The very origin of their tribal name, Arya, meant plowman or worker on the land, a root-word preserved to this day in *acre, area,* and *Iran,* the native name of Persia.

It was a marvelously prolific people—this Aryan throng that slowly moved into the steaming valleys of Southern India. Every race of modern Europe, except the Turanians, such as the Turks, and the Semitics, such as the Jews, is a descendant of this ever-conquering race. They themselves, with true national egotism, gave to themselves an antiquity not at all justified by the evidence at hand. To judge by their own legends, one would naturally conclude that for tens of thousands of years, they had possessed the Punjab, the valley of the Ganges, the uttermost recesses of

India; but the fact remains that their records are so vague as to be almost worthless historically until the conquest by Darius in 512 B.C.

It is not that there is a lack of early literature; for the writings of the Hindus are the most plentiful of all national records that have come down from ancient days. Nor is it a matter of difficulty interpreting the writings; for there have been no problems of deciphering and translating, such as are found in Egyptian hieroglyphics. But the farther the Aryans descended, the more dreamy, the more speculative, the more indifferent to accuracy they became. Then, too, their main religions, Brahmanism and Buddhism, taught a philosophy so abstract and so scornful of the transitory incidents of this earthly life, that mortal existence came to be looked upon as an evil, something to be forgotten and not emphasized through historical documents. To a people longing only for reabsorption into the Eternal, the Nirvana, the details of what this king did, or what that army performed, were an obnoxious nuisance, certainly unworthy of the energy required for placing upon papyrus or clay tablet or stone monument. To the investigator of chronology or of history their constant answer would have been, "What's the use?"

Their first books apparently originated sometime between 2000 B.C. and 1600 B.C., but as they were written on palm leaves or some other form of dried vegetable matter they soon perished, and to-day we must depend upon copies and other much later relics of their writing. We know, however, the original language of those ancient records of Hindu thought and emotion. Well was it called Sanskrit—"Perfected"—for it was a noble tongue, dignified, accurate, facile, the virile forefather of most of the languages of modern Europe and Asia.

It lent itself well to the high thoughts of a people deeply interested in philosophy and religion, and long did the upper class of India, the priests and the scholars, cherish it. But, like all other earthly things, its day of service passed, and there came into existence a corrupted form of speech known as Prakrit or "mongrel" tongue. This Prakrit was the natural and necessary outcome of the Hindu's mingling with the less intellectual tribes of Southern India, and it was more serviceable for trade and daily affairs. But, though Sanskrit ceased to be a spoken language more than twenty centuries ago, we may find to this day its high-bred, pure idiom in the sacred and genuinely classical literature of the Hindus.

THE VEDAS

What Bible or Bibles, what hymns, what prayers, what commentaries on sacred lore did these people descending from the northern highlands to the fetid jungles of the South produce?

The *Vedas*—it is a title often heard, but seldom understood. Yet the four books comprising the Vedas are among the world's greatest and highest philosophical writings—the source of the religious faith of hundreds of millions of people living to-day, and the springs from which have flowed bounteous streams of fable, legend, and poetry.

Veda—the word itself signifies knowledge—not puny human knowledge, but that divine, unwritten knowledge which comes from the Eternal Energy, the

Self-Existent, the God, the Brahma. The root of that ancient word, Brahma, means strength, and well has it justified its original meaning. For though the centuries have passed, and religions and sects have risen and fallen, still Brahmanism flourishes and the Brahman priests feed with spiritual food their tens of millions of Oriental believers. Buddhism, its greatest rival for some centuries after the sixth century B.C., spread with almost incredible speed and strength; but at length the elder faith completely exiled the younger from India. To-day Buddhism sinks its roots deep into such lands as China, Japan, Siam, and Ceylon, but is destroyed, trunk and branch, in the land of its birth.

Strange, is it not, that in spite of the innumerable conquests of invading armies from the days of Alexander and Tamburlaine to this hour of British possession, in spite of the prolonged onslaughts of Buddhism, Mohammedanism, and Christianity, this ancient faith, Brahmanism, stands seemingly invincible? Seldom seeking conquest itself, it has been the "credo" and the spiritual strength not only of countless millions of humble laborers, but of the leaders in philosophy and things intellectual throughout Mother India. There must be in such a religion certain eternal principles of justice, certain theories of spiritual consolation, certain high ideals of righteousness that offer solace and comfort to the harassed soul of man. What are the offerings, then, of these ancient Vedas—the Bible of a vast proportion of this globe's inhabitants?

There is an old Hindu word, *Sanhita,* which means "collected" or "put together." The *Vedas* consist of four Sanhitas, and their names are the *Rig-veda,* the *Sama-veda,* the *Yajur-veda,* and the *Atharva-veda.*

The second and third of these are, in a sense, liturgies
—chants and formal recitals for certain ceremonies and
occasions, and are therefore interesting as revealing
not only customs, but also that inevitable tendency of
religion to stiffen into formalism. But the first and
last of these vedas, the *Rig-veda* and the *Atharva-veda,*
are philosophical and quasi-historical, and reveal the
imagination of a people of no mean intellect working
upon the problems of this life and the next.

In the *Rig-veda* we find nearly eleven thousand
stanzas, simple in meter and for the most part easy of
translation—the whole comprising a dignified body of
worship of the Divine. To those primitive tribes
gradually creeping down from the North and at all
times keeping close to the soil, Nature was *the* God.
Theirs was, in fact, a high type of Pantheism—God in
everything. Necessarily, in such a worship the terms
used are not precise but vague, and the very vagueness
of their noble and often beautiful chants and songs
and prayers permitted to the contemplative Hindu
manifold mystical interpretations.

The folk of India discovered, however, in this very
vagueness, which might delight the imagination, a certain lack of that personal element which the soul longs
to find in religion. They began to desire a more concrete god—or gods. Abstracting this or that attribute
of the original Divine Being, they personified these
traits—strength, wisdom, light, etc.—into gods more
comprehensible, more personal. Have not other religions done the same thing? Have not other religions
their saints personifying this or that attribute of the
Creator? Man longs to remold his God into his own
image.

So with the Hindu; he at length had his Varuna, one of the oldest derivatives of the Brahma; Indra, the monarch of the Heavens; Agni, the god of fire; Soma, the spirit of intoxication, the Bacchus of India. To each of these and others—what hymns and invocations and petitions! To Indra arose, nearly three thousand years ago, such a chant of praise and prayer as—

> Immortal Indra, infinitely wise,
> Remorseless foe of drought and dark,
> Irresistible in might, and
> Relentless crusher of all enemies!
> A fortress to thy worshipers!
> To thee our ardent hymns and praise.
> Thou art our advocate and friend,
> Our brother, father, mother all in one.
> Most fatherly of fathers, we are thine,
> And thou art ours. Oh, may thy soul
> Hear us in compassion as we praise!
> Destroy us not for one sin or for many.
> Spare us to-day, to-morrow, and for aye.
>
> Vainly the demons oppose their strength,
> Vainly to keep from us thy watery treasures.
> Earth quakes with crashings of thy bolts,
> And shattered lies the foe, and crushed his towers,
> His legions fall, his mighty force
> Shattered in dust. Then, the waters,
> Long held back, rush down
> In torrents to the earth, and rivers,
> Swollen, foaming, swirl to the ocean,
> And roar the triumph of the Thunderer.[1]

And to Varuna went up daily from the valley of the Ganges such a hymn as

[1] Adapted from the version by M. Monier-Williams: *Indian Wisdom*, London, William H. Allen & Co., 1875.

May we live safely under thy protection,
O Varuna, far-ruling, Lord of heroes.
Ye sons of Aditi, whom none deceiveth,
Ye gods, in covenant of grace accept us.

Free me from sin, which in bonds has long held me;
May I forever hold to the way of justice.
Tear not the thread of song that I weave;
Break not the poor workmen's staff untimely.

And O thou Varuna, spare me from terrors,
O Righteous One, gaze on me tenderly,
Keep sorrow from me as from a young creature.
Oh, without thee I draw not a breath!

Thou Ruler of worlds sendest forth rivers,
And they flow, Varuna, as thou ordainest;
They fail not nor faint—they never weary;
They pass o'er the earth as birds o'er the heavens.[2]

Are those stanzas so far removed from the hymns of our own chapels and cathedrals? And is the mingling of gratitude and prayer in this chant to Agni, the god of fire, so very different from our own salutations?

Thou art thyself a great god and lord,
The giver of life and immortality,
One in thy essence, but yet three,
Revealing thy undying triple form
As fire on earth, the lightning in the sky,
The sun in heaven. O welcome guest
In every home—thou father, brother, son,
Friend, and protector, all in one!
Deliver, O Mighty God, thy worshipers,

[2] Based on the translation by John Muir: *Original Sanskrit Texts,* London, Williams & Norgate, 1863, Vol. V.

Cleanse us from taint of sin, and when we die,
Be merciful toward us on the pyre
That burns our bodies with their guilt,
And lift our eternal souls aloft
To brighter homes and realms of joy,
Forever there to abide with the righteous.[3]

To the composers of the *Rig-veda* Nature was something in which to delight, and many a song did they chant in honor of that most lovable of all the gifts of Nature—the sunlight. Varuna, the primitive god, had at length become the ruler of the realm of darkness, but the happy god of the Sun was Mitra. And to Mitra the Brahman priests of long centuries ago sang such praise as:

All-seeing Sun, the stars so bright,
Glowing so clear throughout the night,
Now frightened hasten far away,
O'ercome by thy dazzling ray.
Bright God, thou searchest then
The deeds and works of mortal men;
Thou sweepest the sky and with thy rays
Measurest out to us our days;
Thine eye all living things surveys.[4]

There was, also, a special goddess of the dawn, Ushas, the Hindu Aurora, around whose beauties the Indian imagination wove many an amorous and luscious poem.

Fair Goddess, thou smilest softly,
Revealing the beauty of thy youth,
Thy glowing face, thy warm bosom,
The glory of thy bright hair.

[3] Version with some changes, by M. Monier-Williams: *Indian Wisdom*.
[4] Based on John Muir's translation in *Original Sanskrit Texts*, London, Williams & Norgate, 1863, Vol. V.

Thus a happy and loving bride
Bedecks herself in glorious form,
And before her lover's ardent eyes
Proudly displays her charms.

But look, the amorous Sun
Pursues and wins thee soon!
Quickly he grasps thee in his arms—
Thou and he are one![5]

In later ages Brahma became the leading god. Then his emanations, Siva and Vishnu, were the supreme ones, until the more personal, decidedly human god, Krishna, surpassed all others in popular favor.

Such was the spontaneous, joyous religion of the Aryans—"people of the soil." Theirs was a faith based upon daily contact with the elements of Nature, a religion springing naturally from a soul filled with admiration and healthy happiness.

Hindu Philosophy

But time seizes upon religions as upon all other organisms, and at length brings upon them weakness, senility. Such a degeneracy is revealed in the *Sama-veda*, containing the songs sung to the Soma, the spirit of the soma plant, from which an intoxicant was made. Such a fading of religion into a dead formalism is shown in the *Yajur-veda*, with its set rituals; such a death of lofty religious idealism is found in the *Atharva-veda*, with its songs of incantations for driving away this or that evil spirit and overcoming this or that devil.

[5] Based on a medley of hymns to Ushas presented in John Muir: *Original Sanskrit Texts,* Vol. V. Numerous translations of Hindu hymns may be found in Muir's *Metrical Translations from Sanskrit Writers,* London, Trübner & Co., 1879.

Though debased by ceremonials and by superstitions, doubtless absorbed from the native races whom the Aryans conquered, this ancient Brahman religion possessed certain principles that any creed must have if it is to appeal to the higher nature of man. Here was, for instance, the ideal of self-denial and reverence for those who renounced the pleasures of the body for the good of the soul. Here, too, was the principle of compensation—a just reward or retribution for every deed done in the flesh. Among the followers of Brahmanism it developed into the theory of transmigration: that the spirit of every mortal would return to earth to live in the condition for which his previous life had prepared him—the glutton in the form of a pig; the cunning in the form of a fox; the gentle, the just, the wise in the form of a highly spiritual man, a little lower than the angels.

Around such a faith, around such vague and beautifully suggestive books as the *Vedas,* grew up an immense literature of religious commentary, philosophy, and legend. How those high-caste Hindus did—and do—love to discuss the subtleties of theology and the psychology of religion! While a Westerner might expend his intellectual energies upon the problems of science or business and industrial organizations, these Indians, with the blood of hundreds of generations of philosophers in their veins, may have come closer to penetrating the veil of the Unseen than we more practical people of the West.

What compilations of religious thought they zealously collected throughout the centuries! The *Brahmanas,* with their maxims, their comments on the venerable Vedic hymns; the *Puranas,* with their col-

lections of traditions and legends illuminating the
Vedas; the *Upapuranas,* with their commentaries upon
the commentaries known as the *Puranas;* the *Upanishads,* with their marvelous writings in prose and
poetry on the philosophy of life here and hereafter;
the *Sutras,* or fantastic explanations of the antique religious ceremonies—all these and other bulky volumes
reveal the soul of a people whose chief interest in life
was to understand that Riddle of the Universe, God.
How sacred all these writings became, how they were
studied, how they were reflected upon and argued
about! How they split the Hindus into this sect and
that!

But the evil days drew nigh—in spite of, or perhaps
because of, much speculation and debate and argumentation. The effort to explain the growing number
of deities as mere manifestations of Brahma was not
altogether a success; it led to more division of opinion,
more stubborn holding to this or that unimportant
tenet. Then came the endeavor to place the Brahman
priesthood closer to God than the layman could ever
hope to be. Thus originated the most blighting influence that ever touched India—the caste system. The
time came—and is—when the highest group—"the
true sons of God"—hastened home to take a bath if
even the mere shadow of a "common" man fell upon
them. The rules governing this caste system grew so
rigid that he who was far from the rank of priest
might scarcely hope, even through the aid of transmigration, to reach in untold ages the blissful state of
Heaven. Pythagoras, the Greek thinker and scientist,
learned in India this theory of the transmigration of
the soul, and established upon it an inspiring philos-

ophy of life; but the lower caste Indian saw in it little aid for his accursed state.

The highest, most subtle philosophy of all the Hindu religious writings is found, it is generally conceded, in the *Upanishads*. What is the gist of it all? What gateways to happiness, or what is perhaps better, contentment, are opened for harassed, bewildered mortals? The essence of the whole matter is found perhaps in the little school girl's explanation of Emerson's poem, *Brahma*—simply "God everywhere." Nothing exists, declares this Brahman philosophy, except Brahma, the universal spirit. Forms of life, so-called substances, souls, the very gods themselves are merely apparently separate existences, creations of our deluded senses, and in reality simply manifestations of the All-Spirit. The so-called universe is a vain, fleeting show, deserving little of the wise soul's energy or attention. The true aim of every human creature should be an early reunion with the Universal Spirit—which is our home.

But how to gain this longed-for consummation? How shall mortal man escape the long, long, chain of transmigrations for deeds done in the body? How shall he pass quickly back into his original source, the "Over-Soul," the All-Enveloping God? Here, from ancient India, come some suggestions that we hurried folk of the Western hemisphere might well consider, if not accept literally. Says this philosophy arising from the *Vedas:* Suppress desire; for desire hinders the progress of the spirit. Withdraw from the world and its temptations, turmoil, luxuries, and destructive influence upon the spirit. Cease to act; for action is largely a vain thing, gains no spiritual results, and only

calls attention more emphatically to the physical.
Contemplate incessantly; contemplate on the Supreme
One until even here in the flesh reabsorption into that
Over-Spirit begins.   Thus and thus only may one hope
to escape the fate of endless returns to this life.

It is a difficult philosophy for Occidentals to understand—and probably a bitter one when understood.

> The world is too much with us, late and soon,
> Getting and spending, we lay waste our powers.

Of all Westerners probably Wordsworth came nearest
to this idea or ideal—as you will—of regaining God
through a concentrated meditation which lifts man
from the bounds of the physical.

The *Brahmanas,* the *Puranas,* the *Upanishads*—
what quaint and curious lore they contain, what gems
of wisdom bought with ages of experience, what
heights and depths of thought!   Here one discovers
hints of tales and legends that have become universal.
We have seen in Assyrian or Babylonian tradition the
story of the Flood; we shall see it again when we come
to the literature of the Hebrews.   Here it is as the
Hindus tell it in the *Brahmana:*

> There lived in ancient time a holy man,
> Called Manu, who by penances and prayers
> Had won the favor of the Lord of Heaven.
> One day they brought him water for ablution;
> Then, as he washed his hands, a little fish
> Appeared and spoke in human accents thus:—
> "Take care of me, and I will be thy saviour."
> "From what wilt thou preserve me?" Manu asked.
> The fish replied: "A flood will sweep away
> All creatures; I will rescue thee from that."

"But how shall I preserve thee?" Manu said.
The fish rejoined, "So long as we are small,
We are in constant danger of destruction;
For fish eat fish; so keep me in a jar;
When I outgrow the jar, then dig a trench,
Then take me to the ocean, I shall then
Be out of reach of danger." Having thus
Instructed Manu, straightway rapidly
The fish grew larger; then he spake again:—
"In such and such a year the flood will come;
Therefore construct a ship and pay me homage.
When the flood rises, enter thou the ship,
And I will rescue thee." So Manu did
As he was ordered, and preserved the fish,
Then carried it in safety to the ocean;
And in the very year the fish enjoined
He built a ship and paid the fish respect,
And there took refuge when the flood arose.

Soon near him swam the fish, and to its horn
Manu made fast the cable of his vessel.
Thus drawn along the waters Manu passed
Beyond the northern mountain. Then the fish,
Addressing Manu, said: "I have preserved thee;
Quickly attach the ship to yonder tree.
But lest the waters sink from under thee,
As fast as they subside, so fast shalt thou
Descend the mountain gently after them."
Thus he descended from the northern mountain.

The flood had swept away all living creatures;
Manu alone was left. Wishing for offspring,
He earnestly performed a sacrifice.
In a year's time a female was produced.
She came to Manu, then he said to her,
"Who art thou?" She replied, "I am thy daughter."
He said, "How, lovely lady, can that be?"

"I came forth," she rejoined, "from thine oblations
Cast on the waters; thou wilt find in me
A blessing, use me in sacrifice."
With her he worshiped and with toilsome zeal
Performed religious rites, hoping for offspring:
Thus were created men, called sons of Manu.
Whatever benedictions he implored
With her, was thus vouchsafed in full abundance.[6]

Interesting, but primitive indeed, you may exclaim. But consider this from the *Upanishads*. It presents a philosophy which the Buddhists rejected, but yet one which every serious mind seeking the light of the spirit may well reflect upon. Perhaps here is that insight into the Eternal and Omnipotent, that realization of the relative importance of things earthy and things spiritual, that inner calm which may, after all, lead to the best that mortals can hope for in this existence— peace and contentment:

The good and the pleasant are two separate aims,
Yet the one or the other all men are seeking.
But only those who seek the good are wise;
Who seeks the merely pleasant misses the highest aim.
The wise know this, but never the fool,
The way of wealth is fatal, bringing death.
The foolish follow ignorance and think
They walk in wisdom, but ever go in circles,
Misguided, like blind men led by blind.
Young man, you, seeking gain alone,
Know but one world, one life; to you the Now
Is all that is, the Future a vain dream.
The greatest theme of study is the soul;
Whoever gains this knowledge is the wisest man.

[6] M. Monier-Williams: *Indian Wisdom*.

For far above life's cares and griefs and joys,
The things of time and sense, he dwells,
And penetrates the very essence of existence.
If the slayer thinks he slays, or the slain
Thinks he is slain, they know not truth;
For soul lives on, nor kills nor dies;
More subtle than the subtlest, smaller than
The smallest, yet greater than the vastest,
Forever moving, sleeping yet awake, and bodiless,
Passing everywhere among bodies.
Oh, never seek to grasp it with your reason;
The sinful know it never; only soul
Knows soul; to soul alone is soul revealed.[7]

These, then, are some of the fruits of the *Vedas*, the Bibles of the Hindu and of many another Oriental worshiper. As the centuries passed, the ancient faith may have become degraded; mere rites and recitals and liturgies may have superseded to some extent the "inner light" of the creed; but at its best and in its purest state Brahmanism was a religion that could— and did—lift the soul far upward toward God.

Man is, however, a destructive creature, especially toward his religions. Paradoxically he both petrifies and breaks his religious principles; he would establish them, fixed and unyielding, for all ages to come, and the result is that he must at length break them to preserve himself under the changed conditions of another age. Just so with Brahmanism. It became a formal thing, coldly correct on the surface, full of corruption underneath. The inevitable revolt came; for the soul of man will not forever grovel in the dust. That revolt occurred in the sixth century, B.C., and its leader

[7] *Ibid., with some slight changes.*

was Gautama, known now for centuries as the Buddha. His followers have made a god of him—an idea he never dreamed of—but his religion, nevertheless, is a noble philosophy which all the superstitions and innate littleness and narrowness of human beings have not been able totally to destroy or to obscure.

Gautama was born in 624 B.C. His father was a wealthy prince, his mother Maya, the wise, the winsome. Reared in luxury, he married his cousin, one of the most beautiful women of her time, and had one son. Heir to a kingdom, possessed of untold riches, living in a day of peace, brilliant in mind, perfect in health, gleaming in personality, it seemed that all earthly happiness was to be his. Tradition declares that for years even the sight of misery, pain, or death was unknown to him. His father even cleared the highways of the beggar, the lame, the halt, the blind, the dead when the young man went out driving.

But suddenly disenchantment entered this earthly paradise in which he was dreaming. In his twenty-ninth year he went out unheralded. The roads were not cleared. He saw the starving, the old and feeble, the suffering, the dying, and the dead. The shock to his gentle soul was so intense that in the depths of the night he fled from his palace, from his wife and child, and sought the hermit's life in the deep forest—to see if perchance he might find "the perfect way," the way to escape the sorrows of repeated earthly lives.

Here he led such an existence of fasting and self-torture that he came near to self-destruction. But the perfect way was not thus found. Convinced that he was not only not gaining in spirituality, but by his manner of living was actually calling more attention to his

SCHOOL OF AMARAVATI, SCENES FROM THE LIFE OF BUDDHA
Metropolitan Museum of Art

physical body, he returned to civilization, ate and drank moderately, did as other men did, and lived a normal life. His few disciples fled from him in disgust.

Under a sacred fig-tree he set him down to wait, in meditation, for the truth to come, and after twenty-eight days of calmness and inner contemplation the truth did indeed come. He became Buddha, "the Enlightened One," "the Perfect One." The cause of suffering and the way of escape were revealed to him. Donning a yellow robe (the garment of poverty) and carrying a beggar's bowl, the heir of a princely realm went forth to live upon alms and to preach the revealed gospel. Strangely enough, his wife and his son were his first converts.

What new tidings was he to bring to the suffering nation? He taught, in all simplicity and humility, the Four Noble Truths and the Eight-Fold Path that lead to Nirvana, the passive, endless peace that can come only through reabsorption into the All-Embracing, Eternal God. "The Four Noble Truths and the Eight-Fold Path"—hear what these mean in the words of Buddha's own disciples, as recorded in their sacred books:

Thus declared the Blessed One to them: "Two extremes there are, O recluses, that should be avoided by him who would give up this world. First, a life wholly given over to pleasures, a life devoting itself to lusts and raptures. This is vulgar, sensual, degrading, unworthy, absolutely without profit. Second, a life given over to mortification of the flesh. This is painful and likewise unworthy and without profit. The Tathagata (wise one) who avoids these two extremes shall gain that knowledge of the Middle Path which leads to wisdom, which leads to calm, to knowledge, to the Sambodhi (Perfect Enlightenment), to Nirvana itself (Peace).

Which is this Middle Path, the knowledge of which the Tathagata may gain, the path which leads to insight, which leads to wisdom, which leads to calm, to knowledge, to perfect enlightenment, to Nirvana? The Eight-Fold Path it is—that is, Right Belief, Right Aspiration, Right Speech, Right Conduct, Right Means of Livelihood, Right Endeavor, Right Memory, Right Meditation. This, O recluses, is the Middle Path, the knowledge of which the Tathagata may gain.

This, next, is the Noble Truth of Suffering. Our very Birth is suffering, our decay is suffering, our illness is suffering, our death is suffering. The very presence of objects that we hate is suffering. The very separation from objects we love is suffering. Failure to obtain what we desire is suffering. In fact, this five-fold clinging to mere existence is suffering.

Again, this is the Noble Truth of the Cause of Suffering: The thirst that leads to re-birth, with its pleasures and lust, its finding of delights here and now. This thirst is three-fold —namely, thirst for existence, thirst for prosperity, thirst for pleasure.

This is the Noble Truth of the Destruction of All Suffering: It ceases with the entire annihilation of this thirst—an annihilation which consists of the complete absence of every passion—with the absolute abandoning of this thirst, with the casting of it out, with emancipation from it, with true destruction of desire.[8]

It is a strengthening ideal this ancient religious philosopher lifts before us—a truth more healing to the harassed, hurrying world of men than we Westerners can realize. Desire for this or that unessential toy, hunger for this or that passing show, ambition for this or that fleeting honor or the continued effort to out-

[8] Author's version. See specimens in T. W. R. Davids' *Dialogues of Buddha,* Oxford University Press, 1910.

shine our neighbor—these are the causes of nine-tenths of the unhappiness of this world. Daily we toil and sweat for things that are not at all needful. This fact Buddha would quietly state to our generation.

And where in all literature is there a philosophy, a code of ethics, a religion that can offer a better road to spiritual health than Gautama's Eight-Fold Path—such as Right Belief and Right Aspiration? Buddha denounced caste; he taught the brotherhood of man-kind; he insisted upon the efficacy of right thinking and right living rather than of rituals and ceremonies. He maintained that no peace could enter the human soul until that soul had learned self-mastery.

Is it any marvel that one-third of the inhabitants of the globe still embrace Buddhism? At first, considered merely as an outgrowth or division of Brahmanism, this new faith was for more than fourteen hundred years permitted to teach its peaceful doctrine in India; but in the eighth century A.D., the Brahmans, realizing fully its destructive effects upon the caste system, tore it from its native soil and cast it out. But it has flour-ished in central Asia; China and Japan number its fol-lowers by the millions; in Ceylon it may be seen in almost a primitive purity; in Tibet, under the name of Lamaism, it has established a mysterious, far-reaching spiritual power and authority comparable to that of the Roman Catholic church in the Western World.

Possibly it is true that theologians can finally ruin any religion. Buddha, like Jesus, left no writings; but the followers of both have amply made up the de-ficiency. The disciples of Gautama recorded his career, his miracles, his sermons; the disciples of his disciples added argument, debate, disputation, legends, hymns, epigrams, moralizing, theology that the simple soul of this original, simple teacher never could have imagined or devised. So great became the confusion from too much theorizing on plain truth, that several councils had to be called to determine just what the Buddhistic doctrines were. The one held at Patna in 250 B.C. framed a canon or bible of sacred books—as momentous an event for the literature of Asia and Europe as that one which formulated our own Bible.

Buddha in his simplicity had made possible for *all*, the way to the higher life. Ignoring worldly distinctions, he had opened a treasury of truth attractive to all spiritual-minded folk, whether nobleman or peasant, rich or poverty-stricken. Briefly, there were two classes of Buddhist followers. One was the Upasukos, who endeavored to perform righteously all duties as members of family and of community. Their compensation was to be at least a favorable rebirth and thus a gradual approach to the Last Reabsorption, Nirvana. On the other hand there were the Bhikshus, the true followers, those who renounced everything, earthly possessions, relationships, worldly loves, banded themselves into brotherhoods or sisterhoods, and dwelt in poverty and utter humility. To these the reward should be escape from rebirth, immediate Nirvana.

The theory of it all was—and is—plain enough. It may easily be illustrated by means of our modern invention, the electric light. Out there in the main trunk line that vast, mysterious, omnipresent thing called electricity vibrates and pulsates. Here in this room the pressing of a button or the turning of a tiny knob —that same electricity darts into a bulb or globe, and there is light. Turn the button or knob—the light is gone, the electricity has been reabsorbed into the great current pulsating in the main line out there. Just so with us mortals. A little vibrating life is emanated from the great Central Current of Light, the God, and we, like the electric bulb, have for a time an earthly radiance—we say we live. But the switch is turned, and all is dark; we have been reabsorbed into that mighty Life Current from which we originally came.

The Pitakas—Fountains of Legend

All this philosophic musing has been fruitful material for Hindu and other Asiatic theologians—and they have made the most of the opportunity presented. Vast indeed is the library that has accumulated around the few candid truths which Buddha Gautama expressed. Of all the confused mass of writings possibly two are at least known among cultivated Westerners. They are an extraordinary collection of hymns, known as the *Dhammapada,* and the Buddhist Bible commonly called the *Three Pitakas,* or Baskets.

What a world of stories have come out of one of these Baskets—the *Sutta Pitaka!* Tales that every child in Europe and America can repeat, fables attributed to Æsop and Lafontaine, folk-lore that Uncle Remus unwittingly retold, legends that Boccaccio and Shakespeare and hosts of other masters rehearsed in novel and poem and drama—these are the fruits taken, all unknowingly, from that marvelously bountiful *Sutta Basket,* written more than twenty-three centuries ago.

The other two *Pitakas*—the *Vinaya-Pitaka,* containing the rules of conduct for the Bhikshus or Elect, and the *Abidhamma-Pitaka,* dealing with the metaphysics, the psychology, the philosophy of later Buddhism—are well enough in their way, and doubtless served an excellent purpose in the hands of old-time Buddhist students. But it is for the first book that Literature owes Gautama lasting gratitude. For it is that first, the *Sutta-Pitaka,* which contains the Buddhist Birth-Stories, the *Jatakas,* the illustrating fables told by Buddha to force home the ethical lesson he was teaching. As Buddha was supposed to have been reincarnated five hundred and fifty times, he had had plentiful opportunity to observe and hear and see earthly experiences, and in the *Jatakas* he relates in never-to-be-forgotten masterpieces of fiction his supposed adventures among countless generations of men and animals.

Have you ever read elsewhere a story similar to this one telling of a decision once made by Buddha?

A woman with her child went to Buddha's pool to bathe. She first bathed the babe and then went into the water to bathe herself. Then a Yakshini (cannibal witch) saw the child and longed to eat it. She came near and asked the mother, "Friend, is this pretty child yours?" Then she inquired if she might nurse the little one. Being permitted to do so, she suddenly went away with the baby. Then the mother ran after her and held her.

But the Yakshini brazenly said, "Where did you get this child? It is mine." And thus arguing, they came to the door of the Buddha's Judgment Hall. Hearing the noise, he inquired as to the cause, and then asked them if they would accept his decision. They consented. Then he drew a line upon the ground, and commanded the Yakshini to take hold of the child's arms, and the mother to take hold of the legs. "Now," said he, "the child shall be hers who drags it over the line." But when they began to pull at it, the mother, noting how her little one was being hurt, grieved as though her heart would break, and let the child loose.

Then Buddha inquired of the spectators. "Whose hearts are tender toward children—those who have borne them or those who have not?" They answered, "Sire, the hearts of mothers are tender." Then he demanded, "Then, whom do you think to be the mother—she who now holds the babe or she who let go?" And they replied, "She who let go is undoubtedly the mother."

And he rebuked the Yakshini with these words, "O foolish woman! Because of your former sins you have been born a Yakshini, and yet you continue to sin." Then he laid a vow upon her to obey the Five Commandments and let her depart. But the mother exalted the Buddha, and exclaimed, "O my Lord! O Great Physician! May thy life be long." And she went forth with her child clasped to her bosom.[9]

Have you not found in your Æsop or your Lafontaine or your Uncle Remus such a tale as this, with possibly the names of the characters changed?

In the forest of Brahma lived an Elephant whose name was White Front. Now, the Jackals said to one another, "If this vast beast would only die there would be food for four months for us from his carcass." Then a Jackal arose and declared he would bring death to the Elephant by his own cunning. He accordingly went to White Front and solemnly saluted him with the reverential prostration of the eight members.

"Noble creature," said he, "grant me the regard of thy glance."

"Who art thou?" grunted the Elephant, "and why comest thou?"

"Sire, I am merely a Jackal," replied the other; "but the animals of the forest are convinced that it is not wise to be without a king. They have had a full council and have sent

[9] Based on translations by T. W. R. Davids: *Buddhist Birth Stories,* London, Trübner & Co., 1880, Vol. I.

me to announce to your Royal Highness that thou, gifted with so many kingly qualities, hast been chosen Lord of the entire forest; for—

> Who is just and strong and wise,
> Who is true to social ties,
> He is born for Empires.

Let your Majesty, then, come at once, so that this fortunate moment may not escape us." Thus speaking, he in great haste led White Front, who was eager to begin his sovereignship.

Soon the Jackal brought him to a deep swamp, and the Elephant plunged in heavily before he could stop.

"O good friend Jackal," cried the Elephant, "what am I to do now? I am sunk deep in the mud!"

"Oh, perhaps your Majesty," impudently laughed the Jackal, "will condescend to hang on to my tail with your trunk, and thus wade out."

Then White Front realized that he had been deceived, and he soon sank in the swamp and was devoured by the Jackals.[10]

The foregoing stories are among the Buddhist Birth Stories. Possibly Buddha never related one of them; they may be simply the accumulated folk-lore of un-numbered generations of Hindus—a folk-lore happily centered around one story-teller, just as Joel Chandler Harris grouped the legends of the black race about one unforgettable character. What boots it whether Buddha had anything to do with the tales? Known for a time as the *Book of the Five Hundred and Fifty Jatakas* (Births), a portion became highly popular as the *Pancha Tantra,* or *Five Books,* and, again, a portion of the latter spread far and wide over the East as the *Hitopadesa* or *Book of Good Counsels.* As the

[10] Author's version. For many specimens from the *Pitakas,* see *Sacred Books of the East* (F. Max Müller, Editor), Oxford, Clarendon Press, 1880, Vol. 10.

centuries passed, fables from these sources became so common that any child along the Ganges was able to tell scores of them.

The *Book of Good Counsels,* the later Sanskrit version of the *Jatakas,* might well be enjoyed by even the Brahmans and all other enemies of Buddha; for in this production all references to Buddha are omitted, and, moreover, the collection has a rather artistically arranged framework. Here the tales are supposed to be told by an old sage to the wayward sons of a king, and are arranged into four divisions: the Winning of Friends, the Parting of Friends, War, and Peace. But they are the same old fables dealing with the cunning of this creature and the stupidity of that. Here is a typical tale of the Vulture and the Cat:

On the banks of the Ganges there is a cliff called Vulture-Crag, and thereon grew a giant fig-tree. Within its hollow trunk lived an old Vulture, called Gray-Pate, who had lost both his talons and his eyes. The birds that lived in the same tree gave him gifts from their own food, for very pity, and thus he managed to live. Now, one day, when the other birds were away, Long-Ears, the Cat, sneaked up to make a meal of the nestlings, and these, frightened at seeing him, set up a cry that roused Gray-Pate.

"Who comes there?" croaked Gray-Pate.

Long-Ears, perceiving the Vulture, thought himself caught; but as retreat was impossible, he made up his mind to trust to his impudence.

"My lord," he replied, "I have the honor to salute thee."

"Who art thou?" demanded the Vulture.

"I am a Cat."

"Be gone, Cat, or I shall kill thee," cried the Vulture.

"If I deserve death," said the Cat, "I am prepared to die. But first hear what I have to say."

"Why hast thou come here?" inquired the Vulture.

"I dwell," said Long-Ear, "on the Ganges. I bathe and eat no flesh, practicing the moon-penance. The birds that are constantly coming there are always praising your worship as one wholly given over to the study of morality, and worthy of all trust. Therefore I have come here to learn law from thee—a person deep in learning and in years. Now, dost thou so read the law of strangers as to be ready to kill a visitor? What say the books about the householder?—

Bar thy door not to the stranger, be he friend or be he foe,
For the tree will shade the woodman while his axe doth lay it low.

And if means fail, what there is should be given with kind words; as—

Greetings fair, and room to rest in; fire, and water from the well,
Simple gifts—are given freely in the house where good men dwell,—

Nor should there be any distinction between persons—

Young or bent with many winters; rich, or young, whoe'er thy guest,
Honor him for thine own home—better is he than the best.

Otherwise there is this rebuke:

Pity them that ask thy pity; who art thou to stint thy hoard,
When the holy moon shines equal on the leper and the lord?

And another like unto it:

When thy gate is roughly fastened, and the asker turns away,
Thence he bears thy good deeds with him, and his sins on thee doth lay.

For verily—

In the house the husband ruleth, men, the Brahmans 'master'
call;
Agni is the Twice-Born Master—but the guest is lord of all."

Now, to all these wise saws Gray-Pate replied,
"Yes, but cats like meat, and these are young birds here.
Therefore I tell thee to go."
"Sir," answered the Cat. And he first touched the ground
and then his two ears, and called upon Krishna to witness his
words. "I have long practiced the moon-penance and have
overcome all passion. I also know the Scriptures, and no
matter how they may differ, they are unanimous in this first
duty of not injuring others. Thus, all of them say:

> He who does and thinks no wrong,
> He who suffers, being strong,
> He whose harmlessness men know,
> Unto Swerga such doth go."

And so, winning the old Vulture's confidence, Long-Ear, the
Cat, was permitted to dwell in the hollow tree. Daily he stole
some of the nestlings and ate them in the hollow trunk. Of
course, the parents sought high and low for their babes, and
when the Cat perceived this, he slipped out from the hole. And
then, when the older birds found the bones of their little ones
in the hollow where Gray-Pate lived, they naturally were convinced that the nestlings had been devoured bv the old Vulture.
Him they immediately slew.[11]

Now, it so happened that in the sixth century, A.D.,
Chosroes, King of Persia, heard that there was in
India a wonderful book entitled the *Pancha Tantra*.
He so desired a copy that he sent his personal physi-

[11] After the story by Edwin Arnold: *Book of Good Counsels,* London, W. H. Allen, 1893. One of the earliest and best translations
under the title, *Hitopadesa*—Sir William Jones: *Complete Works,*
London, John Stockdale, 1807, Vol. 13. For the most modern and
most entertaining translation of *Pancha Tantra,* see Arthur Ryder's
version, University of Chicago Press, 1925.

cian to distant India to obtain it. A fortune, so tradition declares, was spent in the quest before the doctor was able to bribe a Hindu to give him the volume. Back to his homeland the physician, Berzuyet, bore the precious manuscript, and translated it into the Persian. *The Lights of Canopus* became its fitting title; for Canopus was to the Persians the star of wisdom. But, as the stories were told to an Indian king by a philosopher named Bidpai, naturally enough the book at length was popularly called *The Tales of Bidpai*. How often in ancient Persia, the land of Omar Khayyam, did the children—and the grown folk too, you may be sure—sit in the gardens of roses and listen to such a story as this from the *Tales of Bidpai*.

Two friends once resolved never to leave each other, and they always traveled together. One day, however, they reached a deep river at the base of a hill, and the spot was so pleasant that here they decided to rest. At length they began to observe the place more closely, and found a white stone, on which were written in blue letters the following words:

"Travelers, we have prepared a banquet as your welcome; but first you must be bold enough to deserve it before you may have it. Therefore throw yourself bravely into this pool and swim to the other side. There you shall find a lion carved of white stone. Take it upon your shoulders and, stopping not, run with it to the top of yon mountain, nor shall you fear the wild beasts that will surround you, nor the thorns that will prick your feet. For be assured that nothing can harm you. Then, as soon as you reach the top of the mountain, you shall immediately come into great happiness. But if you once hesitate you shall never possess this joy; for the slothful may never gain what is awaiting here for the industrious."

Then Ganem, one of the two friends, said to Salem, the other, "Brother, here is an opportunity presented us to end all our toil and pains. Let us pluck up courage and test whether this stone speaks truly or falsely."

"My brother," answered Salem, "it is senseless to grant credit to such idle writing as this seems to be, and, in vain hopes of some unknown gain, thus throw ourselves into certain danger."

"Brother," said Ganem, "the courageous despise danger in order to make themselves happy; there is no gathering the rose without being pricked by the thorns."

"For all that," declared Salem, "if we have common sense we can see that this is not our business, for the sake of a vague promise to plunge into this water. A sensible man never moves one foot till the other be fixed. As for me, I share with you no danger of this sort, but shall try to dissuade you from such a foolish undertaking."

"Your persuasion shall not change my intention. If, therefore, you will not join me, be pleased at least that I do venture."

"Oh, dearest brother," cried Salem, "if you are so weak-minded as to be determined to enter this foolhardy adventure, give me a last embrace, and then farewell forever. You have declined my advice, and I cannot stand it to stay and behold your ruin."

And Salem embraced him and went forward on his journey. But Ganem went to the edge of the water and plunged in, with grim determination to win the prize or perish. The water was deep, but with courage he swam to the other side. He rested a moment, and then, lifting up the lion, ran, without ceasing, to the top of the mountain. And, lo! he beheld a glorious city, and as he gazed upon it there burst from the stone lion such a terrible roar that the mountain and the places around it shook. And no sooner had this sound been heard in the city when all the inhabitants came running up toward Ganem. Some who seemed superior to the others spoke to him with great ceremony and respect, and after they had addressed him with praises they placed him upon a horse sumptuously adorned, then led him to the city, arrayed him with the royal robes, and proclaimed him King of all that realm.

Now, when the ceremony was over, he requested them to tell the reason of this honor, and they answered, "The learned men of the kingdom had so enchanted the water that he had crossed and the stone lion that he had carried to the top of the mountain that whenever their King died the man who was courageous enough to undertake the hazards as he had done and brought the lion safely to the top of the mountain had this reward for his fortitude: the lion would roar so loudly that the inhabitants would come forth in search of the person who had arrived to be their King. This custom has lasted from antiquity and is intended to insure for our King a man of resolution and boldness. And now, since the lot has fallen upon your majesty, your sovereignty is absolute over us." [12]

Now the Arabs seized upon the collection, and one of their number, Aballah-Ben-Mokaffah, translated it, with many revisions, into the Arabic, and thereby produced one of the most famous and influential books of the eighth and ninth centuries. The Arabs chose to call it *Kalilah and Dimnah* [13] because of the two wise jackals by these names who play such an important part in many of the tales. Thus the original Birth Stories of Buddha had passed through the Sanskrit, the Pali, the various dialects of India, into the Persian, into the Arabic. Great as the vogue of these fables now was, their fame was as yet but in its infancy. For the Jews, in their far travels, were to carry the book or its narratives into Western Europe, and between

[12] Author's version.
[13] I. G. Keith-Falconer's translation is excellent; Cambridge University Press, 1885.

the eleventh and the thirteenth centuries were to translate the work into Hebrew, Greek, and Latin.

Down through the ages had come another Indian or Hindu collection which was to influence the story-telling of all medieval Europe. It was the *Seventy Tales of a Parrot* (*Suka-Saptati*), later to bear the famous title of the *Seven Wise Masters*. With a framework similar to that of *Kalilah and Dimnah,* the collection seems to be composed principally to warn man against the wiles of women and the supposed female tendency toward perfidy.

In brief, the plot or central idea of the book is this: A king's son, having been educated by seven wise men, is directed by them not to speak for a week after returning home. They have discovered by the stars that if he does not remain silent during the period he will certainly perish. On the first day the prince's step-mother, whose improper advances he has repulsed, accuses him to the king of attempting violence upon her, and she demands his execution. She relates to the king a story supporting her demand. Then one of the wise men comes forward and obtains a day's delay for the prince by telling a tale presenting a moral contrary to that revealed in the woman's story. Each day, for seven days, she narrates a romance or legend to strengthen her viewpoint, while the wise men reply with a story nullifying hers. Thus the prince is saved for a week—sufficient time for him to prepare proof of his stepmother's guilt.

Here is one of the tales as it appears at a far later date as a medieval metrical romance, told in my lady's castle by French or English minstrels:

There was a knight in this country, a rich count, who married a young and beautiful wife, the object of his tenderest affection. Such was the happiness of this young couple that the day and night appeared too short for their endearments, and each moment of separation was considered by both as a serious misfortune. One day, while they were examining a new knife, which had been bestowed on the lady as a bridal present, it slipped from the hands of the husband and slightly wounded her. The accident was followed by no bad consequences, but the unhappy knight was seized with such horror at the sight of her blood that he suddenly died.

> He did great folie, certe,
> Or too tender was his heart.

Unfortunately, grief is not, in all constitutions, a mortal disease, and the lovely cause of his death found herself unable to shake off, with the same expedition, the burden of existence. Yet she trusted that she should not long survive him, and, unwilling to tear herself from his remains, ordered a small lodge to be built in the church-yard over the intended place of his grave, and took possession of this sad habitation on the day of his burial. Her friends vainly interposed,

> And saiden, "Dame, gent and free,
> Of thy self have pite;
> For thou art fair and young sans fail,
> And may'st the world mochel avail:
> Some knight thou wed of noblay,
> And have with him much to play;
> Good children beget and fair:
> Gentil dame debonaire,
> Let away thy mourning,
> And take thee to some comforting."
> "That will I do for no weal;
> But die I will on his buriale."

As they perceived that the torrent of her grief only swelled
the more by indiscreet opposition, they now satisfied themselves
with providing, in silence, every accommodation that could be
afforded in the hovel which she thought fit to occupy; and particularly took the precaution of making an excellent fire and
left a supply of fuel to last till next morning.

It happened that on this very day three thieves were executed
within a short distance of the church-yard. The thieves had
been knights.

> A knight of the countre held his fee
> For to watch the three knightes
> Upon the gallows three nightes.
> He com to the gallows, armed wele,
> Both in iron and in steel,
> For to make, the first night, ward.
> The weather was cold and froward;
> He was for-cold, and looked about,
> And was ware, withouten doubt,
> Of fire in the church-yard.
>
> . . . .
>
> She let him in anonright.
> He sat and warmed him by the fer;
>
> . . . .
>
> And said, "Dame, thou art mad,
> That thou moanest for the dead.
> Comfort theyself, pluck up thine heart;
> Such mourning thou hast unright;
> Thou shouldst love some gentil knight."

Then the knight bethought him of the dead bodies of the
thieves, and hastened away to guard them. But one had
already been stolen. In terror he returned to relate his misfortune to the lady. But she offered a remedy.

> She said, "Sir, I will help thee,
> So that thou wilt spouse me."
> "Yes, dame," he said, "precious.
> Gif thou me help, I will thee spouse."

Then she directed him to dig up her dead husband, and this the knight did. But when she commanded that he hang the corpse in the place of the stolen body, he emphatically declined. Then took she the rope, fastened it about her husband's neck and swung him on the gallows. But the knight pointed out that the thief had had a ghastly wound on his head, and that therefore the trickery would soon be discovered. Then the young widow demanded that the knight take the axe or sword and inflict such a wound upon the head of her husband's corpse. "Nay, Dame, not for all my life would I thus smite the dead one!" declared the knight. The woman seized his sword and with her own hands brought it down upon the dead man's head.

> Then the knight well understood
> That false and fickle was her blood;
> And said, "Yet unlike he beth;
> Broken were his fore teeth."

And she took a stone and "smote hem out everish one."
    Now that the deed was done, she exclaimed, "Sire, now I have won thy love."

> "Nay, dame," he said, "by God above,
> For gold ne silver, land ne house,
> Thy false body ne would I spouse:
> For all so wouldest thou serve me
> As thou has done thy lord so free.
> Thou hast taught me a new ran (saying),
> That I shall never believe woman;
> For though they make semblance fairest,
> They will betray you at the last." [14]

[14] George Ellis: *Specimens of Metrical Romances*, H. G. Bohn, London, 1848.

Thus a collection of ancient Hindu folk-tales, compiled probably by an Indian philosopher of the first century, B.C., Sandabar, then translated into the Persian, into the Arabic, and then into the Hebrew by a certain Rabbi Joel of the ninth or tenth century—the same Joel who is said to have translated *Kalilah and Dimnah*—has passed into the Spanish, the Italian, the French, and the English, and has become the common literary possession of all civilized Europe.

Out of the two books, the *Seven Wise Masters* and *Kalilah and Dimnah*—both originally from India and its sacred Buddhist books—grew at length another volume, one whose fame has never been surpassed by any other writing. It is the *Arabian Nights*. In this popular masterpiece, which is not truly Arabian at all, but is of Indian origin through the Persian, we can trace story after story already told in the *Pancha Tantra* and the *Suka-Saptati*. Whether under the name of *Pitakas, Jatakas, Pancha Tantra, Hitopadesa,* the *Lights of Canopus, Tales of Bidpai, Kalilah and Dimnah, Suka-Saptati,* the *Seven Wise Masters,* the *Seven Sages,* the *Arabian Nights,* or the *Book of Sindibad,* they are fundamentally the same ancient tales related twenty-five centuries ago along the banks of the Ganges.

Naturally, as the stories passed through nation after nation, they took unto themselves the characteristics of successive peoples and environments. We detect the emotions of India, the imagery of Persia, the philosophy of the Syrian nature, the fiery spirit of Arabia, the argumentation of the Hebrew. Whether translated from book to book or carried orally from nation to nation, they at length accumulated in Western

Europe as a precious treasury of lore from which poets, minstrels, and romancers were to draw inspiration and rich material for many a literary gem.

Of all the delvers into the quaint tales of Hindu origin we may call attention to only one, who is in many respects the connecting link between these European versions of Asiatic narrative and the more modern European fiction. He was another of those wonderful Jews who flourished as scholars in that remarkable eleventh-century Spanish revival of learning under Moorish leadership. His real name was Moses Sephardi, but for the sake of prudence he assumed the Christian name of Petrus Alphonsus. What a book was that which he produced—the *Clericali Disciplina,* the Lesson-Book of the Scholar! Written in Latin, it may have helped the scholars somewhat, but its stories were too good to be limited to the learned. They swept over Europe. The same old tales that had once enchanted the Orient once more captivated the Occident. The French seized upon the narratives of *Clericali Disciplina* through two translations, the *Proverbs of Peres Anforse* and the *Romance of Peres Aunfour.* And out of such narratives grew those typical tales of medieval France, the *fableaux,* which every troubador, trouvere, and minstrel from Provence to Scotland recited to admiring audiences.

What bountiful, what marvelous fruit from those ancient Hindu *Jatakas* of Buddha Gautama's day and earlier! In the Middle Ages there was to appear in Europe a huge collection of stories, fables, romances, known as the *Gesta Romanorum,* or *Stories of the Romans.* Every priest, every scholar endeavored to own a copy of the *Gesta Romanorum;* sermons were

based on its contents; singers and reciters built their
fantastic romances from its narratives. And yet a
great portion of that famous volume is only the old
Buddhist Birth Stories brought down through centuries of Persian, Arabic, Greek, and Latin.

Boccaccio found here much of the source of his *De-
cameron*. Chaucer, in his *Nun's Priest's Tale,* one of
the most entertaining of his Canterbury series, simply
retold one of the legends. Spenser in his *Faërie
Queene* reëchoed these stories. Shakespeare's *Merchant of Venice,* with its pound of flesh, is from the
same ancient source. Lafontaine in his *Book of Fables*
brings to us in modern guise the animal exploits that
had thrilled India, Persia, and Arabia. The very
Æsop's Fables that every child of our day can relate
are, so far as can be ascertained, mainly Hindu and
not Æsopian. True, there was a Greek fabulist of the
sixth century, B.C., named Æsop, but the fables that
we know to-day are mainly the twice or thrice told
tales of Indian origin translated out of Latin versions
of Persian or Arabic versions, and edited by Planudes,
a learned monk of the fifteenth century.

It is a long journey from the sixth century, B.C., to
the twentieth century, A.D.; it is a long journey from
the ragged story-teller sitting before an ancient temple
by the Ganges to the modern child reading by electric
light in a city apartment, the animal tales of Æsop or
Lafontaine or Uncle Remus. But through many a nation and through many a language that journey was
at length accomplished. The Orient may sing the
praises of Buddha as founder of a high and noble
religion; the Occident may sing his praises as the un-
conscious founder of a vast imaginative literature.

The Hindu Epics

Thus far we have dealt with the First or Religious Period of Indian Literature and its outgrowths. The Second Period is that of Epic—the era (overlapping, of course, the First) in which those huge poems dealing with the history and the mythology of the Aryan or Hindu conquerors were composed. They are indeed colossal—the two epics that have come down to us from those days. Although the one, *Ramayana,* is attributed to a single author, Valmiki, and the other, the *Mahabharata,* to Vyasa, they are clearly folk-productions, the slowly accumulated legends and traditions in poetic form of a whole nation. No one man could have composed the *Mahabharata;* it is eight times as long as the *Iliad* and the *Odyssey* combined. A man named Valmiki may have written the major portion of the *Ramayana;* but beyond doubt the first and the seventh books of the poem are of much later composition than the other sections.

What do these vast collections of epic material deal with? Are they pictures of a nation's mythical heroes and ancient customs, as are the works of Homer? To a certain extent, yes; but they have not the clean-cut characterization, the progressiveness of plot, and the permeating personality of the famous Greek epics. They are too vast to permit of all this; their very bigness creates confusion.

In the *Ramayana* we hear of the mighty battles of the gods. Ravana, ten-headed chief of the evil spirit, through self-discipline, gains invulnerability; it seems that even the powerful dwellers in the Heavens are helpless before him. In his furious strength he threatens the destruction of the very god-seats. The celestial beings called upon one of their number, Vishnu, to assume human form, descend to earth, and vanquish the mad demon. Humiliating himself, humbling himself so far as to give up godhood to become a man, Vishnu is born the son of an earthly king, and takes unto himself the name of Rama. In a contest with numerous suitors he vanquished all by bending the bow of a god, and thus won as his wife the beautiful and faithful Sita.

All the future looked happy for the god-man Rama. But on the eve of his being proclaimed as heir to the throne, the second wife of his father persuaded the old king to banish the young prince to the wilderness for fourteen years. Obedient to his father's decree, he is about to depart to the forest, when his young wife, Sita, pleads to go with him. But let the epic itself tell the episode:

> Master of weapons, lord of deadly strife,
> Hear thou the duty of a warrior's wife.
> Know that the father, mother, brother, son,
> Obtain the lot their former deeds have won.
> The wife alone her husband's fate must share,
> And in thy trouble I my part will bear.
> For not on father, mother, son, or friend,
> But on her husband, must the wife depend.
> And if thou seek the wood, thy wife hath sworn
> To smooth thy path, nor let thy feet be torn.
> No guile is in me: from thy bosom throw
> The dregs of doubt, and give me leave to go.
> I spurn the terrace and the pleasant seat.
> Mine be the joy to guard thy cherished feet.
> Obedient ever to my parents' sway,
> I will not hearken if they bid me stay.

I will go forth the lonely wood to roam,
The lion's dwelling and the tiger's home.
Happy and heedless, from all terror flee,
Careless of empire, caring but for thee.

.   .   .   .

The woe, the terror, all the toil and pain,
Joined with thy love, to me are joy and gain.
Lion and tiger, elephant and boar,
And all the monsters thou hast counted o'er,
Soon as my Rama's glorious form they see,
In trembling fear will turn away and flee.
Not Indra's self, the ruler of the sky,
Would dare to harm me when my lord is nigh.
Long years ago I heard a sage foretell
That in the woods should be my fate to dwell:
The time is come: now make that promise true,
And when thou goest take thy Sita too.[15]

Rama is gone. The old father, stung with remorse, goes down to the grave, and his second son, Bharata, summoned to the throne, rejects the unmerited prize and goes forth into the wilderness to implore Rama to return. But the young prince, with his god-like sense of justice, declines to shorten his own sentence. and Bharata rules for a time in his stead.

Now begins the exploit for which Rama had descended to earth—the conquering of the evil spirit, Ravana. The sister of this monster, attracted by the physical strength and the beauty of Rama, offers herself to him, but is repulsed. Wild with rage and jealousy, she calls upon Ravana to seek vengeance for her. Ravana strikes quickly, decisively. Garbed as a Brahman, he enters Rama's home while the husband is

[15] Version based on R. T. H. Griffith translation: *Ramayana*, London, Trübner & Co., 1870, Vol. III.

away, and seizes the winsome Sita. Here we have one
of the most dramatic descriptions in the epic or in all
Hindu literature:

> The lady, by his garb beguiled,
> With fearless innocence looked up and smiled.
> She bade the seeming Brahman to a seat,
> And gave him water for his weary feet;
> And still intent on hospitable care,
> Brought forth the choicest of her woodland fare.
>
> .   .   .   .
>
> "And now," she said, "declare thy name and race,
> And why thou roamest to this gloomy place."
> She spoke. The stranger thundered in reply:
> "Terror of men and gods and worlds am I,
> Ravan, whose will the giant hosts obey.
> Since I have seen thee, lovely one, to-day,
> Clad in silk raiment, bright as polished gold,
> My love for all my wives is dead and cold.
> Though countless dames of perfect beauty, torn
> From many a pillaged realm, my home adorn.
> Come, fairest, come, my queen and darling be;
> Among a thousand I will love but thee.
> My city, Lanka, like a glittering crown,
> Looks from the high brow of a mountain down
> On restless ocean, which with flash and foam
> Beats with wild rage against my island Home.
> There pleasant gardens shall thy steps invite
> With me to wander when the moon is bright;
> There in new joys thy breast shall ne'er retain
> One faint remembrance of this place of pain."
> Then from her breast the noble fury broke:
> With flashing eyes and quivering lip she spoke:
> "Me! me! the faithful wife of Rama! him
> Before whose glory Indra's fame is dim;
> Rama, who fails not in the battle-shock,

Fierce as the ocean steed, fast as the rock!
Rama, the lord of each auspicious sign;
Rama, the glory of his princely line.
Me, Rama's wife—the dear, fond wife of him;
Him of the eagle eye, the lordly limb—
Me dost thou dare with words of love to press,
A jackal suing to a lioness?
As far above thy impious reach am I
As yonder sun that blazes in the sky.

.   .   .   .

Thou win his wife! With lighter labor try
To pluck the sun from yonder sky;
Safer to wrap within thy robe the flame
Than woo to folly Rama's faithful dame!" [16]

Then suddenly Ravana stood in his true form before Sita—a huge monster, ten-faced, twenty-armed, and in every head a glaring, red, wild eye. Then he seized her and with angry threats bore her away in his magic car.

"Help, Rama, help! O Lakshman, where art thou?

.   .   .   .

Ye happy bowers, ye blooming groves, farewell!
My mournful fate to royal Rama tell.
And Godaveri, thou dear stream, upon
Whose bosom float the mallard and the swan,
Forget not her who loves thee, but relate
To royal Rama Sita's mournful fate!
Say that the fiend has borne away his wife,
His own true Sita, dearer than his life;
He will regain the spouse he loves so well,—
Yea, though they bore her to the depths of Hell!"
Down to her feet her loosened tresses hung,
As, like a creeper, with twisted arms she clung

[16] *Ibid.*

To bough and branch, and, falling on her knees,
Shrieked out for succor to the mighty trees.

. . . .

All nature trembled, faint and sick with dread,
And sudden darkness o'er the world was spread;
The wind was husht, dimmed was the glorious sun;
An awful voice that cried, The deed is done,
Burst from the mighty sire, whose sleepless eye
Saw the fell outrage from his throne on high;
And pure saints, with mingled joy and awe,
Looked on the sinner and his doom foresaw.[17]

Then the strong Rama, through an alliance with
Hanuman, King of the monkeys, wages war against
the demon, and, after many a wild adventure, they
destroy Ravana. There on the battlefield lies the
bloody corpse, while around it wail the many wives
of the dead man. Rama, moved by their sorrow, bade
the kinsman of Ravana, Vibhishana, to take the women
away to the home of their husband and then to return
to prepare the funeral rites for Ravana. But the kinsman declared, "This Ravana was my enemy. He in-
sulted me before all his council, and I have therefore
no desire to perform his funeral ceremony." Then
answered Rama, "I grieved much to hear such words
from you! Ravana is now dead, and he is therefore
no longer your enemy, but your elder brother." And
Vibhishana performed all the rites with that grandeur
which befitted the Rajah of Lanka.

But peace and happiness were not yet to be Rama's.
Sita was accused of impurity, and only after an ordeal
by fire is she returned to her loving husband. Yet
again is she accused by the people, and Rama is forced

[17] *Ibid.*

to exile her from his palace. Strangely enough, she finds refuge in the hut of the hermit, Valmiki, author of the epic, and in that forest shelter are born to her two sons, who at length are so wonderfully trained by the old sage that even the King, their father, hears of their accomplishments. They are called before the monarch; he reads in their faces the likeness of their beloved mother; and, convinced of her innocence, he recalls Sita and her children to the palace, and all is happiness.

In the eleven books of this epic, with their twenty-four thousand couplets, investigation has revealed that hidden in the romantic fiction there is considerable history of the early conquest of Southern India. But what is possibly of more importance to the average reader is the fact that here we have, some centuries before the coming of Jesus, a story with considerable similarity to the Christian story of the Messiah. Vishnu was the son of the Supreme Brahma, the God, just as the New Testament claims for Jesus the supreme sonship. Vishnu, like Jesus, humbled himself and underwent incarnation, earthly birth. Vishnu, like Jesus, came to struggle against the ancient and powerful adversary of man. It is an enchanting idea—this vision of the God's assuming human form to deliver mankind—and among the Hindus, as among the Christians, it has been a fruitful source of poetry, fiction, and drama.

THE MAHABHARATA

And now as to that titantic collection of epic poetry, the *Mahabharata*. Throughout the centuries the Hindus have declared its author to be Vyasa, but

Vyasa is simply an ancient Indian term for "arranger" or "editor." The great epic is indeed a collection— the accumulated legends of the Indian race.

True, it centers about the mighty war between two sets of cousins, the Kaurava Brothers (the Evil Principle) and the Pandava Brothers (the Good Principle), and thus possesses a certain unity. But not more than one-third of the poem is direct narrative, while the remainder is a medley of glosses, speeches, didactic passages, and descriptions. So full of information is it that for centuries it served as a sort of encyclopedia for the Hindu military caste, and he who knew his *Mahabharata* need know but little else.

The time came in Indian civilization when the followers of Brahmanism and Buddhism ceased to glorify the military profession, but when some parts of this epic were first written early Indian poets were in the custom of hobnobbing with warriors and conquering kings. The result was many a vivid description of struggle, praise of war-like leaders, scenes of carnage. When, however, the day came on which the priestly caste gained the ascendancy, how zealously these lovers of peace used their censorship upon the poem! Many indeed are the contradictory statements and comments within the story as a result of their critical editing, but still the martial strain runs throughout much of it.

The Pandavas were descendants of Bharata, himself a descendant of Puru, father of a lunar race. The rightful king of India, Dhritarashtia, was blind, and, not desiring the arduous duties of monarch, persuaded his younger brother, Pandu, to ascend the throne. But Pandu loved hunting above all other earthly pleasures, and soon he forced back upon his blind brother the task of ruling. As best he could Dhritarashtia carried on the work, and then, full of years, went to his rest, leaving behind him a hundred sons, known as the Kauravas.

The old blind king had tenderly cared for the five sons of Pandu, called the Pandavas, and in his last years so clearly realized the superiority of these nephews over his own offspring that he chose a Pandava named Yudishthira as the new monarch. Then indeed there was ire and plotting among the evil Kauravas.

The eldest of these Kauravas, named Duryodhana, was so successful in his plotting that the Pandava brothers fled to the forest. In their exile one of them won a king's daughter, not as his wife alone, but as the spouse of all five—a reminder, by the way, of the polyandry practiced among the early tribes of India. All these things came to pass before the final days of the blind king, and in his despair he at length was persuaded to divide the kingdom between the two sets of cousins, and then gladly laid him down to die.

Scarcely, however, had the old monarch passed away when Duryodhana, eldest leader of the Kauravas, induced Yudishthira, leader of the Pandavas, to risk the throne in a game of dice. The Pandavas lost, and, in addition, by the terms of the wager, they were compelled to dwell in the distant forest for twelve years. After that period they were to receive again their share of the kingdom.

The twelve years passed—thirteen—fourteen. The Kauravas scorned the demand of the Pandavas for the return of the rulership. Then arose a mighty war, with Prince Krishna, the incarnate Son of the High

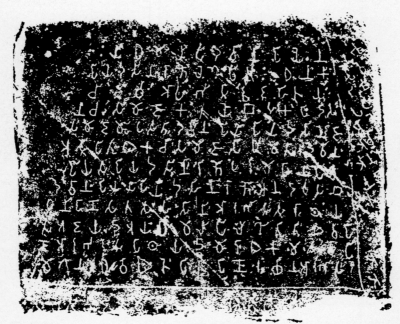

GINÁRA ROCK INSCRIPTION OF KING AŚOKA, AT JUNÂGADH, B.C. 250,
EDICT I

God, aiding the Pandavas. With such heavenly help the Pandavas utterly destroyed the wicked Kauravas, and Yudishthira became king of India.

But Krishna—whom the Hindus at length identified with the god, Vishnu—longed to return to his rightful home among the gods, and death was finally granted to him. Then to Yudishthira there remained nothing worth while in this earthly existence; he would join his beloved friend, Krishna, in the Land Beyond. Bravely he and his four brothers and their wife, Draupadi, set forth for Mount Meru, there to ascend unto Heaven. But the way was long and toilsome, and one after another of Yudishthira's companions fell by the wayside, until only he and his old, faithful dog remained to totter on until the gates of Heaven were reached.

And there—only disappointment. For his dog was refused admittance into the Home of the Blessed. But without this creature, who had suffered all hardship and weariness with him, Yudishthira firmly declined to enter. Then suddenly, like the leper in Lowell's *Vision of Sir Launfal,* the dog stood before him as the god of Justice. A god in the guise of a humble dog had traveled all the long road with him to test his kindness, his perseverance, his mercy!

Again, however, was disappointment to be the lot of Yudishthira. As he was about to pass the celestial gates he discovered that his wife and his brothers had been consigned to the lower regions. Without them Heaven could not be Heaven. He refused to enter; he would join them in the dark realm below. This was the highest test of love; that a man would voluntarily send himself to hell that he might be with those he loved. The gods were radiant with happiness that among mortals such a noble spirit existed; in the twinkling of an eye the wife and the four brothers stood before him. And into the City of God they marched, assured of eternal bliss together.

It is in many ways a magnificent epic—huge, dramatic, vivid, high in its ethics, lofty in its ideals. Here in these hundreds of thousands of lines may be discovered many a picturesque description of the customs of our remote forefathers. Here is a tone of chivalry akin to that of medieval Europe—that deep respect for woman, that glorification of strong manhood, that skill in tournament and contest, that bravery in battle which Malory made so lovable in his *Morte Darthur,* and which Scott in his novels and Tennyson in his poems revived for the modern world. Possibly the vast story was composed or collected in the fifth or sixth century, B.C., but the scenes, the deeds, the manners, the ideals belong to a far earlier period. Here stand revealed our Aryan ancestors.

Stirring episodes abound in this poetical picture of ancient Mother India. Note, for example, the contest for the hand of Draupadi—the Swayamvara, or free choice of a husband, by this entrancing, modest, high-minded Princess.

The day of the contest is at hand, Drupada, the father of Draupadi, has sent his messengers far and wide to invite the sons of royalty to attend. "Princes and chiefs innumerable" responded—among them the hundred sons of blind Dhritarashtia, headed by the haughty Duryodhana. There too were the five Pandava Brothers, quiet, courteous, brave, as befitted high Brahmans. And in a field lay a ponderous bow that only a man of superhuman strength could bend, and

there at a distance revolved on its axle a metal plate
which must be struck by an arrow from that vast bow.
This was the trial; Draupadi was the prize.

Sixteen days of festivities preceded the contest, but
with all the attempts to gloss the occasion with happiness and good fellowship, the ancient Aryan egotism
and haughtiness would break forth. Hard put to it
were the king's officials to keep the peace among these
quick-tempered, jealous sons of the chieftains. And
when Draupadi in all her beauty entered the field then
indeed were bitter looks among the ambitious con-
tenders.

> The hearts of all, Love stung with his unseen arrows,
> And jealousy inflamed each haughty mind.
> Each looked at each with baneful, hating eyes,
> And former friends now met as bitter foes.

Only the Pandava Brothers sat aloof, quiet, dignified, waiting the moment when their eldest Yudishthira, should pit his mighty strength against the bow.
Then what straining of muscles by successive princes,
"in turn to be disgraced." Laughter pealed around
as chieftain after chieftain either threw down the
weapon or tugged vainly at the cord until he fell exhausted. But then came one, vast in bulk, tremendous
of brawn—Karna, said to be the son of a charioteer.
Grasped in his vast hand, the bow bent, and he confidently adjusted the arrow. But the voice of Draupadi
in terror sounded shrilly across the field,

"I wed not with the base born!"

And Karna smiled scornfully, and, having turned
his eyes knowingly toward the sun, whom he considered his sire, he "sternly stalked away." Then

quietly arose from among his brethren and the other
Brahmans the chief of the Pandavas.

> The priestly band, wonder struck, now saw
> One who seemed but a student aspiring
> To victory where powerful chiefs had failed.
>
> .   .   .   .
>
> Then how many of the older men endeavored
> To show the boy the folly of the task;
> But all in vain!

He advanced confidently to the field, "round the
weaponed circle," and called, "with faith inflexible"
upon the Son of God, Krishna. Then lifting the massive bow, he fixed the pointed shaft. The stubborn
cord twanged, the arrow whirred to its mark, the metal
target clanged with the blow! Then

> . . . sudden, wild shouts
> Rose from the hordes so tense. Then Brahman scarfs
> Fluttered and waved, and drums boomed, trumpets blared,
> Heralds called and poets chanted his victory!

The prize—the peerless Draupadi—was to the Pandavas. Pandemonium resulted. The chieftains, the
princes, enraged but not daring to touch the sacred
Brahmans, attacked the very person of Draupadi herself! Battle ensued; but the valiant Five Brothers
drove the brutal competitors from the field.

> Then the trembling hand of Draupadi round the neck
> Of the victor placed the marriage wreath,
> And with the lovely bride, won by his courage,
> The hero passed from the field of bitter contest.

Is there not in all this something of the thrill that
Sir Walter Scott infused into *Ivanhoe,* something of

the romance that Malory and Froissart and many another writer of the days of chivalry gathered in the
pages of their ancient legends?

Once more, let us hear a story from this venerable
Mahabharata of the Hindus. This time it is the majestic legend of the return of the dead to their longing,
loving ones here on earth—"one of the grandest pictures," as Carlyle declared, "ever presented to the
human eye."

The folk sat talking sorrowfully of their kin who
had perished in the great wars of the Bharata, when
Vyasa, the sage, appeared and said, "This day I will
heal all your griefs. Go you all to the river Ganges
and bathe therein, and there each one of you shall
behold the kinsman for whom you have been sorrowing." So they all went down to the river, and chose
a bathing place for themselves and families, and Vyasa
said to them, "You shall see this night whom you desire." And the day passed away so slowly that it
seemed like a whole year to them, and at last the sun
went down, and they all bathed in the river by command of Vyasa, and said their prayers and went and
stood near him; and Yudishthira and his brethren were
on the side of Vyasa, and everybody else stood where
places could be found. Vyasa then went into the water
and prayed and bathed, and he then came out and
stood by Yudishthira, and called out the names of each
of the persons who had been slain, one by one.

At that moment the river began to foam and boil,
and a great noise was heard rising out of the water,
as though all the slain men were once again alive, and
as though they and their elephants and their horses
were bursting into loud cries, and all the drums and

trumpets and other instruments of music of both armies were striking up together. The whole assembly was astonished at this mighty tempest, and some were smitten with a terrible fear when suddenly they saw Bishma and Drona in full armor seated in their chariots, and ascending out of the water with all their armies arrayed as they were on the first day of the Maha Bharta. Next came forth Adhimanya, the heroic son of Arjuna, and the five sons of Draupadi, and the son of Bhima with his army. After him came Kuna and Duryodhana and Sankivar, and the other sons of Drona, all in full parade seated upon their chariots, together with many other warriors and rajas who had been slain. All appeared in great glory and splendor, and more beautiful than they were when alive, and all came with their own horses and chariots, and runners and arms. Every one was in perfect friendship with each other, for enmity had departed from amongst them. And each one was preceded by his bards and eulogists, who sang his praises, and very many singing men and dancing girls appeared with them, singing and dancing. Now, when those warriors had come out of the river, their widows and orphans and kinsfolk were overjoyed, and not a trace of grief remained amongst them, and widows went to their husbands, and daughters to their fathers, and mothers to their sons, and sisters to their brothers, and all the fifteen years of sorrow which had passed away since the war of the Maha Bharata were forgotten in the ecstasy of seeing each other again.

Thus the night passed away in the fullness of joy; but when the morning had dawned, all the dead mounted their chariots and horses, and disappeared; and those who had gathered to behold them prepared to depart, and Vyasa the Sage said that the widows who wished to rejoin their dead husbands might do so, and all the widows went and bathed in the Ganges, and came out of the water again and kissed every one the feet of Yudishthira and his wife Gandhavi, and went and drowned themselves in the river, and through the prayers of Vyasa they all went to the places they wished and obtained their several desires.

Many another story from the ancient epic, *Bhabharata,* might be related—how, for instance, the king's daughter, Savitri, married a prince who she was aware must die on a fixed date, how on the fated day she saw the god of death draw the soul from his sleeping body, how she followed that god over hill and through forest, ever beseeching him either to return the soul to the body or to permit her to follow that soul into the World Beyond, and how at length her prayers overcame death itself and restored to her her beloved husband. It is a sermon in narrative form on the power of faith and love. Or one might revive the marvelous description of the seaside frolic of Vishnu (Krishna) and his sixteen thousand wives—how the ocean became sweet water, upon which floated boats shaped like dolphins and peacocks and cranes, how dancers danced upon the waves, how birds sang on the shore, and how the fawn-eyed nymphs joyed all the day long under the smiles of Vishnu or Krishna. It is a ravishing scene—voluptuous, sensuous, but not sensual.

Such, then, is the *Bhabharata*—longest of the

world's epics, encyclopedia of Hindu legend and tradition, inspiration of story-teller and philosopher of many a century of Indian life. In it are bound in one mighty sheaf the dreams, the romance, the longings, the aspirations of an ancient race.

NALA AND DAMAYANTI

Strangely enough, two episodes in this vast epic have become better known to the Western World— especially in America—than the original from which they came. These two sections or divisions are *Nala and Damayanti,* and the *Bhagavad-Gita.*

The first of these is indeed an interesting story— one to charm the longing in all of us for the romantic and the mysterious. Nala, a prince, a marvelous "tamer of the steed," while wandering in his garden seized a waterfowl and was about to destroy it when the bird spoke and offered, if spared, to carry to a certain beautiful princess, Damayanti, a message of his worthiness to be her husband. And thus it happened that the princess, longing for this suitor, caused her father to declare the date of her Swayamvara, or customary choosing of a husband by the lady. Nala, of course, prepared to be among the suitors, but the gods, to test his virtues, came down to earth and accosted him as he hastened along the highway toward the scene of the choosing.

Then indeed was a hard task laid upon him. Like John Alden in the *Courtship of Miles Standish,* he, the lover of the Princess, was commanded to go before Damayanti and bespeak her favor for one of the gods as a husband.

But Nala, hearing that, joined palms again,
And cried, "Ah, send me not, with one accord
For this, most mighty Gods! How should a man
Sue for another, being suitor too?
How bear such errand? Have compassion, Gods!" [18]

But the gods were obdurate, and, spiriting him secretly into the palace grounds, he stood before the Princess,

In majesty and grace surpassing all,
So exquisite, so delicate of form,
Waist so fine-turned, such limbs, such lighted eyes,
The moon hath meaner radiance than she.
Love at the sight of that soft smiling face
Sprang to full passion, while he stood and gazed. [19]

But duty demanded that he carry out the command of the Almighty Ones, and he urged her to choose from among the "immortal four," Indra, Varuna, Yama, Agni. But the Princess softly replied,

"Pledge thyself faithfully to me, and I
Will seek, O Raja, only how to pay
That debt with all I am, with all I have;
For I and mine are thine—in full trust thine." [20]

In agony he pointed out that it was impossible for him to speak as his heart inclined. "Silence is here my duty." Then Damayanti declared that he must stand among the gods on the day of the choosing, the Swayamvara, and through the powerful guidance of love she would choose him. And so it came about that, although the four gods made themselves the exact

[18] Edwin Arnold: *Indian Idylls*, Robert Bros., Boston, 1883.
[19] *Ibid.*
[20] *Ibid.*

image of Nala, her prayer at the moment of choice was so passionate, so pathetic that the Immortal Ones disclosed themselves, and Nala was hers.

But one of the gods was filled with anger at this weakening of his fellows, and vowed to fill her husband with the spirit of a demon. The hour came when that demon destroyed for many a weary day the union of Nala and Damayanti. For the evil spirit caused him to gamble at dice until all was lost, and forth into the woods he and his faithful wife had to wander, naked but for one poor bit of cloth with which she partly concealed her nakedness.

Nor was the demon yet through with his work. At length in the depths of the night the evil one prompted Nala to steal from his wife this miserable rag and to flee farther into the wilderness, leaving her frightened and desolate. After long travail she reached at last the home of her father, while Nala wandered into a strange kingdom and became a monarch's chief horse-trainer. Though the demon within him had by this time withered one of his arms, yet in all the world was no man his equal in conquering steeds.

Repeatedly men, urged on by huge prizes offered by Damayanti's father, sought throughout the world for Nala, but for years all search was in vain. At length, however, one messenger brought back secretly the word that out in a far realm was a horse-trainer, a charioteer, who bore some resemblance to the lost Prince. Then a trap was set by this messenger and the father of the Princess; another Swayamvara for the "widow" should be declared; she should choose a new husband. The proclamation reached the king of the far-off realm, and Nala was ordered to speed the monarch to the choosing. Thus for the second time Nala was destined to aid another in an effort to gain his own beloved one as wife. But conscience-stricken, he dared not reveal the facts that rankled in his soul, and with all skill and safety he brought the king to the Swayamvara.

And there in the courtyard of his own wife's home Nala slunk about among the horses and the common servants. But love has a way of finding out. Damayanti spied that lonely, abashed charioteer and sent servant after servant to discover who he was. Long he denied his identity, but at length Damayanti herself came.

> And when Prince Nala's gaze fell on his wife,
> He stood with beating heart and tearful eyes.
> And when sweet Damayanti looked on him
> She could not speak for anguish of keen joy
> To have him close.[21]

Then from his breast burst a woeful cry: "The Kali (The Demon)! The Kali!" That was the cause. "Desolate, night and day, grieving me, possessing me, he dwelt!"

Joyous was that reunion. The king whom Nala had brought from afar lavished gifts upon him. The brother who had cheated Nala of all in the dice-playing crept back for forgiveness—and was forgiven; for had not the Evil One urged him to it? And Nala and "his pearl of women" returned to their lordly realm, and he dwelt in happiness long years,

Ruling well his realm reconquered, like a just and perfect king.

[21] Edwin Arnold: *Indian Idylls.*

It is such a story as even in these sophisticated days of realistic fiction "warms the cockles of the heart." For many a century in India it was told before the door of hut and in the chamber of palace; to all, Brahman and commoner, it made its appeal.

THE BHAGAVAD-GITA

The other episode, the *Bhagavad-Gita,* is even better known, and certainly in America is gaining a surprisingly wide reading.   Probably, with the exception of the Bible, there may not be found in any other book of all time so much concentrated wisdom.   The whole work is simply a long conversation between the incarnate god, Vishnu, and one of the Pandava Brothers, as they stand in their chariot waiting for the great battle between the Kauravas and the Pandavas to begin.   The horror of war flashes upon the young Pandava; he resolves not to destroy his fellow-man. And thus it is brought about that Vishnu (incarnated as Krishna) reveals to him the philosophy of life and death.

> . . . The wise in heart
> Mourn not for those that live, nor those that die.
> Nor I nor thou nor any one of these
> Ever was not, nor ever will not be,
> For ever and for ever afterwards.
> All that doth live lives always.   To man's frame
> As come infancy and youth and age,
> So come there raisings-up and layings-down
> Of other and of other life-abodes,
> Which the wise know, and fear not.[22]

[22] These and other selections presented here from the *Bhagavad-Gita* are from Edwin Arnold's translation called by him *The Song Celestial: Poetical Works,* Boston, Roberts Bros., 1883.   The same

With this knowledge,

> The soul which is not moved,
> The soul that with a strong and constant calm
> Takes sorrow and takes joy indifferently,
> Lives in the life undying. That which is
> Can never cease to be; that which is not
> Will not exist. . . .
>   Indestructible,
> Learn thou, the life is spreading life through all;
> It cannot anywhere, by any means,
> Be anywise diminished, stayed or changed.

For there is no death, declares the god; as Emerson maintained in his *Brahma,* so this Celestial One of India maintained that life itself is indestructible.

> He who shall say, "Lo, I have slain a man!"
> He who shall think, "Lo. I am slain!" those both
> Know naught. Life cannot slay. Life is not slain.
> Never the spirit was born; the spirit shall cease to be never;
> Never was the time it was not; End and Beginning are dreams.
> Birthless and deathless and changeless remaineth the spirit
>   for ever;
> Death hath not touched it at all, dead though the house may
>   seem.

And what of creeds, rites, regulations for this or that kind of pious life? They are not the true way to light and life; they are for petty souls who live by "rule of thumb."

version may be found in the *Complete Poetical Works,* London, Kegan, Paul, Trench, Trübner & Co., 1904, and also in *Sacred Books and Early Literature of the East* (edited by C. F. Horne), Park, Austin & Lipscomb, New York, 1917, Vol. IX. Translations of the *Bhagavad-Gita* may be found in the *Sacred Books of the East* (F. Max Müller, Editor), Oxford, Clarendon Press, 1880, Vol. VIII, and the *Harvard Classics,* Vol. XIV. Arthur Ryder is one of the latest translators, University of Chicago Press, 1929.

> Much these teach
> From Veds, concerning the "three qualities";
> But thou be free of the "three qualities,"
> Free of the "pairs of opposites," and free
> From that sad righteousness which calculates;
> Self-ruled, Arjuna, simple, satisfied. . . .
>
> Find full reward
> Of doing right in right. Let right deeds be
> Thy motive, not the fruit which comes from them.

And pious deeds, philanthropy, the doing of this or that so-called good act with the hope of repayment in the World Beyond—these are not to be compared with that inner goodness, goodness of heart, the source and spring of all worthy things.

> The right act
> Is less, far less, than the right-thinking mind.
> Seek refuge in thy soul; have there thy heaven.
> Scorn them that follow virtue for her gifts.
> The mind of pure devotion—even here—
> Casts aside, equally aside, good deeds and bad,
> Passing above them. Unto pure devotion
> Devote thyself; with perfect meditation
> Comes perfect act . . .

Self-control, calmness based on an absolute faith that there is a wise Providence guiding all toward a Desirable End—that gives the soul the peace which passeth all understanding.

> In sorrows not dejected, and in joys
> Not overjoyed; dwelling outside the stress
> Of passion, fear, and anger; fixed in calms
> Of lofty contemplation—such an one
> Is Muni, is the Sage, the true Recluse.

He who to none and nowhere overbound
By ties of flesh, takes evil things and good,
Neither desponding nor exulting, such
Bears wisdom's plainest mark.

It is the life of the senses, an existence swayed by passions, pleasures, prejudices, that brings havoc to the rightful peace of the soul.

The mind
That gives itself to follow shows of sense
Seeth its helm of wisdom rent away,
And like a ship in waves of whirlwind, drives
To wreck and death.

All this does not mean inaction, sitting inert, motionless in constant meditation. Such an existence is against all nature. "No jot of time, at any time, rests any actionless." All must labor; for the sanity of one's mind and soul one must work. But such toil with its only inspiration being the grasping of power or the exploitation of one's fellows is, possibly, worse than inactivity.

But he who, with strong body serving mind,
Gives up his mortal powers to worthy work,
Not seeking gain, Arjuna, such an one
Is honorable. Do thine allotted task.
Work is more excellent than idleness;
The body's life proceeds not, lacking work.
There is a task of holiness to do,
Unlike world-binding toil, which bindeth not
The faithful soul; such earthly duty do,
Free from desire, and thou shalt well perform
Thy heavenly purpose.

He, however, who works only for himself, who grasps and hugs to himself for his own use only, the possessions of this work, he that spreads a feast all for himself, eats sin and drinks of sin.

> Existing for himself,
> Self-concentrated, serving self alone,
> No part hath he in aught; nothing achieved,
> Nought wrought or unwrought toucheth him; no hope
> Of help for all the living things of earth
> Depends on him.

And remember, pleads Krishna, God is all—that is the Supreme Fact of the universe. The genuinely wise

> Have sense of one pervading Spirit's stress,
> One Force in every place, though manifold.
> I am the Sacrifice. I am the Prayer.
> I am the Funeral-Cake set for the dead.
> I am the healing herb. I am the ghee,
> The Mantra, and the flame, and that which burns.
> I am—of all this boundless Universe—
> The Father, Mother, Ancestor, and Guard.
> The end of Learning. . . .
> Death am I, and Immortal Life I am.
> .   .   .   .
> I am alike for all. I know not hate,
> I know not favor. What is made is Mine.
> But them that worship Me with love, I love;
> They are in Me, and I in them.

God, declares Krishna, must be considered the beneficent source of all things; otherwise life is inexplicable.

Whatever Natures be
To mortal men distributed, those natures spring from me.
Intellect, skill, enlightenment, endurance, self-control,
Truthfulness, equability, and grief, and joy of soul,

And birth and death, and fearfulness, and fearlessness and
    shame,
And honor and sweet harmlessness, and peace which is the
    same
Whate'er befalls, and mirth, and tears, and piety, and thrift,
And wish to give, and will to help—all cometh of My gift.

The secret of the "good life," that is, a life of contentment and fruits which bring the greatest satisfac-
tion, is, after all, a very simple secret. But human
ambition, petty jealousies, stubborn opinion growing
into mad prejudice—these are what keep the mortals
of this world from realizing the simplicity of happiness.

The Doors of Hell

Are threefold, whereby men to ruin pass—
The door of Lust, the door of Wrath, the door
Of Avarice. Let a man shun those three.
He who shall turn from entering
All those three gates of Narak, wendeth straight
To find his peace, and comes to Swarga's gate.

These, then, are some of the noble thoughts in that
one section of the *Mahabharata* known as the
Bhagavad-Gita. It is an idealistic philosophy—an
idealism that, even after three thousand years, the
most civilized of nations have not attained. Only a
nation with a genius for ethical meditation could have
created such a summary of the principles of the "good
life."

With its multitude of legends, its stories of reincar-
nation, its tales of the living of gods among men, its
ethics, its revelations of the long, long inner life of a
people, is it any marvel that for untold generations

the Hindu races have looked upon the *Mahabharata* as something inspired, sacred, healing? One of the last declarations of the majestic poem is this: "The reading of this *Mahabharata* destroys all sin and produces virtue, so much so that the pronunciation of a single section is sufficient to wipe away much guilt. It has bound human beings in a chain, of which one end is life and the other death. If a man reads the *Mahabharata* and has faith in its doctrines, he is free from all sin and ascends to Heaven after his death."

Hindu Drama

Like almost all other nations, the Hindus thus passed in their literary evolution through religious and epic creations to dramatic productions and finally to lyric poetry. Why the order of development has so often been such among both ancient and modern peoples is rather difficult to understand; but it may be that, as the civilization of a nation progresses, more of the population is to be found in cities, and cities in themselves are dramatic.

Be this as it may, it seems certain that the theater did not arise in India until long after the epic period. Because of the vagueness of chronology in Asia, the exact dates of the dramas of the Hindus are beyond ascertaining. Probably the sixty or more plays now known to scholars belong to an era beginning approximately a century before the Christian period and closing possibly in the sixth century, A.D. There is indeed considerable probability that the original idea of the drama or theater was introduced into India by the Greek or by Indian travelers who had visited Athens.

Like the Attic comedies, most of these plays of the Hindus have a prologue, but, in general, these performances presented in the valley of the Ganges were much more romantic than even the later Greek plays. The love theme is exceedingly prominent, and the dénouement is often one of extreme happiness. Not unlike the productions of Shakespeare's days, these Indian comedies frequently possess a fool, a buffoon, or a courtier who is attached to some monarch and who functions as a foil or contrast to this ruler. Not infrequently, as happened in the later Greek, Latin, and French theater, the priesthood came in for a goodly share of ridicule. And, lastly, just as in the later Elizabethan drama, these plays are not infrequently a mixture of prose dialogue and lyrical poetry.

How astonishingly modern some of the plays of old India sound! With a slight change in names and background, several of them might seem rather natural productions of the twentieth century. Here is the same sort of analysis of emotions and motives that we expect to find revealed on the stage of to-day. Here are the same intrigues, the same good and bad characters that people our better dramas of the hour. Here is the same clear, familiar, unforced dialogue that carries a present-day performance to success.

But it was that same dialogue, natural as it may sound in translation, which finally stifled and destroyed Hindu drama. For in the original *two* languages sounded across the boards. Kings, gods, the high and mighty of this world talked always in Sanskrit, while the lowly, the minor characters, and the women talked in the "dog language," Prakrit. No drama could long survive the ordeal of requiring two distinct tongues.

For a time the nobility in the courts of kings, the priests, the scholars, the Brahmans might understand and tolerate such bi-lingual exhibitions, but to the great masses of the common people the theater under such a restriction could make no appeal. Hindu drama destroyed itself through its own rigid standardization, its insistence upon a tradition.

In our day the stage appeals not only to the ear, but also to the eye; indeed, the setting, the scenery, the costume are frequently so attractive as to draw our attention somewhat from the tragedy or comedy attempting to reveal itself across the footlight. There are certainly no such distractions in the theater of the early Hindus. Scenery was almost unknown; whatever the environment was supposed to be was expressed by the actors themselves. Again, in our times there is a freedom of speech so excessive in dramas as to draw down the wrath of many who esteem morality and decency. Here, once more, the Indian stage was different. A strict censorship demanded, for instance, that no scene of death or violence occur before the eyes of the audience; eating and drinking and simulated sleep on the part of the actors were taboo; no lady on the stage might speak directly to her lover; a third person should be used as a convenient recipient of such remarks.

And yet, with all the restrictions as to language, scenery, deeds, and conversation, how thoroughly human are these plays performed centuries ago in the Hindu court theaters! Take, for example, the *Toy Cart,* or *Clay Cart,* as the title is sometimes translated —the earliest of the Indian dramas we now possess, written by King Sudraka, supposedly as late as the fifth century, A.D. But dates in early India, it should be remembered, are largely conjectural; some students have ventured to place Sudraka as far back as the first century, B.C.

Be the time what it may, the ten acts of this play reveal a romantic atmosphere and a sharp delineation of characters and an analysis of character highly pleasing even in these days of such skilled dramatists as Barrie, Shaw, and Eugene O'Neill.

It is a story of a merchant whose character, generosity, and idealism are such that even a courtesan, a woman of the street, is moved through admiration to aid him and indeed finally to save his life. How human and at the same time how skillful is the opening scene, which gives the drama its title! The little boy of Charudatta, the merchant, enters with his nurse, Radanika. The child is discontented with his cart of baked clay—the best that his father can now afford him; for Charudatta, through excessive generosity, has reduced himself almost to the state of poverty. Radanika and the child enter.

Rad. Come along, my child, let us ride in your cart.

Child. I do not want this cart; it is only of clay. I want one of gold.

Rad. And where are we to get the gold, my little man? Wait till your father is rich again, and then he will buy you one. Come, let us go and see Vasantasena. Lady, I salute you.

Vasantasena (the courtesan). Welcome, Radanika. Whose charming boy is this? Although he is ill attired, his lovely face quite fascinates me.

Rad. This is Rohasena, the son of Charudatta.

Vas. (stretching out her arms). Come here, my little dear, and kiss me. (*Takes him on her lap.*) How like his father!

Rad. He is like him too in disposition. Charudatta dotes on him.

Vas. Why does he weep?

Rad. The child of our rich neighbor, the great landholder, had a golden cart, which this little fellow saw and wanted. I made him this of clay, but he is not pleased with it, and is crying for the other.

Vas. Alas, alas, this little creature is already mortified by another's prosperity! O Fate, thou sportest with the fortunes of mankind like drops of water trembling on the lotus leaf. Don't cry, my good boy, and you shall have a gold cart.

Child. Radanika, who is this?

Vas. A handmaid purchased by your father's merits.

Rad. This is your lady mother, child.

Child. You tell me untruth, Radanika. How can this be my mother when she wears such fine things?

Vas. How harsh a speech for so soft a tongue! (*Weeping, she takes off her ornaments.*) Now I am your mother. Here, take this trinket and go buy a gold cart.

Child. Away, I will not take it; you cry at parting with it!

Vas. (*wiping her eyes*). I weep no more. Go, love, and play. (*Fills his cart with her jewels.*) There; go, get you a golden cart.[23]

This good-hearted courtesan delicately endeavors to relieve Charudatta's wants by entrusting to him a casket of her jewels; in reality she intends them as a gift. But in the night a burglar steals the casket from the merchant's sleeping servant, Maitreya, and the noble master, burdened with his own troubles as he is, tries to shield Maitreya by taking upon himself the entire blame. This woman of the world, however, is too keen-witted to be deceived by the simple-hearted

[23] Horace H. Wilson: *Select Specimens of the Theater of the Hindus,* Calcutta, V. Holcroft, 1827, Vol. I; an excellent translation by Arthur Ryder, Harvard University Press, 1905.

Charudatta, and by means of some genuinely clever
detective work she recovers the jewels, and again
presents them to the merchant.

But now the courtesan is set upon by the very person
who had stolen the wealth, and is supposedly murdered
by him. Covering her body with a heap of leaves by
the roadside, the rogue goes his way, thinking an evil
job well done. But the woman has disappeared, and
the law demands its recompense. With that same
subtle intellect displayed by the average twentieth-
century police force, the Hindu officers seize Charudatta, prove what needs no proof, that he had received
jewels from the victim, and upon such circumstantial
evidence condemn him to execution.

What a scene is that of the march to death!—just
such a scene as has been enacted in the yard of many
a county jail in America. Here are the court officials,
swollen with dignity, flattered by the conspicuous position they occupy for the moment. Here are the
buffoons who would make a farce of a tragedy. Here
is the innocent prisoner, patient, calm, dignified, endeavoring to hide his agony from his little boy, who
clings in sorrowful amazement to the father. Thus,
possibly two thousand years ago, the conscience of man
cried out against the doubtful right of the State to
destroy the life of a human being.

Hear a few lines from this tragic scene of centuries
long gone, yet so horribly similar to what yet takes
place in the name of the law in the modern world.
Enter Charudatta with two Chandalas as executioners.

1st Chan. Out of the way, sirs, out of the way; room for
Charudatta, adorned with the Karavira garland, and attended

by his dexterous executioners; he approaches his end, like a lamp ill fed with oil.

Char.   Sepulchral blossoms decorate my limbs,
Covered with dust, and watered by my tears,
And round me harshly croak the carrion birds,
Impatient to enjoy their promised prey.

2d Chan.   Out of the way, sirs, what do you stare at? A good man whose head is to be chopped off; a tree that gave shelter to gentle birds to be cut down.—Come on, Charudatta.

Char.   Who can foresee the strange vicissitudes
Of man's sad destiny? I little thought
That such a fate would ever be my portion,
Nor could have credited I should live to be
Dragged like a beast to public sacrifice,
Stained with the ruddy sandal spots and smeared
With meal—a victim to the sable goddess.
Yet as I pass along, my fellow-citizens
Console me with their tears, and execrate
The cruel sentence that awards my death;
Unable to preserve my life, they pray
That heaven await me, and reward my sufferings.

1st Chan.   Stand out of the way.—What crowd you to see? There are four things not to be looked at. Indra carried forth —the birth of a calf—the falling of a star—and the misfortune of a good man. Look, brother Chinta—the whole city is under sentence! What! does the sky weep, or the thunderbolt fall, without a cloud?

2d Chan.   No, brother Goha; not so: the shower falls from yonder cloud of women. Let them weep—their tears will at least help to lay the dust.

Char.   From every window lovely faces shed
The kindly drops, and bathe me with their tears.

1st Chan. Here, stop, strike the drum, and cry the sentence
—Hear ye—Hear ye—This is Charudatta, son of Sagaradatta,
son of Provost Vinayadatta, by whom the courtesan Vasantasena has been robbed and murdered: he has been convicted and
condemned, and we are ordered by King Palaka to put him to
death: so will his Majesty ever punish those that commit such
crimes as both worlds abhor.

> *Char.* Dreadful reverse—to hear such wretches herald
> My death, and blacken thus with lies my fame:
> Not so my sires—for them the frequent shout
> Has filled the sacred temple, where the crowd
> Of holy Brahmans to the Gods proclaimed
> The costly rite accomplished—and shall I,
> Alas, Vasantasena, who have drunk
> Thy nectared tones from lips, whose ruby glow
> Disgraced the coral, and displayed the charms
> Of teeth more pearly than the moon's chaste light,
> Profane my ears with such unworthy draughts,
> Or stain my enslaved spirit with the pledge
> Of poison, brewed by infamy and shame?
> *(Puts his hands to his ears.)*

1st Chan. Stand apart there—make way.

> *Char.* My friends avoid me as I pass, and hiding
> Their faces with their raiment, turn away.
> Whilst fortune smiles we have no lack of friends,
> But scant their number in adversity.

(Voices behind.) Father! Father! My friend—my friend!
Char. My worthy friends, grant me this one indulgence.
1st Chan. What, will you take anything of us?

> *Char.* Disdain not my request; though basely born,
> You are not cruel, and a gentle nature
> Ranks you above your sovereign. I implore you,
> By all your future hopes, oh! once permit me
> To view my son, ere I depart to death.

1st Chan. Let him come.—Men, stand back, and let the child approach—here, this way.

Enter Maitreya with Rohasena.

Mai. Here we have him, boy, once more; your dear father, who is going to be murdered.

Roha. Father—Father!

Char. Come hither, my child.

(*Embraces him and takes his hands.*)
These little hands will ill suffice to sprinkle
The last sad drops upon my funeral pyre.—
Scant will my spirit sip thy love, and then
A long and painful thirst in heaven succeeds.
What sad memorial shall I leave thee, boy,
To speak to thee hereafter of thy father?
This sacred string, whilst yet 'tis mine, I give thee.
The Brahman's proudest decoration, boy,
Is not of gold nor gems, but this—with which
He ministers to sages and to Gods,
This grace my child, when I shall be no more.
(*Takes off his Brahmanical cord, and puts it round his son's neck.*)

1st Chan. Come, you Charudatta, come along.

2d Chan. More respect, my master. Recollect; by night or day, in adversity or prosperity, worth is always the same. Come, sir, complaints are unavailing; fate holds her course, and it is not to be expected that men will honor the moon, when Rahu has hold of him.

Roha. Where do you lead my father, vile Chandala?

Char. I go to death, my child; the fatal chaplet
Of Karavira hangs around my neck:
The stake upon my shoulder rests, my heart
Is burdened with despair, as, like a victim
Dressed for the sacrifice, I meet my fate.

1st Chan. Hark ye, my boy, they who are born Chandalas are not the only ones—those whose crimes disgrace their birth are Chandalas too.

Roha. Why, then, want to kill my father?

1st Chan. The king orders us; it is his fault, not ours.

Roha. Take and kill me; let my father go.

1st Chan. My brave little fellow, long life to you!

Char. (*Embracing him.*)

> This is the truest wealth; love equal smiles
> On poor and rich: the bosom's precious balm
> Is not the fragrant herb, nor costly unguent—
> But nature's breath, affection's holy perfume.

Mai. Come now, my good fellows, let my worthy friend escape: you only want a body—mine is at your disposal.

Char. Forbear—Forbear.

1st Chan. Come on. Stand off; what do you throng to see? A good man who has lost his all, and fallen into despair, like a gold bucket whose rope breaks, and it tumbles into the well.

2d Chan. Here stop, beat the drum, and proclaim the sentence.   (*As before.*)

Char. This is the heaviest pang of all; to think

> Such bitter fruit attends my closing life.
> And, oh! what anguish, love, to hear the calumny
> Thus noised abroad, that thou wast slain by me!

(*Exeunt.*) [24]

But, lo, as the solemn procession nears the place of execution, a ghastly figure totters down the highway toward the throng! Running, stumbling, waving its blood-stained arms, it draws near. It is Vasantasena, clotted with her own gore, begrimed, lacerated—but alive! Charudatta, who in his days of prosperity had saved so many others, is now saved in the hour of his bitter adversity by an outcast from society.

[24] *Ibid.*

It would have been a remarkable piece of literature in any age—this king's drama, the *Toy Cart*. It is all the more remarkable as coming from a country far removed from the inspiring stage of Athens, and coming also from among a people who had for so many generations given themselves to philosophic and religious meditation that the dramatic element in their nature might well be supposed to have been long since stifled.

From those distant days along the Ganges have come specimens and traditions of other unusual plays. Another king, Sri Harsha-diva, of the seventh century, A.D., may have written three that have been handed down to our day. Rama of the *Ramayana*, Krishna of the *Mahabharata*, and other earthly deities of the ancient religion evidently furnished many a scene or indeed whole plot for the stage of the early Hindu theater. It was seemingly a sudden and rather brief outburst of dramatic genius among a people distant from the centers of this type of literary culture.

Among all these dramatists of fifteen or twenty centuries ago one stands forth preëminent—Kalidasa, sometimes termed "the Hindu Shakespeare." *Sakuntala,* or the *Fatal Ring*—what a sensation this play of Kalidasa's made in literary Europe when Sir William Jones translated it in 1789! Goethe read it, and in his enthusiasm wrote:

> Spring's blossoms, Autumn's harvest-gold
> In one large word wouldst thou enfold?
> All that delights and satisfies
> In single phrase wouldst thou comprise?
> I "Sakuntala" name, and there
> At once speak all that's good and fair.

Written about 550 A.D., this play possesses emotionalism, a vividness of characterization, a strength of plot that should satisfy even the most cultured audience of the twentieth century. Other dramas, of course, were produced by this Hindu of long ago, notably *Vikramorvasi,* but it is through *Sakuntala* that Kalidasa has gained fame, not only in India, but throughout the Western World. The fact that several English translations have been made of it since the first by Sir William Jones—notably those by Sir Monier-Williams in England and Professor Arthur Ryder in America—is evidence that this early masterpiece of Eastern drama is losing none of its charm for modern readers.

Let us rehearse the story and feel for ourselves the romantic beauty of the play.

King Dushyanta, young, vigorous, handsome, is on a hunting trip. Having stalked an antelope far, he comes upon a sacred grove of the Hindu sages, and, discovering that this is "holy ground," he instantly desists from the chase. Walking reverently through the grove, he suddenly comes upon a group of beautiful young women playing under the trees. It is Sakuntala and her friends—Sakuntala, daughter of a king and a heavenly nymph. Dushyanta, smitten with love, hides in the underbrush and looks and listens. A bee buzzes dangerously close to Sakuntala's face.

Sak. (*moving her head*). Oh, a bee has left the blossom and is fluttering about my face.

Dush. (*aside with affection*). How often have I seen our court ladies affectedly turn their heads aside from some roving insect, merely to display their graces. But this rural maid knits her brows, and gracefully moves her eyes through fear only, without art or affectation. O happy bee, who touchest the corner of that eye so beautifully trembling! Who, approaching the tip of that ear, murmurest as softly as though thou wert whispering a secret of love, and who sippest nectar, while she waves her graceful hand, from that lip which contains all the treasures of delight! While I am solicitous to know in what family she was born, thou art enjoying bliss which to me would be extreme felicity.

Sak. Free me, I entreat, from this importunate insect, which quite baffles all my efforts!

Pri. What power have we to deliver you? The King Dushyanta is the sole defender of our consecrated grove.

Sak. This impudent bee will not rest. I will remove to another place. (*Running aside and looking about.*) Away! away! He follows me wherever I go. Deliver me, oh! deliver me from this distress.

Dush. (*advancing hastily*). Ah! While the race of Puru govern the world and restrain even the most profligate by good laws well administered, has any man the audacity to molest the lovely daughters of pious hermits?

Anu. Sir, no man is here audacious; but this damsel, our beloved friend, was teased by a fluttering bee.

Dush. (*approaching her*). Maiden, may thy devotion prosper. (*Sakuntala looks upon the ground, bashful and silent.*)

Pri. Stranger, you are welcome. Go, my Sakuntala; bring from the cottage a basket of fruit and flowers. The water that we brought will serve to bathe his feet.

.   .   .   .

Sak. (*aside*). At the sight of this youth I feel an emotion scarcely consistent with a grove devoted to piety.

Dush. (*gazing at them alternately*). How well your friendship agrees, holy damsels, with the charming equality of your ages and of your beauties.

Anu. Your sweet speech, Sir, gives me confidence. What imperial family is embellished by our noble guest? What is his native country? Surely it must be afflicted by his absence from it. What, I pray, could induce you to humiliate that exalted form of yours by visiting a forest?

Dush. Excellent lady, I am a student of the Veda, dwelling in the city of our king, descended from Puru, and, being occupied in the discharge of religious and moral duties, am come hither to behold the sanctuary of virtue. . . . In my turn, holy damsels, allow me to ask one question concerning your lovely friend.

Both. The request, Sir, does us honor.

Dush. The sage Canna, I know, is ever intent upon the Great Being, and must have declined all earthly connections. How, then, can this damsel be, as it is said, his daughter?

Anu. Let our lord hear. There is in the family of Cusa a pious priest of extensive power, eminent in devotion and in arms.

Dush. You speak, no doubt, of Causica, the sage and monarch.

Anu. Know, Sir, that he is in truth her father; while Canna bears that reverend name because he brought her up, since she was left an infant.

Dush. The word excites my curiosity and raises in me desire to know her whole story.

Anu. You shall hear it, Sir, in few words. When that sage king had begun to gather the fruits of his austere devotion, the gods of Swerga became apprehensive of his increasing power, and sent a nymph, Menaca, to frustrate, by her allurements, the full effect of his piety.

Dush. Is a mortal's piety so tremendous to the inferior deities?

Anu. In the bloom of the vernal season Causica, beholding the beauty of the celestial nymph, and wafted by the gale of desire— (*She stops and looks modest.*)

Dush. I now see the whole. Sakuntala, then, is the daughter of a king by a nymph of the lower heaven.

Anu. Even so.

Dush. (*aside*). The desire of my heart is gratified. (*Aloud.*)

How indeed could her transcendent beauty be the portion of mortal birth? Yon light that sparkles with tremulous beams proceeds nor from a terrestrial cavern. (*Sakuntala sits modestly, with her eyes upon the ground.*)

Dush. (*aside*). Happy man that I am! Now has my fancy an ample range. Yet I am divided with anxious doubt whether she be not wholly destined for a religious life.

Pri. Hitherto, Sir, our friend has lived happy in this consecrated forest, the abode of her spiritual father; but it is now his intention to unite her with a bridegroom equal to herself.

Dush. (*aside, with ecstasy*). Exult, oh my heart, exult! All doubt is removed, and what before thou wouldst have dreaded as a flame may now be approached as a gem inestimable.[25]

Later comes a scene depicting a courtship as tender as one might desire to see on the stage, and then follows the blessing of the sages upon the couple and their marriage. Suddenly, however, the King is called away by urgent affairs of the empire. But he leaves with his young wife a magic ring—the symbol of his love and constancy—and he bids her never to lose it lest misfortune fall upon their union.

Misfortune, however, was fated to come. A holy Brahman sage, a wandering, self-important philosopher, comes to the sacred grove, and, not receiving from the lonely, absent-minded Sakuntala that instant attention and reverence which he considers due such a guest, he departs in a rage, hurling at her a curse:

> He, even he of whom thou thinkest, he
> Shall think no more of thee, nor in his heart
> Retain thy image. Vainly shalt thou strive

[25] Sir William Jones' translation, *Complete Works*, London, John Stockdale, 1807, Vol. 9.

To waken his remembrances of the past;
He shall disown thee, even as the sot,
Roused from his midnight drunkenness, denies
The words he uttered in his revellings.[26]

At length the wandering sage is appeased to the extent that he will permit her to win back her husband's memory and affection provided she wears, upon meeting Dushyanta, the ring that he had given her. But there, alas, is the trick of the prophecy.

Sakuntala, waiting vainly for the return of her king, starts with some of the hermits and sages for the distant court. The way is long, the days are hot, and as the weary woman stoops to drink from a spring the magic ring slips unnoticed from her finger. On to the court she goes, and there the king, warned of the approach of holy men from the sacred grove, is seated in dignity on his throne.

Chamberlain. Victory to the king! So please your majesty, some hermits, who live in a forest near the Snowy Mountains, have arrived here, bringing certain women with them. They have a message from the sage Kanwa, and desire an audience.

(*Enter the Hermits, leading Sakuntala, attended by a matron, Gautami; and in advance of them the Chamberlain and the Domestic Priest.*)

Sak. Heaven avert this throbbing of my right eyelid!

Gaut. Heaven avert the evil omen, my child!

Hermits. Victory to the king!

King. Accept my respectful greeting. I trust the venerable Kanwa is in good health.

Hermits. The venerable Kanwa bids us say he feels happy in giving his sanction to the marriage which your majesty

[26] *Ibid.*

much abridged

contracted with this lady, his daughter, privately and by mutual agreement... Since, therefore, she expects soon to be the mother of thy child, receive her into thy palace, that she may perform with thee the ceremonies prescribed by religion.

King. What strange proposal is this?

Hermit. What do I hear? Dost thou hesitate?

King. Do you mean to assert that I ever married this lady?

Sak. (*aside*). O my heart, thy worst misgivings are confirmed!

Gantami (*to Sakuntala*). Be not ashamed, my daughter. Let me remove thy veil: thy husband will then recognize thee.

King (*gazing at Sakuntala. Aside*).

> What charms are here revealed before mine eyes!
> Truly no blemish mars the symmetry
> Of that fair form. Yet can I ne'er believe
> She is my wedded wife; and like a bee
> That circles round the flower whose nectared cup
> Teems with the dew of morning, I must pause
> Ere eagerly I taste the proffered sweetness.

Hermit. Great king, why art thou silent?

King. Holy men, I have resolved the matter in my mind, but the more I think of it the more I am unable to recollect that I ever contracted an alliance with this lady.

Sak. If, then, thou really believest me to be the wife of another, and thy present conduct proceeds from some cloud that obscures thy recollection, I will easily convince thee by this token.

King. An excellent idea!

Sak. (*feeling for the ring*). Alas! alas! woe is me! There is no ring on my finger! (*Looks with anguish at Gautami.*)

Gaut. The ring must have slipped off when thou wast in the act of offering homage to the holy water of Sachi's sacred pool.

King (*smiling*). People may well talk of the readiness of woman's invention! Here's an instance of it!

Gaut. Speak not thus, illustrious prince: this lady was brought up in a hermitage, and never learned deceit.

King. Holy matron,
    E'en in untutored brutes, the female sex
    Is marked by inborn subtlety,—much more
    In beings gifted with intelligence.

Sak. (*angrily*). Dishonorable man, thou judgest others by thine own evil heart; thou at least art unrivaled in perfidy, and standest alone—a base deceiver, in the garb of virtue and religion—like a deep pit whose yawning mouth is concealed by smiling flowers!

    (*The Hermits depart and leave Sakuntala; the King will not receive her, so the Priest leads her away weeping. Then a voice behind the scene cries, "A miracle!"*)

Priest (*entering with astonishment*). Great Prince, a stupendous prodigy has occurred! Sakuntala, as soon as Kanwa's pupils had departed, was bewailing her cruel fate,

    When suddenly a shining apparition
    In female shape descended from the skies,
    Near the nymphs' pool and bore her up to heaven.[27]

Sakuntala is gone, and King Dushyanta marvels at the miracle, but, with no memory of his marriage to her, he feels no twinge of conscience. But a poor fisherman finds the ring, is accused of stealing it, and is brought into court by policemen possessed of just about as much acumen as those in the previous play we have examined. With the ring once more in the king's hand, the enchantment is broken; he recalls the wedding with Sakuntala. But Dushyanta is of this earth, and she is of the heavens. Years of vain regret

[27] *Ibid,* Act V.

(M-W)

and longing pass, and then at length the king is called upon by the gods to aid in the war against the race of giants. The battles are won, and the king is returning in triumph, riding in the chariot of the god of gods, Indra. Rounding a curve on a sacred mountain he comes upon a child playing with a lion. In the features of this child he discerns so strong a resemblance to Sakuntala that he halts the chariot and begins to question the boy and the attendants. Then appears the mother, Sakuntala, and all ends joyfully.

This, then, is the sort of drama that gained the favor of kings and Brahmans in the royal courts of India fifteen centuries ago. After all, is it not the theme of love and misunderstanding and reconciliation that to-day satisfies the theater-goer in New York or in London? Are not the heroine and the hero of this play of the earlier Hindus composed of the same human fiber as those that strive and suffer and conquer on the far more gorgeous stage of our times? After all, not only human nature but the portrayal of human nature changes so little throughout the ages. If only those high-born and high-bred Brahmans of hundreds of years ago had condescended to hear the plays in the language of the common folk, instead of in a mixture of dying Sanskrit and Prakrit—who knows but what those Indian valleys and highlands might have produced a dramatic literature as vital and as enduring as that of England or France or Germany?

LYRIC POETRY

During this same period when the Hindu theater was flourishing, there was being composed a lyric poetry of rather exceptional skill and romantic atmosphere.

Possibly the invasion of Persian and Arabian literature had something to do with the birth of this type of verse in India. Totally different in style and tone from the ancient hymns which the priests still chanted, it often had a lightness of touch and a sweetness of sentiment comparable to the best in our modern poetry. Hymns, of course, were still composed— lengthy ones, often running into hundreds of lines. More frequently, however, the verse dealt with some emotional state of the author or some personal re- action inspired by a scene or incident, and in such instances the lines are imbued with a genuine romantic beauty. Of this character is the *Ritu-Samhara,* long a famous composition among the Hindus, and one that has frequently been compared, justly and favorably, with Thomson's *Seasons.*

Kalidasa himself wrote a large number of just such poems of sentiment, and one of them, *Meghaduta,* or the *Cloud-Messenger,* has gained especial notice from students of Eastern literature. A demi-god, banished from among the celestial beings, entrusts to a wander- ing cloud a message to his wife, still dwelling in the heavenly realm among the Himalaya Mountains:

> O gentle Cloud! long be thy days of bliss!
> Speak softly to her—be thy message this:—
> "Lady! thy dear One in great Rama's Grove
> Mourns the sad fate that parts him from his love;
> Asks—doth thy strength with lonely weeping fail,
> Is thine eye dim, and doth thy cheek grow pale?
> Far, far away by hostile fate's decree,
> In fondest fancy he is still with thee;
> Wasted with woe, to him thy form appears,
> An image of his own, all worn with tears;

In sympathy with his thy longing soul,
And bursting tears that neither can control;
Far from thy sight and from thy willing ear,
He trusts to me alone thy breast to cheer;
Yet oh! what bliss, might he but touch thy cheek,
And in thine ear himself thy message speak!
I see thy graceful form in every flower
That freshest, fairest, twines around my bower;
When from my path the startled roe-deer fly,
In their soft glance I see thy gentle eye;
The peacock's brilliant plumes to me recall
Thy long dark tresses glittering as they fall;
The small brook wavelets arching in their flow,
Seem but the shadow of thy slender brow;
And when the Moon illumes my weary night,
Thy pure, pale cheek is ever in my sight.
In each fair thing an emblem faint I see
Of beauty centering alone in thee!" [28]

Of all these later Hindu poems, however, by far the most famous and most beloved among the people of India seems to have been *Gitagovinda,* a piece of lyrical drama or dramatic lyric frequently called "the Hindu Song of Songs." It is not unlike the *Song of Solomon,* not only in its fervor, but in its meeting the same fate at the hands of commentators, who have persisted in finding in it a religious symbolism that probably its composer never dreamed of. Strange, is it not, that so often religious zealots feel duty-bound to spoil a good song or story by attaching a library of ethical nonsense to it?

The author of this lyrical composition, a poet named Jayadeva, evidently intended to relate the spirited nar-

[28] H. H. Wilson's translation, with some changes, Calcutta, P. Perivia, 1813.

rative of the love-philanderings of that jovial god, Krishna. For Krishna, possibly the ancient god, Vishnu, had to become in his later days—because of the inevitable desire of the public for fun—a sort of celestial wearer of the cap and bells. He became what in ultra-modern parlance we would style a "lady's man," and during one of his frequent lives on earth evidently forgot rather often his faithful spouse, the milkmaid, Radha. But, woman-like, she always forgave him when he crept back penitent.

In the *Gitagovinda* we find, however, a serious and beautiful portrayal of the emotions of the unfaithful god and his patient Radha, and with it all a luxuriance and voluptuousness of description only possible, perhaps, in a production of the passionate tropics.

> Beautiful Radha, jasmine-bosomed Radha,
> All in the spring-time waited by the wood
> For Krishna fair, Krishna the all-forgetful,
> Krishna with earthly love's false fire consuming—
> And some one of her maidens sang this song.[29]

And what a song of luxurious, passion-laden spring she does sing!

I know how Krishna passes these hours of blue and gold,
When parted lovers sigh to meet and greet and closely hold
Hand fast in hand, and every branch upon the Vakul-tree
Droops downward with a hundred blooms, in every bloom a
    bee;
He is dancing with the dancers to a laughter-moving tone,
In the soft awakening spring-time, when 'tis hard to live alone.

[29] Excerpts from Edwin Arnold: *Indian Poetry*, Boston, Roberts Brothers, 1883.

Where Kroona-flowers, that open at a lover's lightest tread,
Break, and, for shame at what they hear, from white blush
     modest red;
And all the spears on all the boughs of all the Ketuk glades
Seem ready darts to pierce the hearts of wandering youths and
     maids;
'Tis there thy Krishna dances till the merry drum is done,
All in the sunny spring-time, when who can live alone?

Where the breath of waving Madlavi pours incense through
     the grove,
And silken Mogras lull the sense with essences of love—
The silken soft pale Mogra, whose perfume fine and faint
Can melt the coldness of a maid, the sternness of a saint—
There dances with those dancers thine other self, thine Own,
All in the languorous spring-time, when none will live alone.

And then Radha herself sees afar the errant husband frolicking under the trees with the voluptuous
nymphs of the woods. It is an enchanting scene—to
the reader, but one to shoot darts of jealousy and
agony into the heart of the wife.

One, with star-blossomed champak wreathed, woos him to rest
     his head
On the dark pillow of her breast so tenderly outspread;
And o'er his brow with roses blown she fans a fragrance rare,
That falls on the enchanted sense like rain in thirsty air,
While the company of damsels wave many an odorous spray,
And Krishna, laughing, toying, sighs the soft spring away.

   .   .   .   .

The third one of that dazzling band of dwellers in the wood—
Body and bosom panting with the pulse of youthful blood—
Leans over him, as in his ear a lightsome thing to speak,
And then with leaf-soft lip imprints a kiss below his cheek;
A kiss that thrills, and Krishna turns at the silken touch
To give it back—ah, Radha, forgetting thee too much!

But with the coming of another morning the sated
Krishna returns—disgusted, ashamed, humiliated.

> . . . in the glad light he came, and bent
> His knee, and clasped his hands; on his dumb lips
> Fear, wonder, joy, passion, and reverence
> Strove for the trembling words, and Radha knew
> Joy won for him and her; yet none the less
> A little time she chided him, and sang:

> Krishna!—then thou hast found me!—and thine eyes
>   Heavy and sad and stained, as if with weeping.
> Ah! is it not that those, which were thy prize,
>   So radiant seemed that all night thou wert keeping
> Vigils of tender wooing?—have thy Love!
>   Here is no place for vows broken in making;
> Thou Lotus-eyed! thou soul for whom I strove!
>   Go! ere I listen, my just mind forsaking.

> Krishna! my Krishna with the woodland-wreath!
>   Return, or I shall soften as I blame;
> The while thy very lips are dark to the teeth
>   With dye that from her lids and lashes came,
> Left on the mouth I touched. Fair traitor! go!
>   Say not they darkened, lacking food and sleep
> Long waiting for my face; I turn it—so—
>   Go! ere I half believe thee, pleading deep.

But the longed-for, expected, inevitable reconciliation comes, and

> Radha, abasing still her glorious eyes,
> And still not yielding all her face to him,
> Relented; till with softer upturned look
> She smiled, while the Maid pleaded; so thereat
> Came Krishna nearer, and his eager lips
> Mixed sighs with words in this fond song he sang:

O angel of my hope! O my heart's home!
My fear is lost in love, my love in fear;
This bids me trust my burning wish, and come,
That checks me with its memories, drawing near;
Lift up thy look, and let the thing it saith
End fear with grace, or darken love to death!

  ·   ·   ·   ·   ·   ·

But Radiant, Perfect, Sweet, Supreme, forgive!
My heart is wise—my tongue is foolish still:
I know where I am come—I know I live—
I know that thou art Radha—that this will
Last and be heaven: that I have leave to rise
Up from thy feet and look into thine eyes!

Commentators may declare that it is only a symbolical picture of the return of the erring soul to the safe haven of God—a return to the peace of religion after satiation with the passions and lusts of the world. Maybe so; but it is a marvelously tender story—without the commentaries—of love that suffereth long and is patient—the kind of love that many a woman in the many centuries which have passed since *Gitagovinda* was written, has experienced for the sake of a man whose susceptibility outran his reason. And does it not prove again what has already been revealed in our study of other ancient literatures, that romantic love is not, what some dry-as-dust scholars have declared, a strictly modern emotion? Before the pyramids were built the way of a man with a maid was mysterious—and charming.

We must pass from this view of the long vistas of Indian literature. There came a day, as in most national literatures, when the springs of inspiration seemed to dry up. There were philosophers—Sankara, probably the greatest that the Hindu race ever produced. There were grammarians, excellent in their way. There were scientific writers of genuine merit—Varahamihira, for instance, the worthy astronomer. But wars, invasions, the inevitable decay of national vigor, perhaps the enervating climate—all these took their toll of the intellectual vigor of the people.

Then followed a period of dearth of inspirational work, and then, as all the world knows, a remarkable reawakening of the poetic and philosophic spirit of the Hindu. There was Toru Dutt, who gained in the nineteenth century a far too meager hearing in the Western Hemisphere for her ballads of her native land, and there were others like her in genius and in the failure of the Occident to recognize their genius. There is to-day that remarkable Indian woman, Sarojini Naidu, whose volumes of verse, *The Broken Wind, The Bird of Time,* and *The Golden Threshold,* reveal vividly the growing nationalism of her people. And there has also come out of that ancient civilization one whose genius is so compelling that readers of all nations have hailed him as a true master. Tagore stands to-day almost without a peer in grace, depth of thought, versatility as essayist, dramatist, and poet.

This, then, is the tale of the long ages of song and story, drama and meditative prose in India. That Aryan stock, with its noble Brahman steadfastness of ideals, is a remarkable example of the manner in which the human intellect can sustain itself on a high plane in spite of the earthward pull of existence in this world. With such a heritage of ethics, genuinely deep philosophy, and poetry that has persisted in spite of its wrappings of a dead language, the Hindu may justly be expected, perhaps at no very distant date, to add greatly to the ever increasing treasury of man's literature.

IV

THE DAWN IN PERSIA

They say the Lion and the Lizard keep
The Courts where Jamshyd gloried and drank deep:
And Bahram, that great Hunter—the Wild Ass
Stamps o'er his Head, but cannot break his Sleep.[1]

PERSIA, the land of wine and song, the land of
love, the land of Omar Khayyam—the ancient
glory of it all is gone, but still the world senses
the fragrance of its rose gardens, and, in imagination
at least, drinks the wine of passion with Saki "among
the guests star-scattered on the grass." If in our
dreams there is one spot on this terribly realistic globe
where "youth's sweet-scented manuscript" never closes
and the nightingale still sings under the moon of our
delight, it is Persia. It may be, according to the history text-books, that

Iram indeed is gone with all its Rose,
And Jamshyd's Sev'n-ringed Cup where no one knows;
But still the Vine her ancient Ruby yields,
And still a Garden by the Water blows.

Such is the alchemy of Literature—that it can make
a country which is now a mere shadow of its former
self a source of dream and romantic melancholy and
sentimental meditation for the entire modern world.
Whether Persia shall ever again pour out for mankind
new wine of song and story it is not necessary to con-

[1] Excerpts from Edward Fitzgerald's translation of *The Rubaiyat
of Omar Khayyam,* First Edition.

166 The Dawn of Literature

jecture; she long ago presented to us a goblet so overflowing with emotional fervor that this alone should
justify her existence.

But the folk whose name old Omar has glorified were
not always such pleasure-lovers and such sentimental-
ists. When they first toiled down out of that lofty
mountainous section known to them as Bactria, now
Afghanistan, they were of that same stern, high-
handed, and high-minded Aryan stock which descended
into Southern India. Those early Hindus and Persians
were indeed brothers in blood; they herded the sheep
and cattle on the same high table-lands; they probably
centered their political interest in the same ancient
capital city, upon the ruins of which the modern Balkh
stands; they spoke a language so closely akin to the
Sanskrit, long heard in India, that scholars first inter-
preted the old Persian tongue by means of this early
Hindu one.

Whether it was the pressure of invading tribes, or
the desire for exploration, or the friction of religious
differences that caused these two great branches of the
Aryan family to split and go their separate ways we
shall never know. But certain it is that some twenty-
four centuries before the Christian era the one went
south into the steaming jungles of India, and the other
wandered westward to the highlands of Iran or Persia.
This very name of their new homeland, *Iran,* is indicative again of their relationship to the ancient
Aryan race; for *Iran* is simply a derivative of *Aryan,*
and both connote the idea of *land*—a people who found
sustenance and joy in the soil.

The high philosophic religion of the early Hindu,
as we have seen, degenerated in spite of the efforts of

Brahman and Buddhist. Not so with the faith of those sturdy Persian forefathers—at least for many a century. In a land unplagued by an enervating climate, and unencumbered with an ever encroaching tropical vegetation, these Iranian herders and farmers long escaped that pessimism, fatalism, and inactive meditation which soon afflicted the dwellers in India. The Persian faith was indeed singular for its comparative simplicity and for its association of piety with good deeds and service to mankind. Doubtless even the human soul's attitude toward God and His commandments may be infinitely influenced by the mere fact of climate.

One of the original gods—perhaps *the* original god —of this Persian branch of the Aryan stock seems to have been Varuna (the Greek Ouranos). In this deity they worshiped the All—not only the Creator but His created universe. Probably the early Hindus possessed much the same conception of God, but, as has been indicated, their religion degenerated into pantheism and polytheism. Not so much so with the less speculative Persians. Slowly they evolved from this single Supreme Being seven traits, each of which gradually became a god in itself. And Varuna himself, being thus divided, fell from his high station and became but one of the seven, whose father or chief god became Aditi, the Infinite One.

Varuna now was known as Ahura-Mazda or Ormund, and his companions became the Amshaspunds— the Immortal and Holy Ones. To Ahura-Mazda was attributed spiritual enlightenment; he was indeed the Spiritual Wise One. And wisdom here, as in many other countries, was best symbolized by light. But light has always had its opposite, darkness, and thus there came into existence the idea of a god of darkness or evil, Angra-Mainya. And just as darkness is in eternal conflict with light, so does wisdom or goodness wage age-old battle with evil. But among this healthy folk of the high table-lands and mountains of Persia optimism reigned instead of the hopelessness so frequently found in the hot valleys of India; in some far-off day, so the Iranians believed, Ahura-Mazda would overcome Angra-Mainya, and the good should reign supreme.

At length, in the intellectual development of the Persian people this idea of wisdom and goodness as the gist of religion became so prominent that the companion gods of the Spiritual Wise One practically ceased to be even minor gods; Iran was swinging back, apparently, toward a splendid type of monotheism. Good deeds, purity in thought and word and action, holiness—these were the elements that constituted true piety and that gave the hope of immortality. And as the four elements of the universe, earth, air, water, and fire, had been created by Ahura-Mazda, it was the duty of mankind to reverence and even worship them.

Especially should man worship in the presence of fire; for it is light, and light is the symbol of the chief attribute of the Spiritual Wise One. Thus has arisen the popular belief that the ancient Persians were fire-worshipers. But is it not highly probable that these early people simply prayed and chanted before fire as a symbol, and no more worshiped the symbol than the orthodox Catholic of to-day worships the image or the painting of the saint before which he kneels? In both instances it probably was—and is—merely a psychological aid toward concentration of the attention in worship.

As those Aryans were so proud of their relationship with the land, it is but natural that they should have looked upon cultivation of the soil as the most praise-worthy of all occupations. In fact, idleness, disinclination to labor on the land or in any other trade apparently was looked upon as positive sin.

What does a nation or a race believe concerning its god or gods? If that question be answered we have a rather fair gauge whereby we may measure the ethics, the spirituality of that nation or race. To those ancient Persians Ahura-Mazda meant the sum-total of certain qualities that would adorn any conception, ancient or modern, of the Deity. Wisdom, Good Judgment, Divine Order, Righteousness, Perfection, Immortality—these were some of the attributes of the Supreme Being whom these simple-minded highlanders of Iran worshiped.

Fortunately indeed for the Persian, religion and earthly conduct were intimately related. His happiness or woe in the World Beyond depended with inexorable exactitude upon the good or evil of his deeds in this earthly existence. He might not always overcome evil, but his religion insisted that he at least resist evil with all his power. There was an insistent demand that he strive for purity of mind and body. Labor, especially agriculture, is good for the soul. Ahura-Mazda demanded that his believers show the utmost kindness toward all useful animals, and that the cow, as the chief source of national wealth, should receive the most careful treatment possible. And, lastly, God, the true God of the Persians, was worthy

of adoration and demanded it. Thus, with purity as
the moral duty of man, holiness as a guarantee of
heaven, and labor with the living things of Nature as
an aid to faith in the God of Nature, those primitive
Aryans possessed a religion reasonable, spiritual, and
highly efficient for their particular stage of civilization.

From those far-distant days on the Persian plains
has come down one curious custom deriving from that
primitive Aryan faith. The religion of Ahura-Mazda
forbade the burial or burning of the human body; for
hundreds of years the ancient Persians placed their
dead upon lofty pedestals or piles, for the winds and
the rains and the fowls of the air to destroy. But when
Iran fell as an independent kingdom, and an attempt
was made to stamp out the old religion, a great horde
of the faithful—two millions, it is estimated—fled to
India, and there, as the Parsis, clung tenaciously to
their ancient belief. And thus it has happened that
one may see in India of to-day those weird, awe-
inspiring "Towers of Silence," about which hover at
all hours a cloud of vultures expectant of their daily
food of man's flesh.

Zoroaster

In the evolution of every national or racial religion
there comes at length a spiritual leader to clarify the
faith of the people. Such was Buddha to the Hindus,
Confucius to the Chinese, Moses to the Hebrews.
And to the Persians came Zarathushtra—the Zoroaster
whose teachings attracted, long after his death, the
admiration of such philosophers as Plato and Aristotle.

Much the Iranian poets and preservers of legends
wrote of him, but legend it mainly was. To this hour

Zarathushtra remains one of the most shadowy of the world's famous leaders. According to Persian tradition he lived most of his mature life at Balkh in ancient Bactria, the parting place of the early Hindus and the Iranians, and taught his gospel under the reign of King Vishtaspa. Probably he was born at Shiz in Media, but the time of his ministry is really so vague that some Orientalists have placed it around 1000 B.C., while others, basing their estimate upon the statements of Greek writers, especially Plato and Aristotle, conjecture that he lived in the sixth century, B.C. Certainly some of the ancient hymns or prayers attributed to him reveal a civilization changing from a nomadic to a pastoral stage, and this fact might make the earlier date more plausible. But in spite of the inclination of most of the investigators to believe the declaration of the Greeks that he was an actual historical person, there are those who hold to the theory that this word, Zarathushtra, is merely a general title for a series of priests who impressed upon the folk the principles of an exceptionally high religion.

Be all this as it may, the early Persians held firmly to the belief that the greater part of their Bible, the *Avesta,* was composed by this same eminent teacher, Zarathushtra. Not that he himself wrote the books comprising it. In fact, it is thought that, like Jesus, he left little or nothing in writing; his faithful disciples zealously recorded his sayings at the time or shortly after his death. To-day it is generally conceded by scholars that the hymns known as the *Gathas* are probably the actual expressions of this noble soul who lived and preached among these primitive people. As such these chants or supplications are, therefore, of

unusual importance, linguistically, as the earliest specimens extant of the Persian language.

Now, as time went on, the theologians went on
also, and around and about this original core of
Zarathushtra's religious principles, the *Avesta,* they
wove the usual huge fabric of commentaries and
opinions. And the commentaries they called the *Zend.*
Thus resulted the *Zend-Avesta,* or, as it is in the original, *Avistak va Zend,* the Text and Commentary.

Whether the *Avesta* as we have it now is the complete or authentic Bible of the ancient Persians is indeed doubtful. For in the troubled centuries of
Iranian history from the days of Zarathushtra to the
era of the Mohammedan invasions, these Scriptures
were scattered hither and thither, and it long seemed
that never again could the nation have in its entirety
this Guide Book of religion. But in the third century,
A.D., the Sassanids, a great dynasty of Persian
monarchs ruling from 224 to 641, ordered every fragment of the *Avesta* to be collected, and further directed
that to these bits of the teachings should be added all
the portions retained in the memory of the priesthood.
Thus slowly, painstakingly, in the course of centuries,
the text was reassembled in the form in which we now
possess it.

And what is that form? What elements compose
this sacred writing that governed the morals, thinking,
and spiritual life of a nation for possibly fifteen centuries? The *Avesta* consists, first, of a very ancient
section called the *Yasna* (meaning sacrifice and worship), which includes liturgies and hymns or *Gathas.*
Then, secondly, is the *Vispered,* a group of prayers and
invocations to all the gods. (Strange how nations,

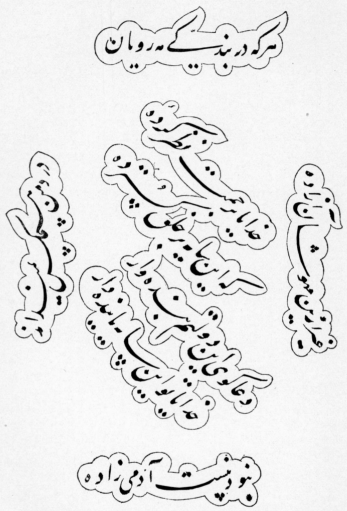

SPECIMEN OF THE PERSIAN WRITING KNOWN AS
NASHK-TALIK

ancient and modern, have feared lest they omit or forget a single god, saint, or angel!)

Next in this old Iranian Scripture we find the *Yashta,* a collection of twenty-one hymns, the title, like *Yashna,* signifying worship. Finally, there is a section, possibly of much later date than the others, named the *Vendidad,* which consists largely of the law against demons. As in the case of Brahmanism and Buddhism, we find here that inevitable tendency of a noble religion to degenerate into a type of hoodooism to drive out devils and other evil spirits. Strange, is it not, that man has never been content to let his creed or faith remain simply a meditative adoration of the Maker of the Universe?

That there is a simple nobility in the fundamental principles of Zoroaster's teaching is clear to any one who reads the prayers and sayings attributed to him. Does he not search down to the very foundations of all true piety and spiritual wisdom in such bits of supplication as these?

Approaching thee, O Mazda, with deepest veneration, I pray for the primal blessing of thy bountiful Spirit. May my attitude toward all beings be one of Righteousness. And with this I pray for a true understanding of thy Good Spirit in order that I may satisfy the Soul of the Kine.

O great living, creative God, inspired and guided by thy Good Spirit, I draw near and pray for a blessing for both the worlds—the world of the body and the world of the mind— those gifts that are gained only through Righteousness from Above; for only through it may man attain blessedness and felicity.

O Righteousness! when shall I behold thee, with full knowledge of the Goodness of the Mind of God? And, above all

else, when shall I realize that Obedience in life which leads
to the path of the most blessed Ahura-Mazda? These things
I beseech, for through prayer we may indeed ward off the
flesh-devouring fiends, the truest symbols of foulness of the
spirit.

Therefore, O God, Mighty Creator! satisfy my longing
with the attainments that are born of the grace of thy Good
Mind—that grace which Thou knowest to be the child of
Righteousness—that grace which is indeed sublime. For never
have I known thine instructions to be vain in the struggle for
our daily food and all other worthy objects of desire.[2]

"The grace of thy Good Mind"—it is a goodly
phrase, akin to that prayer of Cotton Mather—"a
trembling walk with God." A mind, a heart, a soul
cleansed and prepared for the wisdom from on high—
it is probably the most desirable thing that a wise man
can pray for. But to obtain this state, this attitude,
the soul must be cleansed, purified.

"Purity is the best, the fairest of all things, even as thou
hast declared, O wise Zarathustra." With these words the
blessed Ahura-Mazda made happy the holy Zarathustra.
"Purity is, next to life, the greatest of all goods—that purity
which is given by Mazda to him who cleanses himself with
good thoughts, good words, good deeds."[3]

This was the simple, practical faith that the
Mohammedan Arabs invading Persia in the eighth
century discovered and destroyed. Yes, the world and
mankind are evolving; but evolution too often means,
not progress, but retrogression.

[2] Author's version.
[3] Author's version. A version by L. H. Mills may be found in his
The Gathas, Oxford University Press, 1900, and in *Sacred Books of
the East,* Oxford, Clarendon Press, 1887, Vol. III. For the *Zend-
Avesta* see *Sacred Books of the East,* Vol. IV.

THE ARAB ENTERS PERSIA

There is nothing more dramatic in the history of literature than the meteor-like rise—and fall—of Arabian civilization. Before that mighty prophet and founder of one of the most far-flung religions in the world, Mohammed, died in 632 A.D., he had transformed these wandering, solitary tribes of Arabs into a vast, united surge of fanatical humanity sweeping from one country to another, filled with the faith of the Koran, and thirsting for the blood of the infidel. Westward into Egypt, leaping across the Mediterranean into Spain, besieging the very walls of France until halted by Charles Martel at Tours in 732, they threatened to change the entire course of European civilization. Northward they swept over Syria, Assyria, Mesopotamia, and on toward India, and their religion of Allah crushed all other creeds and dogmas in their path.

The first fervor of annihilating the unbelievers having burnt itself out, these Arabs or Moors or Semitic followers of the virile Mohammed now rapidly became the most intellectual, the most learned people of their day. Those who two centuries before had been riding in wild marauding bands across the sand of the desert, singing fierce songs of passion and battle, now became the lavish patrons of scientist, poet, musician, and artist. It was these earnest believers in the Koran who literally saved culture in the so-called Dark Ages. It was such a Moslem as Haroun al Rashid, or Aaron the Just, Caliph of Bagdad in 786, who preserved mathematics, chemistry, astronomy, geography, the art of story-telling, architecture from passing into oblivion.   And it was his son, Al Mamoun, succeeding him as Caliph in 813, who saved from total destruction the manuscripts of antiquity, saved for posterity the poetry, the legends, the philosophy, the wisdom of the East.   And it was the Moor in Spain who perpetuated for the modern world the idealistic learning which Western Europe, busy with its petty feuds and materialism, was permitting to perish from among men.

Persia, like almost every other nation of Asia, came under the spell of these reborn Arabs.   Sweeping over Iran in the eighth century, they sternly suppressed the ancient religion of Zarathushtra, all but killing it root and branch.   Secretly the "Fire-worshipers," as they were called, might creep far back into the hills and now and then practice the rites of their fathers, but never again could the teachings of Zoroaster gain the ascendancy.   In the centuries that followed this Arabian invasion the Iranians became, in fact, entirely devoted to the faith of Mohammed, and to this hour there is scarcely a more zealous Moslem nation than Persia.

But the Persians accepted the Koran—with a difference.   And in that difference lies the literary genius of the land of Omar Khayyam.   Back and forth over that land swept the ebb and flow of many a philosophy and creed, and each left its sediment of thought and opinion.   The far-wandering Hebrew left there the lore of the Old Testament and the Talmud; the Greek from Athens and Alexandria brought the subtle philosophy of his ancestors; the Brahman of India, the Buddhist of Ceylon and the Mongolian country, the Christian of Europe—each and all impressed the theories of morals and ethics and religion upon this much-visited people.

The result—one of the broadest, most tolerant types of religious faith and practice in all the Eastern World. "Great argument about it and about" led to innumerable sects, and their very number compelled mutual respect and tolerance lest the nation be destroyed by a war of fanatics. The Koran had strictly forbidden the drinking of alcohol; these Persians twisted the commandment into almost a glorification of drink. The Koran had cast forbidding eyes upon the charms of women; the Persians made the love of woman the theme of themes for poet and story-teller. The Koran had demanded a stern, almost ascetic type of life; the Persians praised the gratification of every sense of the human body.

And with all this broadness, liberalness of view, and tolerance came a depth of brooding philosophy scarcely approached by that found among Mohammedans in any other section of Asia or Africa. Consider the teachings of such a sect as the Shiites, the followers of Ali, Mohammed's nephew, and read their prophecies of the coming of a Redeemer who will establish the kingdom of righteousness on earth—understand these and you will understand a religious creed that stands high among the visions of man. Study the principles laid down by the Sufites, the Mystics, with their uncompromising demand for an all-embracing devotion to God and to the Good, and you will discover a faith that causes many a Christian creed to appear cold and barren.

It was from such a breadth of religious experience and from such a broad interpretation of man's relationships to his fellowmen and God that so brilliant a galaxy of poets and romancers and philosophers arose.

But it was not without travail and struggle that Iran gained the right to express herself in song and story. The fanatical Arabs who had swept over the country had brought a Koran written in Arabic, and therefore any literary effort not in Arabic was for nearly two centuries after the invasion looked upon as sacrilegious. At length in the tenth century the Persian rulers had so far freed themselves from the sovereignty of the Caliphate that local poets and romancers dared to use for literary purposes their native language. Even after such linguistic liberation the Arabic types of poetry and even Arabic subjects of song persisted until the bold spirit of the father of later Persian literature, Rudagi, led the way to true Persian themes and modes.

Then, naturally, as the pride of the reviving nation increased, there arose a desire to relate once more the stories of a glorious national past. Rulers brought to their luxurious palaces poets from the "provinces" for the express purpose of encouraging them to tell in epic and in lyric the tales of the fore-fathers. And the result finally was one of the most romantic narratives ever composed in verse—the *Shahnameh,* or *Book of Kings,* by that tremendously fertile and tremendously energetic poet, Firdausi. His scope was so vast and his success so far-reaching in its influence that Persian poets combed the traditions, not only of their own nation, but of many others for ma-terial for similar poetical stories. Alexander the Great, Mohammed, his nephew Ali, the Old Testament heroes, Jesus, the Crusaders—all became subjects of fiction in either verse or prose.

The land of Omar the Tentmaker became a nest of song-birds. Persian monarchs lavished wealth upon men who could compose panegyrics that pleased royal ears; humorous verse, biting satires, keen epigrams brought local fame to minor poets long since almost hidden in oblivion; all Iran listened willingly to the multitude of short poems dealing with love and wild adventures. Then, too, there were those religious or mystical poets, such as the Sufites, who composed legends, fables, and devotional songs that might be accepted to this day by followers of almost any living creed. But in all this discussion pro and con of religion there were, of course, those who gave it all up in despair, and, as free-thinkers or skeptics, attempted to hide this despair behind a cynical indifference or flippancy. And one of those despairing souls, but cheerful in his despair, the English-speaking world seems destined never to forget—Omar Khayyam.

With such a flood of poetic feeling pervading the soul of Iran, with such a wealth of opportunity for reading and traveling and observing, these Persians readily adopted, adapted, and invented for their poetry, forms sometimes natural, sometimes artificial, frequently surprisingly intricate. Thus the rubaiyat, or four-line stanza, with its unrhyming third line, is ideal for its purpose; for what a world of thought or sarcasm or satire or sorrowful comment may be packed into that free third line! Then, these poetical Persians had another unusual form called the Ghazal, consisting of not less than five nor more than twelve couplets, the second line of each couplet after the first two lines of the poem continuing the rhyme of the first couplet. And in the last couplet the poet must introduce his own name! Thus the author's fame was literally interwoven with his production. Obviously all names are not romantic or poetic, and the result was that in Persia almost every writer assumed for himself a charming pen-name—Rudagi, Firdausi, Khayyam, Rumi, Hafiz.

But who were all these poets and romancers, and what deeds did they sing and relate? Are their emotions and words so foreign to our modern life that we cannot attune ourselves to their songs and stories?

RUDAGI

There was a ninth-century Persian with the high-sounding, almost terrifying name of Hakim Mohammed Farideddin Abdellah, but as he was born at Rudag he chose to call himself simply Rudagi. And it is a revered name in Persian literature; for Rudagi holds about the same relation to the poetry of Iran as Chaucer does to the poetry of England. Both are literary fathers.

Now, this Rudagi was so learned in many fields and so skillful as a musician that he became the favorite of Nasir Ahmed, monarch of Khorostan. Indeed Nasir lavished wealth upon him, so much so that the poet's homes were palaces, his servants numbered more than two hundred, and his movable property was so great that four hundred camels were necessary to transport his possessions from one of these homes to another. And yet, like the traditional Homer, he was totally blind all the days of his life.

Well did he deserve his bountiful store of this

world's goods; for he poured forth epics, romantic
legends, and lyrics for his royal patron and for the
nation in general. But that royal patron, like all
mortals, at length passed from this world's joys and
sorrows, and Rudagi awoke one morning to find himself an outcast from the royal court, destitute of favor
and in dire poverty. Thus the last days of his life
passed in humiliation and misery until in 954, in his
seventy-fourth year, death brought release. Humiliation and misery were indeed his in those last years;
for he lived long enough to see many of his epics and
romances forgotten and even utterly lost. To-day
only a few of his lyrics remain. *Sic gloria mundi.*

And yet one poem of his is said to have caused a
monarch to change his royal home. When Nasir removed temporarily from Bokhara to the more pleasant
Herat the ruler became so enamored of the latter city
that he extended his visit month after month. His
courtiers, far from their homes and kinsmen, became
so despondent and indeed alarmed that they devised
the scheme of having the blind court-poet sing to Nasir
of the charms of the "old home place." Tradition
declares that Rudagi had scarcely finished reciting the
third stanza of his lyric when the ruler announced his
decision to return to Bokhara. Such is the power of
song. And this is the poem that saved Bokhara as
the capital of the nation.

> The gale whose breath such joy imparts,
>   Comes from the gentle stream
> Where they reside, to whom our hearts
>   Return in memory's dream.
> The precious odor that its wings convey
> Is their regret for us—so far away.

The sands are rough along that shore
  Where glides our native Amu's stream;
But when we tread its banks once more,
  Like velvet those rude sands will seem.
O pitying Oxus, let thy waves divide,
And yield us passage down thy opening tide!

All hail, Bokhara, land of flowers!
  Our prince moves proudly on;
He goes to glad thy sunny bowers,
  He asks thy smile alone.
The waving cypress seeks his native groves,
The rising moon the firmament it loves.[4]

ASADI

It was a Persian poet of the tenth century, Asadi or Essedi, of the town of Tus, who caused one of the longest and most stirring of national epics in the world's literature to be created. The nobility of Persia were by this time exceedingly desirous of having the glorious exploits of the nation's past put into permanent and artistic form, and the great monarch, Mahmud, turned to his court-poet, Asadi, as the genius to undertake the *Shahnameh, or Book of Kings.*

But the bard was old and pleaded to be excused from so gigantic a task. He recommended in his stead his young pupil, Firdausi, as one who had the ability and the temerity for it, and Firdausi set to work collecting the vast store of national traditions and legends, and transforming them into poetry. But even Firdausi, with his youth and vigor, at length despaired of completing so huge an epic, and was about to decline further effort when hoary-headed Asadi came to him

[4] Version in Louisa Costello's *Rose Garden of Persia,* London, Longman, 1845.

with the declaration that if the pupil died before the poem was finished he, the ancient teacher, would complete it. Then it was that Firdausi rather scornfully reminded him of his earlier refusal to accept the task because of age. "My life," said Asadi, "is as God wills; but I am certain that I can finish the epic." And setting to work that very hour, he is declared to have written four thousand lines of it in two days.

So filled with fresh enthusiasm was Firdausi at this unexpected fertility and perseverance in his old master that he returned to the work with renewed vigor and, after many years of inspired toil, completed the national epic of Iran. And, strangely enough, the venerable teacher lived to see it finished—and to weep over the death of his pupil.

Asadi doubtless composed a great mass of verse for his court audiences, but to-day only a small amount remains. One notable thing he did: he either invented or introduced from Europe the so-called dispute in verse form, the *tenson,* as the Provençal singers afterwards called it. This argument or debate in poetry at length swept Europe of the Middle Ages, and thousands of *tensons* were composed, not only in France, but in England, Spain, and Italy.

One of Asadi's that may be taken as typical is *The Dispute of Day and Night.*

> Day and Night, who each can yield
>   Joy and solace to the race,
> Thus contended for the field,
>   Claiming both the highest place.
> Night spoke frowningly: " 'Twas I
> Who from all eternity
> Ruled the chaos of the world,

When in dire confusion hurled.
The fervent prayer is heard at night;
Devotion flies day's glaring light.
'Twas night the Mount when Moses left;
    At night was Lot avenged by fire;
At night the moon our Prophet cleft,
    And saw Heaven's might revealed entire.

   .   .   .   .   .   .

"Day is with toil and care oppressed,
Night comes, and, with her, gentle rest.
Day, busy still, no praise can bring;
All night the saints their anthems sing;
Her shade is cast by Gabriel's wing.
The Moon is pure; the Sun's broad face
Dark and unsightly spots deface.
The sun shines on with changeless glare,
The Moon is ever new and fair."

   .   .   .   .   .   .

Day rose and smiled in high disdain:
    "Cease all this boasting, void and vain;
The Lord of Heaven and earth and thee
    Gave me a place more proud than thine;
And men with joy my rising see,
    And hail the beams that round me shine.

   .   .   .   .   .   .

"I sprang from Heaven, from dust art thou;
    Light crowns my head with many a gem;
The collier's cap is on thy brow,
    For thee a fitting diadem.
My presence fills the world with joy;
Thou com'st all comfort to annoy.
I am a Moslem—white my vest;
Thou a vile thief, in sable dressed.
Out, negro-face!—dar'st thou compare
Thy cheeks with mine, so purely fair?

"What canst thou, idle boaster, say
To prove that Night excels the Day?
If stubborn still, let Him decide
With whom all truth and law abide;
Let Nasur Ahmed, wise as great,
Pronounce, and give to each his state." [5]

FIRDAUSI

Let Nasur Ahmed, wise as great,
Pronounce, and give to each his state.

How much depended upon the favor of the king in those days of Persia's literary renaissance! Poets and musicians, historians and romancers, one and all, looked to the sovereign for that financial recompense which enabled genius to live and create.

If it had not been for the munificence of the Sultan Mahmud, who came to the throne of Khorastan in 997, probably the gifted romantic poet, Firdausi, would never have been heard of, and his astounding epic story, *Shahnameh*, would have been lost to the world. When one remembers the genius that those early potentates nourished and developed one is prone to forgive them for being potentates.

It is indeed an astounding task—this *Shahnameh*, or *Book of Kings*. Consider the research that was involved—the thousands of legends that had to be collected and unified, the vague traditions that were to be verified, the musty manuscripts that were to be read, the gathering of this vast accumulation of narrative into one coherent, sweeping story. It required, not

[5] Version in Louisa Costello's *Rose Garden of Persia*. A recent edition of the *Rose Garden* is that of Gibbings & Co., London, 1911. See also Dole and Walker: *Flowers from Persian Poets*, New York, T. Y. Crowell & Co., 1901.

only the light of genius, but "the perseverance of the saints." Asadi had declined it; the poet Dakiki had attempted it but had been assassinated before he had fairly started. But Firdausi, through toil that was titanic, accomplished it.

The history of this man's life is a vivid romance in itself. His real name was Abul Kasim Mansur, and he was born at the ancient town of Tus in 911. He early became an antiquarian and poet, and was turning old Persian legends into verse when word of Dakiki's death reached him. Then and there he determined to take up the task of writing the epic of his nation's history. Although he had been receiving some patronage from the ruler of Tus, he felt that only at the great court of Mahmud could the huge work be accomplished.

To the sultan's palace he therefore betook himself. But how to gain audience with this mighty monarch— that was the problem. He found the court, yes, the very courtyard itself thronged with sycophants, soliciting visitors, fawning, jealous parasites. How could he, a green provincial rhymester, gain the ear of the monarch? He told those about him of his ambition and received scornful laughter for his pains. Three of the court poets, thinking to have sport with this country clown, solemnly came to him and offered to test his skill in versifying. They had thought of three rhyming words for which they believed there was no fourth rhyme in the Persian tongue. Firdausi accepted their challenge.

Then said the first of the poets:

Thy beauty eclipses the light of the sun.

And the second continued with the line:

The rose of thy cheek would comparison shun.

And the third triumphantly capped it with:

Thy glances pierce through the mailed warrior's johsun.

Instantly Firdausi completed the quatrain with the verse:

Like the lance of fierce Giv in his fight with Poshun.

The three court poets stood for a moment dumb with astonishment. "Giv!" "Poshun!" Who were these? They condescended to ask for an explanation, and that moment Mansur's famous career as epic writer began. For there in that crowded courtyard he recited so energetic and thrilling a story of a forgotten battle of long ago that the trio of poets, loud in their praises, went at once to the mighty Mahmud. Called before the sovereign, he chanted another poetic legend with such skill that Mahmud immediately directed him to join the seven other poets engaged in the task of composing the history.

So charmed did the sultan become with this poet of Tus that he one day declared that Mansur's creations made the court a genuine paradise and that henceforth the writer's name should not be Mansur but Firdausi, meaning paradisaic. The ruler at length turned over to him the entire task of composing the *Shahnameh,* and Firdausi, in a wild burst of gratitude, wrote a most flattering panegyric to his master. The sultan, not to be outdone in generosity, ordered the State Treasurer to grant the bard a thousand gold pieces for every thousand completed couplets of the *Book of Kings*.

Firdausi, however, was evidently afraid of himself in the presence of so steady and so great an income. He secretly had a plan for using the whole sum for the construction of a dike to protect Tus from the annual floods, and he thought it safer not to tempt himself with regular installments, but to have the payments held in his name until the poem was completed. Far better for him if he had taken the recompense as it came due. For the more orthodox Mohammedans looked upon him as an infidel, and frequently influenced the changeable Mahmud against him, while the presents sent him by other rulers were used by Mahmud's courtiers as a means of arousing that monarch's jealousy.

Then came at last the climax of insults to the sensitive poet. After thirty years of slavish toil the *Shahnameh* stood completed—sixty thousand couplets packed, overflowing, with the lore, the legends, the traditions of Iran's existence. Firdausi, now an old man, had it presented to the sovereign by the king's own favorite, Ayaz. It was read amidst the unbounded enthusiasm of the court. Mahmud, greatly affected, ordered his treasurer to send to the poet the sixty thousand gold pieces, an elephant's load. But that treasurer, like a good many financial experts, had little poetry in his soul, and he persuaded the sultan that sixty thousand silver pieces were amply sufficient for a mere poet.

The bulky bags of money were delivered, and the elephant driver was scurrying away on his beast when Firdausi, opening the sacks, discovered the sorry trick.

Pale with humiliation and rage, he called the driver back, demanded that the fellow accept one-third of the treasure for the bringing of it, loudly ordered a bartender to bring a mug of beer and gave that boniface another third of the silver for the drink, and then, seeing a bathhouse keeper looking on, gave that lowly gentleman the last third for nothing at all. Caring naught for the risking of his own life, Firdausi then hastened to write a bitter note to Mahmud, reproaching the ruler for his broken pledge, and declaring that the epic had not been composed for mere lucre.

Then was there hot disputing at court, stern words from the monarch to his treasurer, and it looked for the time being as though the proud poet would indeed receive his rightful pay. But the wily wizard of finance at length convinced the sultan that the matter would soon blow over and that, besides, Firdausi had offered the king a gross insult in thus nonchalantly disposing of sixty thousand pieces of royal silver. Mahmud's anger was thus turned upon the maker of the national epic, and Firdausi, now rather cooled, and alarmed for his own safety, hastened to the court and begged forgiveness.

The pardon was graciously granted by the monarch, but, aware of the perfidy of most Oriental rulers, Firdausi prepared for his final *coup*. He destroyed hundreds of his poems, prepared a most insulting satire to be delivered after twenty days to Mahmud, wrote upon the walls of the mosque a fierce farewell to that gentleman, and then fled in the garb of a dervish. A price was placed upon his head, and he passed from court to court of foreign rulers. For some time the caliph of Bagdad sheltered him, because of his flattering eulogies to this monarch, but Mahmud so persistently insisted upon his surrender that at last he fled from Bagdad to Kohistan, where his boyhood companion was now the governor. Here he could rest with some sense of security.

And now, as the years passed and Mahmud the Great grew older and the fame of the *Shahnameh* grew greater, many friends of both parties began to intercede, and the sultan proclaimed that if the aged poet wished to return he might do so safely and would also receive more than the number of gold pieces originally promised to him. Back to Tus came, then, the eighty-year-old Firdausi, infirm but steadfast in his determination not to compromise with his sovereign. And there in the year 1020 Mahmud's elephants came, bearing upon their backs not only a royal robe and a humble letter of apology, but also one hundred thousand pieces of gold, a regal fortune. But as the great animals went down the streets of Tus they passed a solemn funeral procession—Firdausi was dead!

The repentant sultan offered the treasure to the poet's daughter, but that high-spirited woman, a true product of her father, indignantly spurned the gift. The aged sister of Firdausi, however, aware of her brother's long cherished plan of aiding his native city with the money, accepted it, and by means of it built not only the protecting dike, but a great caravanserai.

"A glorious monument of Eastern genius and learning"; thus the Orientalist, Sir William Jones, has described the *Shahnameh*. There are said to have been four hundred poets in Mahmud's palace, but so much greater than they was this poet of Tus that most of them are now absolutely lost in oblivion; his fame simply eclipsed theirs.

To the Westerner the *Book of Kings* is utterly impossible as history; it is nothing more than an amazing collection of wild and romantic tales almost destitute of a foundation of facts. But to the Easterner it is history, something upon which to base national pride. Moreover, to the philosophical Asiatic it offers a wealth of wise sayings, ethical reflections, epitomes of the long experience of mankind. Whether actual history or only fantastic romance, it is a literary production in which any nation might glory.

That Firdausi was indeed delightfully human may be proved by his two famous or infamous poems to Mahmud. When that monarch smiled upon him the poet could indite such a eulogy as this:

> Praise, praise to Mahmud, who, of like renown
> In battle or in banquet, fills the throne!
> Lord of the Realms of Chin and Hindustan,
> Sovereign and Lord of Persia and Turan;
> With his loud voice he rends the flintiest ear;
> On land a tiger fierce, untouched by fear,
> And on the wave he seems the crocodile
> That prowls amidst the waters of the Nile.
> Generous and brave, his equal is unknown;
> In deeds of princely worth he stands alone.
> The infant in the cradle lisps his name,
> The world exults in Mahmud's spotless fame.
> In festive hours Heaven smiles upon his truth;
> In contest deadly as the dragon's tooth;
> Bounteous in all things, his exhaustless hand
> Diffuses blessings through the grateful land;
> And of the noblest thoughts and actions lord,
> The soul of Gabriel breathes in every word.

May Heaven with added glory crown his days.
Praise, praise, to mighty Mahmud, everlasting praise! [6]

When, however, the sultan played upon him the
shabby trick of sending silver instead of gold, then
Firdausi's lyre sounded to a different key, and insult
and invective came as a result.

In Mahmud shall we hope to find
One virtue to redeem the mind?
A mind no generous transports fill,
To truth, to faith, to justice chill.
Son of a slave! His diadem
In vain may glow with many a gem.
Exalted high in power and place,
Outbursts the meanness of his race.

.   .   .   .

Hadst thou, degenerate prince, but shown
One single virtue as thy own,
Had honor, faith, adorned thy brow,
My fortunes had not sunk as now;
But thou hadst gloried in my fame,
And built thyself a deathless name.
O Mahmud, though thou fear'st me not,
Heaven's vengeance will not be forgot!
Shrink, tyrant, from my words of fire,
And tremble at a poet's ire! [7]

It is no idle boast—that expression "words of fire."
Some of those stories that Firdausi told in his *Book of
Kings* have become part of the literary inheritance of
mankind. He it was who revived the age-old tale of
Jemshid the Wanderer and that tragedy which Mat-

[6] James Atkinson's version, London, Oriental Translation Fund,
1832. Also in Dole and Walker: *Flowers from Persian Poets*. Spirited translations of these later Persian poets may be found in *Sacred
Books of the East* (F. Max Müller, Editor), Vol. VIII.
[7] James Atkinson's version in Costello's *Rose Garden of Persia.*

thew Arnold has made so familiar to the English-speaking world—Sohrab and Rustem. It so happens that through frequent translation these characters out of this Persian romantic epic are best known to the Western reader; but there are many others that should be as famous—the harum-scarum King Kaus, for instance, who was forever endangering his life by fantastic escapades.

There is no more bitter-sweet romance than that of Jemshid's fateful meeting with the Princess of Zabul. Long he had wandered, a deposed king, when in the spring season he sank down by the gates of the garden of King Gureng of Zabul. Then passed a slave-girl of the Princess, and, struck by his forlorn look, asked, "Who art thou?" "I was once possessed of wealth," answered Jemshid, "and lived in great luxury, but now I am abandoned by fortune and have wandered from a far country. Would to heaven I might be blessed with a few cups of wine; then might my weariness and sorrow be relieved!"

And the servant, hastening to her mistress, gave such an entrancing description of the man that the Princess was half in love with him before she had seen him. "He asks only wine," she declared, "but I shall give him both wine and music, and a beautiful princess besides." She hastened to the gates, and

> . . . seeing him,
> She thought he was a warrior of Iran
> With spreading shoulders, and his loins well bound.
> His visage pale as the pomegranate flower,
> He looked like light in darkness.[8]

[8] Excerpts are from James Atkinson's translation, London, Oriental Translation Fund, 1832.

With her heart filled with "warm emotions," she urged him to enter the palace grounds. After much suspicious hesitation on his part—for he had suffered much from treachery—she took him by the hand and led him to a fountain within the garden, and called for music and wine.

> Three cups he drank with eager zest,
>   Three cups of ruby wine;
> Which banished sorrow from his breast,
>   For memory left no sign
> Of past affliction; not a trace
> Remained upon his heart or smiling face.

More and more in love with him, the Princess offered him dainty food, but he called only for more wine. "What!" she at length exclaimed, "is your desire for wine so great?" With Omar-like spirit he replied:

> Whilst drinking wine I never see
> The frowning face of my enemy;
> Drink freely of the grape, and nought
> Can give the soul one mournful thought;
> Wine is a bride of witching power,
> And wisdom is her marriage dower;
> Wine can the purest joy impart,
> Wine inspires the saddest heart.

The more the Princess looked upon this elegant wanderer the more she became convinced that this was the famed King Jemshid of whom her nurse had often told her. She had heard of his marvelous skill as an archer; she commanded a slave to bring a bow and arrows. Two doves were on the garden wall, "whose amorous play had caused her cheeks to be overspread with blushes." "Point out which of them I shall hit," she requested of the young man. Jemshid took the weapon from her hand, and, fitting an arrow, he said softly, "Now for a wager. If I hit the female shall the lady whom I most admire in this company be mine?" Silently she nodded her assent. The bow twanged, and the arrow transfixed both wings and body of the female bird. This can be no other, thought the Princess, than King Jemshid, called the Binder of Demons. Then took she the bow from him and quietly said, "See, the male bird has returned. If my aim be as successful, shall the man whom I choose in this company be my husband?" But at that moment the old nurse appeared, and, appraising Jemshid as one might a slave offered for sale, she turned to the Princess and declared, "All that I foretold is now about to be fulfilled. God has brought Jemshid to be your spouse. The Almighty will bless you with a son destined to be conqueror of the world."

Then the nurse directed a picture of Jemshid to be brought, and compared it with the young man, and placed it in his hands. But upon seeing it he burst into tears. Yet he protested that he himself was not Jemshid, but that he wept only through pity for the misfortunes of the young king. "He must now be dead, devoured, perhaps, by the wolves and lions of the forest." But the nurse, not to be tricked, took him aside and begged him to state the truth. Nothing, however, would he reveal until the Princess, taking him farther into the park, poured out her heart to him, told how the nurse had for years been prophesying his coming and their marriage, and then weeping exclaimed:

How long hath sleep forsaken me? how long
Hath my fond heart been kept awake by love?
Hope still upheld me—give me one kind look,
And I will sacrifice my life for thee;
Come, take my life, for it is thine for ever.

Unable longer to dismiss her entreaties, he confessed that he was the wandering King Jemshid, driven from land to land with a price upon his head. Overjoyed with the disclosure, the Princess secretly took him to her rooms, where they were married according to the simple custom of the day.

Then was King Gureng wroth as the wind at the discovery, and only the sturdy defense of the shrewd old nurse saved Jemshid from instant death. But at length the father relented, and the young couple were for a little season happy in their love. But there came too soon a day when Jemshid had cause to believe that perfidy was in the heart of the monarch, and he fled the court, leaving the Princess prostrate with grief. And scarcely had he departed from the gates when he was captured by an enemy, and, being delivered to the king who had usurped his throne, he was sawn asunder.

Much more familiar to Western readers is the ancient legend of Sohrab and Rustem, probably because of Matthew Arnold's masterly adaptation of it. It is the tragic story so often repeated in world literature, of a father's unwitting slaying of his own son.

King Kaus of the Persians is so alarmed about the reports of the progress of a young Sohrab, leader of the invading Turanians, that he begs the assistance of the mighty Rustem, son of Jemshid and King Gureng's daughter. Rustem, the greatest of Persian warriors, mature and seasoned in many a conflict, so scorns the

fame of the young Sohrab that he delays eight days
before coming to Kaus. For this the hot-headed and
utterly foolish king orders him and another soldier,
Giv, to be impaled alive.

But as the officers of the monarch seek to lay hands
upon the great Rustem he dashes them aside, vaults
upon his horse, and angerly upbraids Kaus.

> Weak and insensate! take not to thy breast
> Devouring fire; thy latest actions still
> Outdo the past in baseness. Go thyself,
> And, if thou canst, impale Sohrab alive!
> When wrath inflames my heart, what is Kaus?
> What, but a clod of earth? Him must I dread?
> No, to the Almighty power alone I bend.
> The warriors of the empire sought to place
> The crown upon my head; but I was faithful,
> And held the kingdom's laws and customs sacred.
> Had I looked to the throne, thou would'st not now
> Have had the power with which thou art surrounded.
> To injure one who is thy safest friend.
> But I deserve it all; for I have ever,
> Ungrateful monarch! done thee signal service.[9]

A friend of both at length effects a reconciliation,
and preparations are made for the battle. Rustem
secretly invades the enemy's camp and takes a look at
Sohrab. Unbounded is the admiration with which he
describes him to Kaus.

> No Tartar ever boasted such a presence;
> Turan, and even Persia, cannot show
> A hero of his bold and gallant bearing.
> Seeing his form thou would'st at once declare
> That he is Sam, the warrior; so majestic
> In mien and action!

[9] Excerpts from James Atkinson's translation, London, Oriental
Translation Fund, 1832.

Early in the morning Sohrab ascends to the top of the Turanian fortress to gaze upon the camp and pavilions of the Persian host. Curiously he inquires concerning the owner of tent after tent. For his mother had long since told him that he was the son of the most famous warrior of Iran, the unconquerable Rustem. He had hoped to hold that father in his arms at some time during this adventure, but the captives with him on the fort this morning deceive him and cause him to believe that Rustem is not among the Persian hosts.

Then goes forth the young Sohrab to challenge the Iranian army to send its greatest champion to single combat. Rustem answers that call, but as he stands before the youth his heart speaks against the conflict, and he says to Sohrab:

> Compassion rises in my heart;
> I cannot slay thee—let us part!
> Thy youth, thy gallantry demand
> A different fate than murderous brand.

"Perhaps," says Sohrab, "thou art Rustem!"

"No," replies Rustem, "I am only the servant of Rustem."

Thus fate turns again against father and son, and they begin their fierce struggle. With spear, with sword, with bow and arrow they fight, and then they betake themselves to wrestling. "Rustem applies as much force as might shake a mountain" to raise Sohrab from the ground, but he cannot move him. Then Sohrab seizes his ponderous mace and strikes Rustem such a blow that he reels with pain. Then says Rustem, "Let there be a truce to-night," and the weary Sohrab agrees.

All that night the father prays to the Almighty for strength to overcome the young man on the morrow. And that evening Sohrab in his tent remarks, "This old man has the strength and bearing of Rustem. God forbid that, if the signs my mother gave be true, he should prove to be my father!" Then these two meet again on the battlefield, and the heart of Sohrab goes out in a strange love for the older man.

> Affection fills my breast with hopes and fears,
> For thee my cheeks are overflowed with tears;
> How have I ceaseless sought to know thy name,
> Oh, tell it now, thou man of mighty fame.

But Rustem puts aside the plea, and the wrestling match begins. "Like lions they together tug, and strain their sinewy limbs." Suddenly Sohrab seizes his father with such force that he dashes Rustem to the ground and springs, "fierce as a tiger," upon him. The victorious boy is on the point of beheading his father when Rustem points out that it is the custom to kill the loser only after the second fall. Thus spared and sparing, each returns to his tent in the twilight.

Another night Rustem spends in prayer to God, and a second night Sohrab sits in his tent wondering who this man may be, to whom his affection goes forth so strangely.

Then the third battle. Suddenly in the wrestling Rustem has him down and "like lightning quick he gives the deadly thrust." Writhing in his pain, Sohrab cries out his father's name.

> Rustem, with vengeance armed, will reach thee there,
> His soul the prey of anguish and despair!

Horror seizes upon the soul of the elder man. Opening the armor of the dying youth, he discovers the secret bracelet of gold known only to the father and the distant mother. In frantic sorrow Rustem cries out for death.

> Frantic, in the dust, his hair
> He rends in agony and deep despair.

With a remorse unbearable the father endeavors to take his own life, but is restrained by the Persian leaders, who have rushed to the scene. Then one of these warriors thinks of a sovereign balm that King Kaus possesses, and a messenger rushes to the royal pavilion to obtain it in an effort to save the young man. But Kaus, brainless and cruel as ever, repulses the messenger and sends back the word, "Let the serpent die!" And death comes upon Sohrab, and the darkness falls, and the lonely night wind sighs across the wide plain. Then the great Rustem draws his cloak over his head and sits beside the body of his son while night sinks over the wide plain, and the campfires of both armies flicker in the far-away lines on either side of them. And thus "all the warrior's pride in dust and ashes lay." [10]

It is such stories as this that have made the *Shah-nameh* a classic of the East, and have brought to Firdausi a lasting fame among the poets of Persia. Here the heroic and the romantic mingle with a skill akin to that of Sir Walter Scott at his best; here valiant manhood and gentle womanhood, the refinements of palace and the beauty of sylvan scenes, the sentiments of chivalry, and the music of poetry unite

[10] For the story in detail see E. D. Remminner: *Story of Rustem,* New York, Scribner, 1909.

to charm the mind and the heart of the reader. This *Book of Kings* which Firdausi composed nearly a thousand years ago in far-off Persia still makes its subtle appeal.

OMAR KHAYYAM

The fame of Omar Khayyam has echoed throughout the English-speaking world. So fortunate has been this Persian in his translator that his name now seems undying. Edward Fitzgerald granted Omar Khayyam a miraculous rebirth.

Omar is by no means the greatest of the poets of Iran. Indeed in his own day he was probably far better known as an astute algebraist and learned astronomer. His Arabic treatise on algebra was copied far and wide, while his revision of the Mohammedan calendar was considered a marvel of skillful calculation. But now his learning is all forgotten; his reflections on life and its seeming futility have touched a kindred chord in the souls of millions.

His real name was Giyathuddin Abulfath Omar, and he was born early in the eleventh century at the town so often mentioned in his writings—Nishapur. To his name he added the pen name, Khayyam, meaning "tent maker," which was what his father probably was. There is a most agreeable tradition that while in school he and two other boys vowed that whichever one should first rise to power and prosperity would help the other two. One did indeed become a Governor, and immediately presented to one companion the office of Chamberlain, and to Omar a yearly pension so that he might devote himself to his beloved mathematical studies.

And thus freed from the ordinary economic cares of this world, Omar Khayyam, during his long career ending in 1123, engaged leisurely in his scientific pursuits, reflected much on man and man's relations to life here and hereafter, and wrote in marvelous quatrains or rubaiyats his conclusions as to the meaning of it all. Those conclusions are none too happy; a subtle disappointment or pessimism runs through them all; they close at length with the sorrowful belief that we can be certain of nothing in the life beyond, and that here we can but "eat, drink, and be merry; for to-morrow we die."

But this mechancholy, this frank pessimism has somehow found response in every reader of the famous poem. Is it not because of that hidden despair which all thinking human beings feel in the presence of the thought of the mystery of death? Who in that presence can sincerely declare, "I know"? Only faith, a valiant "I believe," can offer any consolation whatever.

So many Western readers have missed or overlooked this subtle, sorrowful despair in the *Rubaiyat*. They have found only the cynical laugh of the unbeliever, the call for the pleasures of the flesh, the praise of wine, woman, and song. Yet there is genuine spiritual agony in some of that desperate questioning of the old Persian poet.

> After a momentary silence spake
> Some Vessel of a more ungainly make:
>   "They sneer at me for leaning all awry;
>   What! did the Hand then of the Potter shake?" [11]

[11] Excerpts from Edward Fitzgerald's *The Rubaiyat of Omar Khayyam*, first edition.

And again:

> O Thou who didst with pitfall and with gin
> Beset the Road I was to wander in,
> Thou wilt not with Predestin'd Evil round
> Enmesh, and then impute my Fall to Sin.

It is the age-old question of theology: Shall the God who made us weak punish us for our weakness?

> Ne'er a peevish Boy
> Would break the Bowl from which he drank in joy;
> And He that with his hands the Vessel made
> Will surely not in after Wrath destroy.

Omar had thought long and deeply over it all. Certain definite conclusions he had reached—conclusions at least about happiness and unhappiness:

> I sent my Soul through the Invisible,
> Some letter of that After-life to spell:
> And by and by my Soul return'd to me,
> And answer'd, "I Myself am Heav'n and Hell":

> Heav'n but the Vision of fulfill'd Desire,
> And Hell the Shadow from a Soul on fire
> Cast on the Darkness into which Ourselves,
> So late emerg'd from, shall so soon expire.

But the darker mystery of death and what comes after the fateful hour—ah, that is the mystery which defies all solution:

> Up from Earth's Center through the Seventh Gate
> I rose, and on the Throne of Saturn sate,
> And many a Knot unravel'd by the Road;
> But not the Master-knot of Human Fate.

> There was the Door to which I found no Key;
> There was the Veil through which I might not see:
>   Some little talk awhile of Me and Thee
> There was—and then no more of Thee and Me.

This pretense of knowledge on the part of mankind, this high talk in pedantic words in the midst of this pathetic ignorance—it fills Omar with scorn. What can science, theology, philosophy, learning of any type reveal concerning the Riddle of the Universe?

> Myself when young did eagerly frequent
> Doctor and Saint, and heard great argument
>   About it and about: but evermore
> Came out by the same door wherein I went.

And these so-called great and mighty and famous! Fate laughs them to scorn.

> They say the Lion and the Lizard keep
> The Courts where Jamshyd gloried and drank deep:
>   And Bahram, that great Hunter—the Wild Ass
> Stamps o'er his Head, but cannot break his Sleep.

But there is one thing that man can at least do to show the god-like nature in him; forth can he go at the final hour, bravely, firmly to face the Great Uncertainty, the Unanswered Question:

> So when the Angel of the darker Drink
> At last shall find you by the river-brink,
>   And, offering his Cup, invite your Soul
> Forth to your Lips to quaff—you shall not shrink.

But the pity of it—the pity of it! Why is it so? Why is there such loss here on earth, such mystery beyond? Why could not the Mighty Maker have

shared his master idea with us? Why should we helpless mortals, without our request to enter the world,
without our request to leave it, be tossed into it, tossed
heedlessly about it, tossed nonchalantly out of it?
There is a smothered cry in the pessimistic expression
of it:

> But helpless Pieces of the Game He plays
> Upon this Chequer-board of Nights and Days:
>   Hither and thither moves, and checks, and slays,
> And one by one back in the Closet lays.

You and I, my brothers—declares Omar—human
as we are, could and would have worked out a more
logical, a more pleasant, a more humane plan than this.

> Ah, Love! could you and I with Him conspire
> To grasp this sorry Scheme of Things entire,
>   Would not we shatter it to bits—and then
> Re-mold it nearer to the Heart's desire!

What, then, under the circumstances, is left for man
to do? Nothing but to "drown the insolence" of it all
in drink. There is but one certainty—and that is this
moment. Enjoy it, then: seek not fame, fortune,
power; seize now the pleasures of the senses—while
you may.

> Come, fill the Cup, and in the fire of Spring
> Your Winter-garment of Repentance fling:
>   The Bird of Time has but a little way
> To flutter—and the Bird is on the Wing.

Then, when that last hour comes and you and I go
forth to meet Nothingness, let those who linger on
"turn down an empty Glass," as a symbol of life fully
spent—drained to the last dregs.

It is a fascinating—and dangerous—philosophy of life. Built upon despair, it leads to personal, national, and universal stagnation and ruin. The acceptance and following of the doctrine by any considerable portion of the world's population would lead to barbarism within a decade. Civilization and the happiness of mankind are not founded upon the individual's ignoring of his share of the toil and the responsibilities of this globe, but upon a certain amount of social burden-bearing.

Nevertheless, in all this dark pessimism and at times bitter cynicism of Omar Khayyam there are solid foundations of facts. The fine scorn that he spends upon our pathetic strivings for the baubles of this earth is a well-founded scorn. That somber Hebrew writer of *Ecclesiastes* had faced the same tragic situation—man's senseless pursuit of the nonessentials of the "good life." Both Omar and the Preacher of *Ecclesiastes* cried out over a world mad for materialistic luxuries and ephemeral fame. But in the one case the poet reaches agnosticism, in the other the poet sounds a clear call for faith in a logical, observing, planning God: "Remember thy Creator in the days of thy youth."

Whatever we may think of Omar Khayyam's philosophy of life, we must acknowledge his supreme art—his condensation, his ability for brilliant summary, his flashes of inspired insight, his skill in the making of images that suggest a multitude of thoughts, his capacity for appealing to emotions and ideas that are universal. Is it not passing strange that out of the rugged plains and mountains of a remote, small, conquered and reconquered area of Asia should have sounded a voice that finds response in the hearts of men of all ages, all conditions, all creeds, all nations?

KHAKANI

In the twelfth century, Persia produced a group of poets who devoted what talent they possessed to the financially successful, but poetically futile work of praising sultans and other rulers. Consequently these singers, who were more interested in the flesh-pots than in art, are well-nigh forgotten to-day. Possibly only one of them, Anwari, deserves any attention, and that because of the fact that his genius simply could not be held down by the atmosphere of obsequious flattery.

It was in the thirteenth century that poetry began to arise once more above mere panegyric and took unto itself not only a deeper tone of serious philosophy, but even the character of the mystical. National humiliation and suffering it was that brought about this profound change. Over Asia there swept, like the scourge of God, that barbarous, vindictive, terrifying Tartar chief, Genghis Khan. Cities were left as smoldering ruins; hordes of captives were driven like mere cattle; the nation lay prostrate. Bagdad and Samarkand, famed for their high culture under Mohammedan leadership, now were wrecks of their former selves—their libraries burned, their schools destroyed, their scholars and artists and poets driven into exile.

But amidst all this darkness there shone one bright ray of safety and civilization. Over in Asia Minor at the hitherto unimportant town of Iconium there was reigning a highly intelligent Turk, Alauddin Kaikubed, a lover and a patron of all that was artistic and scholarly. This was his opportunity. The word went forth that poets, musicians, teachers, and artisans would be welcomed at this court, and hither the exiles flocked. For a period it is probable that no other one spot on earth possessed so much genius as did this city of Iconium. There the father of Rumi, one of the most thoughtful of Persian poets, founded a college. There Sadi abode for a part of his feverish life and there he may have written some parts of his famous *Gulistan* or *Rose Garden*. There many a song was composed that, but for the protecting hand of Alauddin Kaikubed, would never have been created.

Before Iran was laid waste by the ruthless barbarians under Genghis Khan there dwelt in the court of the Prince of Shirvan one of the most learned of the lyrical writers of Persia. His name was Efsal-ed-din Hakaiki, but he chose as his poetical or pen name Khakani. Like most court poets of his era, his was a life of prosperity so long as he obeyed implicitly the commands of his royal master. But evidently on one occasion he grew weary of the palace life and went away without permission of the ruler, and for this act of disobedience was cast into prison for several months.

There he fell among Christian captives and was so influenced by their doctrine that apparently the whole trend of his future thinking was affected by it, and he even dared to publish a poem in favor of their religion. Whether or not he found no basic conflict between the teachings of Jesus and Mohammed we cannot tell, but it is certain that to his dying day he remained a devout Moslem. His poetical work, therefore, presents a soul opened to and sympathetic toward two religions, and a result is, naturally, a broadness, a tolerance, a magnanimity not commonly found among followers of either Bible or Koran.

Khakani, however, was not always the profound scholarly writer. Like Omar Khayyam and many another Persian poet, he found the physical charm of woman a theme worthy of song, and some of the most pleasing of his verses deal with this very theme. For instance, having seen one day a woman of surpassing beauty, he wrote a vivid description that might have been a credit to Poe at his best:

> O waving cypress! cheek of rose!
>   O jasmine-breathing bosom! say,
> Tell me each charm that round her glows;
>   Who are ye that my heart betray;
> Tyrant unkind! to whom I bow,
> O life destroyer!—who art thou?

> I saw thy form of waving grace!
>   I heard thy soft and gentle sighs;
> I gazed on that enchanting face,
>   And looked in thy narcissus eyes;
> Oh! by the hopes thy smiles allow,
> Bright soul-inspirer!—who art thou?

> Wher'er she walks, amidst the shades,
>   Where perfumed hyacinths unclose,
> Danger her ev'ry glance pervades—
>   Her bow is bent on friends and foes.
> Thy rich cheek shames the rose—thy brow
> Is like the young moon—who art thou?

The poet-slave has dared to drain
    Draughts of thy beauty, till his soul,
Confused and lost in pleasing pain,
    Is fled beyond his own control.
What bliss can life accord me now
But once to know thee!—who art thou?[12]

Nizami

Far more romantic, perhaps *the* greatest romantic poet that Persia ever produced, was Nizami, a mingling of Sir Walter Scott and Lord Byron in one man, without, however, the latter's cynicism. You who have not read his stirring epic, *Khosru and Shireen,* or his tender and sorrowful *Laili and Majnun* have indeed missed two of the most affecting romances of either the Orient or the Occident. And when we of the Western World have caught, if only through translation, some of the beauty and fervor of his love-songs, and the depth of understanding in several of his philosophical poems, we are forced to the conclusion that here was what Persia has proclaimed him to be—one of the world's literary masters.

Is not the following legend, for instance, something entirely worthy to stand beside the other traditions of the deeds and sayings of Jesus of Nazareth?

One evening Jesus lingered in the market-place,
Teaching the people parables of truth and grace,
When in the square remote a crowd was seen to rise,
And stop with loathing gestures and abhorring cries.

[12] Version in Louisa Costello's *Rose Garden of Persia,* London, Longmans, 1845.

The Master and his meek disciples went to see
What cause for this commotion and disgust could be,
And found a poor dead dog beside the gutter laid;
Revolting sight! at which each face its hate betrayed.

One held his nose, one shut his eyes, one turned away;
And all among themselves began aloud to say—
"Detested creature! he pollutes the earth and air!"
"His eyes are blear!" "His ears are foul!" "His
    ribs are bare!"

"In his torn hide there's not a decent shoe-string left!
"No doubt the execrable cur was hung for theft!"
Then Jesus spake, and dropped on him this saving wreath,—
"Even pearls are dark before the whiteness of his teeth!"

The pelting crowd grew silent and ashamed, like one
Rebuked by sight of wisdom higher than his own;
And one exclaimed, "No creature so accursed can be,
But some good thing in him a loving eye will see." [13]

And is there not a simple dignity and yet a world of
meaning in the following story from Nizami's last
poem, *The Alexander Book?* Alexander the Great,
searching for the sources of the Nile, came at length
to a steep mountain. Soldier after soldier was sent up
this tremendous mass to bring back word of what lay
beyond, but none ever returned. At length Alexander
directed a father to ascend the mountain and to throw
down from the lofty cliffs to his son waiting at the
bottom a written report of the mysterious land on the
other side. And the son came back to Alexander with
this message explaining adequately the disappearance
of all who had gone to that tall summit:

[13] See S. Robinson's *Persian Poerty for English Readers,* Glasgow,
1883.

When I arrived at the rocky mound of the summit,
I was in an utter strait from the straitness of the way.
All that I beheld on the side which I had seen tore my heart
    to pieces,
And my judgment was annihilated by its perilous aspect.
But on the other side the way was without a blemish,
Delight upon delight, garden upon garden,
Full of fruit, and verdure, and water, and roses;
The whole region resounding with the melody of birds,
The air soft, and the landscape so charming,
That you might say, God had granted its every wish.
On this side all was life and beauty,
On the other side all was disturbance and ruin;
Here was Paradise, there the semblance of Hell—
Who would come to Hell and desert Paradise?
Think of that desert through which we wended,
Look whence we came, and at what we have arrived!
Who would have the heart from this lovely spot
Again to set a foot in that intricate track?
Here I remain, King, and bid thee adieu;
And mayst thou be happy as I am happy![14]

It is, however, upon Nizami's poetic love romances
that his fame in the East has been established, and
these, though sounding somewhat extravagant to
Western ears, may yet, when properly translated, gain
him a wider hearing in Europe and America. For
there is in such poems a tenderness, a concentrated
tragedy that should be attractive to the human heart
anywhere. Long centuries ago, for example, the story
of *Laili and Majnun* captivated Persia, and its beauty
of sentiment and tragic ending still give it charm.

The two lovers are parted and mourn the loss of
each other with all the passionate abandonment of the

[14] *Ibid.*

Orient. Against her vehement protest Laili is married
to a man who won over her father through the glitter
of gold. Then unexpectedly that husband dies, and
Laili, free once more, hastens to Majnun. In unre-
strained joy the lovers meet, and are experiencing not
only the rapture of the present but thoughts of a long
future together, when suddenly Majnun remembers
the Arab law forbidding the marriage of a man to a
widow! They stand apart, gasping with the despair
of it all, and then Majnun suddenly flees from the
temptation of gazing upon her longer. And she returns to her childhood home, there to die of her sorrow. Majnun, hearing of her death, begs to see the
corpse of the one whom he has so long and vainly
loved, and, weeping beside her beautiful body, he too
expires.

It is fit material for grand opera—this old Persian
romance of two doomed lovers. But even more forlorn, even more bitterly tragic is the fate of the lover
in Nizami's other famous epic romance, *Khosru and
Shireen*. The sad tale had been told before this poet's
day; it was known in various versions by high and low
in Iran; but the genius of Nizami gave it the artistry
and depth of sentiment that place it among the masterpieces of Eastern Literature.

Here we have a literary ancestor of Victor Hugo's
Toilers of the Sea. Ferhad, a young but famous sculp-
tor, has fallen in love with the beautiful Princess
Shireen, but she is the king's chosen one, and Ferhad
must be removed, by fair means or foul, from the
court. The monarch sneeringly demands of him the
seemingly impossible: he may have as his bride the
matchless Shireen if he shall hew through the gigantic

mountain of Beysitoun a channel for the river, and shall, moreover, decorate the borders of that channel with sculpture. Ferhad, trusting in the inspiration of his love, accepts the challenge and immediately commences the titantic task.

The mountain trembles to the echoing sound
Of falling rocks that from her sides rebound.
Each day, all respite, all repose, denied,
Without a pause the thundering strokes are plied;
The mist of night around the summit coils,
But still Ferhad, the lover-artist, toils,
And still, the flashes of his ax between,
He sighs to every wind, "Alas, Shireen!"
A hundred arms are weak one block to move
Of thousands molded by the hand of love
Into fantastic shapes and forms of grace,
That crowd each nook of that majestic place.
The piles give way, the rocky peaks divide,
The stream comes gushing on, a foaming tide,—
A mighty work for ages to remain,
The token of his passion and his pain.[15]

The years had passed in unremitting toil, and at last the masterpiece of engineering and artistic skill stood completed. The river roared its flashing torrent through the polished chasm of marble and granite; sculptors and artisans from all the known world wandered along the galleries, marveling at the statues, the tracery in stone, the polished pillars. And there stood Ferhad, chisel in hand, mortally weary, but victorious at last. An old woman suddenly appeared before him with a message—a false message from his rival, the King: "Shireen is dead!" To Ferhad it meant the end

[15] James Atkinson's version, London, 1836, in Louisa Costello's *Rose Garden of Persia*, London, Longmans, 1845.

of all. Was this the reward for the ceaseless moil
of the years?

> He spoke not, moved not, stood transfixed to stone.
> Then, with a frenzied start, he raised on high
> His arms, and wildly tossed them toward the sky;
> Far in the wide expanse his ax he flung,
> And from the precipice at once he sprung.
> The rocks, the sculptured caves, the valleys green
> Sent back his dying sigh,—"Alas, Shireen!" [16]

Such is the type of story—a strong mingling of the
sentimental and the tragically sorrowful—that has
gained for Nizami a place in the Persian heart similar
to that which Scott once occupied in the European
heart. All the world loves a lover, and this Persian
of long ago could portray the sufferings of the lover
with a skill convincing and overpowering. "Gentle
melancholy" and the tone of inevitable fate—these
won for Nizami, as they have for Omar Khayyam,
the affection of millions who had loved and suffered.

RUMI

In the thirteenth century there arose a poet destined
to become one of the seven greater bards known as
"the Persian Pleiades." His name was Jelaleddin,
but, as he lived long in Asia Minor, still called by the
Moslems "Rum" (Roman), he assumed the pen name
of Rumi. This man Rumi, like five others of the Persian Pleiades, belonged to that mystical sect called
Sufis.

Their *credo* was a type of pantheism—God in everything. In fact, this Sufism went so far as to declare
that nothing except God really exists, and that the

[16] *Ibid.*

individual soul is nothing but a temporary emanation from God, to be reabsorbed ultimately into the Divine. Naturally such believers would often write in a highly religious and even exalted or rhapsodical strain, and, though they might compose verses on such earthly subjects as wine, woman, and song, there was frequently hidden in such common themes a symbolism understood by other members of the cult.

So with Rumi. The Persians found in his lightest line a meaning deeply significant. That he possessed a philosophy or a religion spiritual beyond our expectations cannot be doubted; his is a theology equal at times to the highest presented in Christianity or in Judaism. For example, is not this portion of one of his poems the very essence of sincerity in religion?

> For the true spiritual Caaba is the heart,
> And no proud pile of perishable art.
> When God ordained the pilgrim rite, that sign
> Was meant to lead thy thoughts to things divine.
> A thousand times he treads that round in vain
> Who e'en one human heart would idly pain.
> Leave wealth behind; bring God thy heart,—best light
> To guide thy wavering steps through life's dark night.
> God spurns the riches of a thousand coffers.
> And says, "My chosen is he his heart who offers.
> Nor gold nor silver seek I, but above
> All gifts the heart, and buy it with my love;
> Yea, one sad contrite heart, which men despise,
> More than my throne and fixed decree I prize."
> Then think not lowly of thy heart, though lowly,
> For holy is it, and there dwells the Holy.
> God's presence-chamber is the human breast;
> Ah, happy he whose heart holds such a guest! [17]

[17] E. H. Whinfield's version, *Masnavi*, London, Trübner & Co., 1887.

Rumi was the product of a long line of scholars and thinkers. Born at the ancient city of Balkh in 1207, he early was taken by his father to that refuge of students and poets, Iconium. There that father became principal or president of a college, and there Rumi succeeded him in this office. In Iconium doubtless the young professor and poet would gladly have spent his day quietly and earnestly in the pursuit of learning. But there came one day to this city one of these wandering Sufis, apparently a most zealous, even fanatical preacher, named Shamsuddim. Great must have been the personality of this same Shamsuddim; he seemed to make every one his hot enemy or his hot disciple. He captivated Rumi. The poet became an ardent follower of Sufism.

But the foes of Shamsuddim rose against him; a riot occurred; Rumi's son was killed in the street fighting; the Sufi preacher was executed. The poet Rumi, far from being crushed and dismayed by these catastrophes, not only exulted in such sacrifices for his new faith, but at length founded a brotherhood or a religious order long famous for its pious attitude and its stern puritanical demeanor and method of living. Strangely enough, however, there was added the custom or rite of mystic dances, representing the vibration of the loving soul in unison with God. It was evidently a forerunner of the physical demonstration of exultation shown long afterwards by the Shakers and certain early groups of the English Quakers. To this very hour the brotherhood thus established by the devout Rumi exists in Turkey, and the leadership, after more than six centuries, still abides in the Rumi family.

Certainly this Sufi poet wrote a large amount, but

the one production that seems destined to keep his fame alive is his *Mesnavi,* a most interesting, even if somewhat formless collection of anecdotes, precepts, reflective poems, and comments on Moslem doctrines. There is a world of noble idealism in this *Mesnavi*—lofty convictions as to the rightful attitude of man toward the storm and stress of life, high theories of the brotherhood, not only of men, but of all God's creatures, inspiring visions of man's possible relationships with that God. In a poem, either his or by his disciples, the title of which is sometimes translated as *Man's Destiny,* we discern that same philosophy known among the Greeks as Stoicism, commonly taught by Brahman and Buddhist leaders of ancient India, found also in the high indifference which Shakespeare apparently urged in his lines:

> We are such stuff as dreams are made on,
> And our little life is rounded with a sleep.

Here indeed is the teaching of Jesus: he who gives his life shall receive it again.

> Seeks thy spirit to be gifted
>   With a deathless life?
> Let it seek to be uplifted
>   O'er earth's storm and strife.
>
> Spurn its joys—its ties dissever;
>   Hopes and fears divest;
> Thus aspire to live forever—
>   Be forever blest!
>
> Faith and doubt leave far behind thee;
>   Cease to love or hate;
> Let not Time's illusions blind thee;
>   Thou shalt Time outdate.

Merge thine individual being
In the Eternal's love;
All this sensuous nature fleeing
For pure bliss above.[18]

To the positive, aggressive Westerner it may be a theory that absolutely fails to appeal, but the Westerner is young in comparison with the Oriental; long centuries of civilization and reflection on what constitutes the "good life" may yet force us of America and Europe to similar conclusions concerning abnegation of self and the control of the emotions.

There is a curious bit of verse by Rumi dealing with a merchant and his captive parrot—a poem which seems to stress the idea found in Coleridge's *Ancient Mariner:* that a wrong to one of earth's humblest creatures may vibrate as a wrong throughout the world, and that "he prayeth best who loveth best all things both great and small."

A merchant departing on a long journey inquired of each of his servants what presents he should bring back to them individually. After all had expressed their wishes the master asked of his parrot, "What gift shall I bring thee?" The bird's answer was a strange but a significant one. When, he said, thou seest in the distant groves the parrots free and happy, tell them a companion, confined in a cage through Heaven's decree, sends greetings, but asks,

Is it right that I in my longings
Should pine and die in this prison through separation?
Is it right that I should be here fast in this cage,
While you dance at will on the grass and the trees?

[18] *Ibid.*

> Is this the fidelity of friends,
> I here in a prison, and you in a grove?
> Oh remember, I pray you, that bower of ours,
> And our morning-draughts in the olden time;
> Oh remember all our ancient friendships,
> And all the festive days of our intercourse! [19]

And the merchant went his way, and a day came when he saw in far Hindustan a group of parrots happy in freedom. And he lifted up his voice and repeated the message of his captive bird. Scarcely had he finished the words when one of the parrots fluttered and fell to the ground and expired. Then the merchant in anguish cried that he had slain an innocent creature; that perhaps this dead parrot and the captive one had been close of kin, "their bodies perhaps were two and their souls one." He resolved ever more to guard his tongue, for words are as sparks of fire.

> The world around is as a cotton-field by night;
> In the midst of cotton how shall the spark do no harm?

At length the traveler returned home, and to each servant he gave a gift. But the captive parrot demanded to know what had occurred on the long journey, and the merchant described to him the scene in the grove. And when he concluded with the words, "It broke its heart and fluttered and died," the bird in the cage also fell in death. The merchant lifted it from its cage and laid it gently upon the ground. And lo! the parrot suddenly came to life, flew to a nearby tree, and proclaimed its message: "The dying companion far away taught me by its own action. It told

[19] *Ibid.*

me to escape from earthly speech, from articulate
voice, to gain freedom by giving up all and going down
into death!"

> Farewell, my master, thou hast done me a kindness,
> Thou hast freed me from the bond of this tyranny.
> Farewell, my master, I fly towards home;
> Thou shalt one day be free like me.

Here is not only the message of the kinship of all
beings in the universe, but that lesson so emphasized
by Jesus: he who would win his life must lay it down,
and only through death is genuine life obtained.
Whether through his wide reading Rumi was influenced
by the doctrines of the early Christians cannot, of
course, be ascertained; but it is certain that many of
his philosophical principles have the very flavor of
the teachings of the Nazarene.

God was indeed near to this devout Persian Sufi.
Well might he have used as a symbol of the joys that
follow death the closing lines of a poem dealing with
a dying lover, written either by Rumi or by one of
his Sufi companions:

> "Ah, when the fair, adored through life, lifts up at length,"
>   he cried,
> "The veil that sought from mortal eye immortal charms to
>   hide,
> 'Tis thus true lovers, fevered long with that sweet mystic fire,
> Exulting meet the Loved One's gaze, and in that glance
>   expire."

SADI

Surely it should not be surprising that out of those
high tablelands of Iran came so many poets who were

philosophers as well as singers. Here was the same
stock, remember, as that which gradually crept down
into India and produced two of the most idealistic religions in the history of man. This, too, was the East
with its leisurely way of living, its long days of calm
meditation, its deep interest in the idea of God, and
its theories of transcendentalism. Many generations
of thinkers along such lines had as certainly created
a genius for philosophy and theology as the few
American generations of a very different type of
thinkers have created the Yankee genius for mechanics
and administrative skill.

Paramount, perhaps, among the numerous philosophers of Persia stands Sadi—a thinker and bard
whose fame still echoes through Iran. All the wild
and disastrous adventures of his stormy life could not
destroy the philosophy of the man; rather, the buffets
of fate apparently made his theories of life stronger
and more clear. Whether teaching youth in a Persian
college or bending under the lash of a European slave-
driver, he was one who saw life clearly and as a whole.

Born at Shiraz in 1184, he was educated in Bagdad
College, and until he was forty years of age led the
quiet, secluded existence of a college professor. Then
came the fierce Genghis Khan roaring down upon Bagdad, and Sadi was forced to flee before the onrushing
hordes of barbarians. He wandered far in those days
—down into Egypt, over into Europe, even into India.
It must have been a weary time for this highly educated, refined bookman, who had previously known so
much of culture and so little of hardship. But far
worse days were to come. He unfortunately roamed
into Palestine, and the Crusaders, with true Christian

zeal against all Moslems, seized him and put him to work laying brick and stone for their fortifications.

There came at length a leading merchant of Aleppo —a Mohammedan—who was amazed to find the most erudite scholar of Iran making blocks of mud under the watchful eyes of a crusading blockhead. The Aleppo chief explained the incongruity of the situation, and by dint of repeated explanations evidently made some impression upon the Christian French and English who were rescuing from the "infidels" the tomb of the Kindest Man that ever lived. They finally released the professor—for a consideration. Back to Aleppo this decidedly philosophic fellow, Sadi, went, and there quietly settled down in the home of the chief.

His quiet was not, however, to be for long. For the chief had a daughter—beautiful, yes, but a born scold. And the philosopher was foolish enough to fall in love with her, and married her. Now, Sadi had essayed matrimony years before, with rather disappointing results, and when this second marriage proved a catastrophe he permitted his philosophic opinions about women to take a most sarcastic turn. His expressions about wives are, in fact, vigorously current throughout Persia of to-day. Only a man with considerable domestic experience could have coined such adages as: "Choose a fresh wife every spring or New Year's day, for the almanac of last year is good for nothing," and "Take your wife's opinion and act just the opposite of it." "Art thou not the slave that my father bought for ten dinars?" sneeringly inquired his wife one day. "Yes," replied Sadi, "he ransomed me for ten dinars and sold me to you for a hundred."

But neither bitter experiences at home or abroad

soured his nature or tore from his soul the high ideals of philosophy that in his earlier years he had taught the boys in the college at Bagdad. In spite of the treatment that he had received at the hands of the Christians he had a genuine love for the personality of Jesus and a deep reverence for the teachings of the Nazarene. He had far less skepticism about the miracles of Christ than has many a modern Christian. In fact, although still a devout Moslem, he held such admiration for the founders of Christianity that he did not hesitate to worship in Christian temples, and even prayed at the supposed tomb of John the Baptist at Damascus.

Possibly it was this broadness of mind, this spirit of magnanimity that caused Sadi to live considerably beyond a hundred years—tradition says even to one hundred and twenty. For at least the last twenty-five years of this long life he dwelt in the seclusion of a hermit, but in his latest days roamed back to his birthplace, Shiraz, there to die. Here was one who could boast neither power nor material prosperity; yet sovereigns condescended to come to him for advice, and thousands of the humbler folk looked upon him as a most wise and loving friend.

Now, Sadi's lyrical poems cannot equal the best that Rumi and his son-in-law, Hafiz, produced, but through two of his books he gained a fame which may even outlast that of his two friends. Those works are the *Gulistan,* or *Rose Garden,* and the *Bustan,* or *Fruit Garden* or *Garden of Perfume*.

The *Rose Garden* is a medley of one hundred and eighty-eight short stories interspersed with verse, while the *Bustan* is composed of ten sections of fable, mainly in poetic form. While obviously intended to show man the way to morality and wisdom, the two volumes are not, as a whole, couched in solemn, prophetic language. On the contrary, there are some rather good jokes amidst the advice. There is, for instance, the anecdote about the Moslem whose voice in reciting the prayers in the mosque was so atrocious that one day a man asked him how much he was paid for reciting. "Paid!" he exclaimed. "I am not paid! I recite for the sake of God!" "Then," responded the other, "for God's sake, don't!"

Again, there was a muezzin whose voice was so harsh that his call to prayer served only to drive the people away from the mosque. The prince of the land, being tender-hearted, gave him ten dinars to go somewhere else as muezzin. But a little later the fellow returned with the complaint that the gift was too small. "At my present place," he declared, "they offered me twenty dinars to go somewhere else." "Don't accept it," laughed the prince; "for if you stay a little longer they will be glad to offer you fifty!"

Then, there was the fellow with sore eyes who went to a veterinary for relief. The veterinary gave him some salve for animals' eyes, and the chap lost his sight. He carried the matter into court, but the wise judge declared, "There are no damages to be recovered. The man would not have gone to a veterinary if he had not been an ass."

Of course, however, this is not Sadi at his greatest. The scholar who had traveled far, who had been a slave in Palestine, a professor at Bagdad, a poet and philosopher at Shiraz, the man who throughout a tremendous stretch of years had seen life in innumerable phases, had gained an insight, a knowledge, a wisdom granted to but few human beings. The depth of thought, the practical philosophy, the epigrammatical expressions of Sadi have made him one of the most widely read authors of the East—a man to be quoted by generation after generation of the intellectual.

> Send to the tomb an ample store;
> None will it bring—then send before.[20]

Those lines are not the resigned pessimism of an Omar Khayyam; they are the counsel of a man who believes that life's struggle is worth while. There is a purpose in it all, he declares, and there is an injunction upon every mortal to find his place in the world's work.

> Oh, square thyself for use. A stone that may
> Fit in the wall is not left in the way.

There is a Ben Franklin shrewdness about this Persian sage. Go to no extremes, keep the middle of the road, consider the consequences before you act.

> When thou contendest choose an enemy
> Whom thou mayest vanquish or whom thou canst fly.

And again:

> Silence is mannerly—so deem the wise,
> But in the fitting time use language freely;
> Blindness of judgment just in two things lies,
> To speak unwished, or speak unseasonably.

[20] The versions of Sadi's poetry given here are based on translations by E. B. Eastwick, several examples of which may be found in *Flowers from the Persian Poets,* New York, Thomas Y. Crowell Co., 1901, Vol. II. Excerpts may also be found in *Persian Literature,* New York, Colonial Press, 1900. An excellent version of *Bustan* is that of A. Hart Edwards, New York, E. P. Dutton, 1911. The translation, by James Ross, published in London in 1823, is reprinted in *Sacred Books and Early Literature of the East,* New York, Park, Austin & Lipscomb, 1917, Vol. 8. The most popular translation of *Bustan* is Edwin Arnold's, New York, Harper, 1899.

These adages of worldly wisdom, however, are set within a framework of poetic fancy, and, at times, gorgeous description. Sadi has an eye for the proper staging and background for the philosopher as he moralizes. Many a time it is a garden at evening:

> A garden where the murmurous rill was heard
> While from the hills sang each melodious bird;
> That, with the many-colored tulip bright,
> These with their various fruits the eye delight.
> The whispering breeze beneath the branches' shade,
> Of blending flowers a motley carpet made.

There is indeed a delicacy of sentiment in Sadi toward even the humblest things of Nature. To him there is a reason for all; the derelict, the wreckage, is to him not lost, abhorrent waste matter.

> I saw some handfuls of the rose in bloom,
> With bands of grass suspended from a dome.
> I said, "What means this worthless grass, that it
> Should in the roses' fairy circle sit?"
> Then wept the grass, and said, "Be still! and know
> The kind their old associates ne'er forego,
> Mine is no beauty, here, or fragrance—true,
> But in the garden of the Lord I grew."

There is indeed in this Sage of Shiraz deep compassion for those human beings who tread life's humble round, burdened, worn, weary. Thus he tells for our consideration a short but significant story of a poor guard who was thoughtlessly mistreated by a certain king:

I have heard that King Toghrul came in his rounds on a Hindu sentinel. The snow was falling thick, and it rained in torrents, and he shivered with the cold like the star Canopus. The heart of the King was moved with compassion, and he said: "Thou shall put on my fur-mantle; wait a moment at the end of the terrace, and I will send it out by the hand of a slave." Meanwhile a piercing wind was blowing, and the King walked into his royal hall. There the sight of a lovely lady so enchanted him, that the poor sentinel entirely slipped his memory. As though the wintry cold was not suffering enough, to his evil fortune were added the pangs of disappointment.

Hear, whilst the King slept in comfort, what the watchman was saying toward the dawning of the morning:

"Perhaps thy good fortune made thee forgetful, for thy hand was clasped in the hand of thy beloved. For thee the night passed in mirth and enjoyment; what knowest thou of how it passed with us? When the company of the caravan are stooping the head over the platter, what concern have they for those who have fallen down in the sand (the desert)? O boatman, launch thy boat into the water, for it hath nearly reached the head of the helpless waders! Stay your steps a while, ye active youths, for in the caravan are weak old men also. Thou who art sleeping sweetly in thy litter, whilst the bridle of the camel is in the hand of the driver, what to thee are plain, and hill, and stone, and sand?—Ask how it is with those who are left behind on the journey. Thou who art borne along on thine high and strong dromedary, how knowest thou how he fareth who is traveling on foot? They who in the quiet of their hearts are reposing at the resting-place, what know they of the condition of the hungry wayfarer?"

It is this same sympathy with "the under dog" so often expressed in his prose and poetry that undoubtedly has helped to make Sadi so beloved and venerated among Eastern readers. Time after time he seems to warn us in story or epigram: Remember the weaker brother, be not vainglorious in your strength and

prosperity. Be magnanimous. Hear this story of a
certain monk and a repentant sinner:

In Jesus' time there lived a youth so black and dissolute
That Satan from him shrank, appalled in every attribute.
He in a sea of pleasures foul uninterrupted swam,
And gluttonized on dainty vices, sipping many a dram.
Whoever met him in the highway turned as from a pest,
Or, pointing lifted finger at him, cracked some horrid jest.
I have been told that Jesus once was passing by the hut
Where dwelt a monk, who asked him in, and just the door
    had shut,
When suddenly that slave of sin appeared across the way.
Far off he paused, fell down, and sobbingly began to pray.
As blinded butterflies will from the light affrighted shrink,
So from those righteous men in awe his timid glances sink;
And like a storm of rain the tears pour gushing from his eyes.

.   .   .   .

The pride-puffed monk, self-righteous, lifts his eyebrows with
    a sneer,
And haughtily exclaims, "Vile wretch! in vain hast thou come
    here.
Art thou not plunged in sin, and tossed in lust's devouring sea?
What will thy filthy rags avail with Jesus and with me?
O God! the granting of a single wish is all I pray:
Grant me to stand far distant from this man in the judgment
    day."
From Heaven's throne a revelation instantaneous broke,
And God's own thunder words thus through the mouth of
    Jesus spoke:
"The two whom praying there I see shall equally be heard;
They pray diverse,—I give to each according to his word.
That poor one thirty years has rolled in sin's most slimy deeps,
But now, with stricken heart and streaming tears, for pardon
    weeps.

Upon the threshold of my grace he throws him in despair,
And, faintly hoping pity, pours his supplications there.
Therefore, forgiven and freed from all the guilt in which he
    lies,
My mercy chooses him a citizen of Paradise.
This monk desires that he may not that sinner stand beside,
Therefore he goes to Hell, and so his wish is gratified."

In God's pure court all egotistic claims as naught are held.
Whose robe is white, but black as night his heart beneath it lies,
Is a live key at which the gate of Hell wide open flies.
Truly not self-conceit and legal works with God prevail;
But humbleness and tenderness weigh down Salvation's scale.[21]

It is a lesson worth considering. In this day when
there is so much talk of the "inferiority complex"—
and so little evidence of it—possibly a little humility
mingled with our power and prosperity may be a most
useful ingredient. At least so thinks Sadi. He makes
his moral decidedly concrete at times; evidence his little tale of two wrestlers:

A man who had reached great skill in wrestling knew three
hundred and sixty splendid sleights in that art, and always
could exhibit something new. He taught his favorite student
three hundred and fifty-nine of the tricks, reserving one, however, to himself. At length the student excelled so greatly in
skill that no one was able to deal with him, and he even
boasted to the Sultan that he permitted his teacher to appear
superior simply out of respect for the master's years.

The Sultan did not at all like this attitude of disrespect and
therefore demanded that there be a test of ability. The state
officials and other notables of the court came to the extensive
grounds to view the spectacle. The young man, entering like

[21] See S. Robinson's *Persian Poetry for English Readers,* Glasgow,
McLaren, 1883.

TOMB OF SADI

From " Ouseley's Travels "

a wild elephant, attacked with a force that would have overturned a mountain of iron. But the teacher, realizing the
pupil's superiority in strength, now used the sleight that he
had kept in reserve. The youth, not knowing how to cope with
it, was lifted high into the air and then flung to the earth.
The multitude burst into loud applause.

The Sultan directed that a robe and money be given the
teacher, and with derision he reproved the boy for presuming
to compete with his instructor and benefactor. The pupil,
however, cried out, "O King, he did not win the victory
through strength or skill, but because he had withheld from
me one small trick in the art!" "Yes," replied the teacher, "I
reserved it for just such an occasion as this; for the wise have
said, 'Beware of putting yourself so much into the power of
a friend that, should he turn enemy, he may be able to effect
his purpose against you.' Have you not also heard what a
man declared who had been injured by one whom he had
educated? Either there never was such a thing as gratitude
or else man now no longer practices it. Never have I taught
any one archery who did not ultimately use me as a target." [22]

This, then, is the sage and poet, Sadi, whose tomb
near the ancient city of Shiraz is a shrine for thousands
of visitors every year. Kindly, sympathetic, shrewd,
but with it all never forgetting the poetry, the romance,
of life, he long ago captured the heart of the Orient
and is steadily gaining the affection of the Occident.
Undoubtedly he prophesied aright when he said of his
Rose Garden:

What use to thee that flower-vase of thine?
Thou wouldst have rose-leaves; take, then, rather mine;
Those roses but five days or six will bloom;
This Garden ne'er will yield to Winter's gloom.

[22] Author's version.

HAFIZ

Shiraz—it is a gem in a desolate waste. As the traveler bursts through the mountainous ranges and unexpectedly looks down upon its broad deep valley in the mellow light of the spring sunshine and gazes upon its mosques and ancient shadowy gardens he is apt to declare with its poets of old, "This is the earthly Paradise!" A nearer inspection of its narrow streets and crumbling grandeur may cause some disillusionment, but under the soft rays of the moon and the stars there returns all the enchantment that inspired Sadi and Hafiz and a host of others of the city's poets to sing of its inspiration.

Yet how many a carnage has been enacted in and about this beloved home of Persian authors throughout the centuries! Over Iran and indeed a great part of Asia Minor there reigned during the last years of the fourteenth century a Sultan named Ilkhani—on the surface a devout Mohammedan, but in reality a cultured beast. Sensitive to poetry, music, and art, a creator himself in these fields, he was at the same time a monster so cruel that the citizens of Bagdad at length invited the Tartar chief, Tamerlane, to snatch the kingdom from him.

Then indeed did Persia feel the ravages of remorseless war. All of Iran fell beneath the bloody feet of the ferocious Tartar chief, and as he swept on to India he left behind him little but smoking ruins and pyramids of human skulls and fields littered with human bones. Beautiful Shiraz knew the bitterness of his rage and trembled at the mention of his name.

And yet, his conquests over, his sway absolutely secured, this same Tamerlane became surprisingly mild, patronized scholarship and the arts, and so encouraged poetry and romance and history that they flourished in his later years as they had scarcely flourished before. And his children and his children's children even increased the encouragement begun by their famous or infamous sire. It was a golden day for the scientific and mathematical genius of the nation, while religion took unto itself a broader liberalism than had seemed possible under the orthodoxy of Moslemism. And Shiraz, the city of roses and poets, glowed under such patronage and appreciation of the nobler expressions of life.

It was at Shiraz "the heavenly" that Hafiz, the greatest lyric writer of Iran, dwelt and sang. Yet when Tamerlane came down upon the city it was only by a sudden flash of the poet's wit that Hafiz's life was saved. Called into the presence of the scowling warrior, he was sternly asked by Tamerlane why he had pretended to possess cities in his line of poetry: "For the black mole on thy cheek I would give the cities of Samarkand and Bokhara." That question from the lips of the most ferocious conqueror whom Asia had ever known might have forever silenced a less ready man. But Hafiz instantly replied: "Yes, your Majesty, and it is by just such acts of generosity that I am reduced, as you see, to my present state of poverty!"

That response was too much for Tamerlane. He laughed, ordered the audacious poet to be presented with costly gifts, and requested that Hafiz should henceforth dwell at court. But the undaunted bard, desiring independence above all favor and wealth, quietly but most firmly declined to comply, and the

Tartar chief, admiring his sturdy character, permitted him to wander as he list.

And Hafiz went his way and sang of wine and women against all the laws of Mohammedanism, and filled Persia with such songs of sentiment and such lyrics of passion that the most unlettered camel-driver and most ignorant herder of goats and sheep in Iran sing bits of the verses to this day. What Anacreon meant to the Greeks, what Horace meant to the Romans, what Burns meant to the Scotch, what Tom Moore meant to the Irish, all this and more Hafiz meant and means to the Persians.

Like many a man who has drunk of the joys of life a little too deeply in his youth, Hafiz changed rather abruptly in his later years, joined the Sufi sect, and wrote verse of such hidden religious symbolism that much of it is incomprehensible to the modern Western mind. But he never ceased to love beauty and happiness in its every form, and whether it was the tints of dawn, the blush on a girl's cheek, the odor of the rose, or the flavor of a wine, he found in everything that gave pleasure to the senses an inspiration for enthusiastic lyrics. The nightingale, the cypress, the mellow moon, his beloved city basking under the sunlight— these thrilled him to poetic expression. But as Emerson has said, "If you mistake him for a low rioter he turns on you with verses which express the poverty of sensual joys, and an heroic sentiment and contempt for the world."

A curious paradox—this man Hafiz. A paradox to his own people and to his own religion. How could this believer in the Mohammedan creed actually have written such poems as his about the joys of wine and

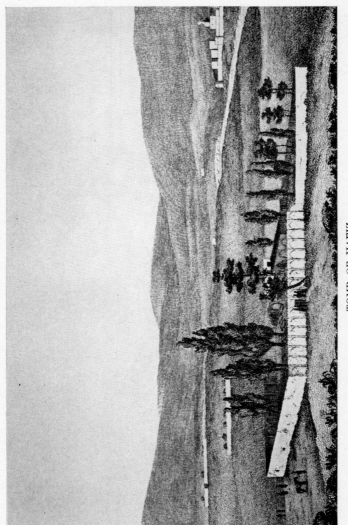

TOMB OF HAFIZ
From " Ouseley's Travels "

woman? It was impossible, declared the commentators and the theologians; these expressions of his were mere symbolism to veil his deep love of Allah and His Righteousness. And commentators and theologians have ever since been trying to spoil the meaning of a perfectly clear, even if rather sensual bard.

. Even the zealous interpreters of his verse had their own doubts, as is evidenced by the fact that when he died in 1388 these Moslems hesitated to grant him the customary funeral services, until some of his friends suggested that some lines from his poetry be placed in an urn and a child be bidden to draw forth some quotation that might throw light upon the question. And lo! the child drew forth this verse: "Withhold not your step from the bier of Hafiz; for, though sunk in sin, he goes to Paradise!"

Perhaps it was such a stanza as this excuse given by a drunkard that caused some of the Mohammedan priests to consider him really "sunk in sin":

Know you the true reason and cause why it is that I drink?
From pride and from folly I strutted and swelled through
the town:
And now those detestable vices, from which the saints shrink,
I will in the depths of the ocean of drunkenness drown.[23]

Or perhaps it was this Anacreontic song of a light-hearted, young and lusty lover that brought the frown of disapproval to the ecclesiastical brow:

My breast is filled with roses
My cup is crowned with wine,
And the veil her face discloses—
The maid I hail as mine.

[23] William Jones' version, Louisa Costello's *Rose Garden of Persia,*
London, Longmans, 1845.

The monarch, wheresoe'er he be,
Is but a slave compared to me.

The honey-dew thy charm might borrow,
    Thy lip alone to me is sweet;
When thou art absent, faint with sorrow
    I hide me in some lone retreat.
Why talk to me of power or fame?
    What are those idle toys to me?
Why ask the praises of my name,
    My joy, my triumph is in thee.

How blest am I! around me swelling
    The notes of melody arise!
I hold the cup with wine excelling,
    And gaze upon thy radiant eyes.

O Hafiz—never waste thy hours
    Without the cup, the lute, and love,
For 'tis the sweetest time of flowers,
    And none these moments shall reprove.
The nightingales around thee sing;
It is the joyous feast of spring.[24]

It would take a deal of theological ingenuity to make
anything symbolical of the joys of piety out of that.
And it would indeed require the services of a score
of religious commentators to put a "heavenly" meaning into this poem on a lute and a drinking cup:

This goblet waited on full many a guest.
Believer, come! the wine-house lures; come, hark,
And drink; with cup and lute be wholly blest.
Their wine and music put to shame the lore
Of Koran, Puran, Ved and Zendavest.

[24] William Jones' version, Louisa Costello's *Rose Garden of Persia*,
London, Longmans, 1845.

Believer, come! feel inspiration's breath
Exhaling through your soul, and through your breast.
And if the world would catch you in her snares,
Reject her with the might of one protest.
Unnumbered sages have rejoiced when soft
This lute's sweet solace has their hearts caressed.
Unnumbered kings have smiled to quaff this cup,
When anxious thought and woe their souls oppressed.
Through these two charmers dear, unnumbered bards
Have drowned their pain when grief their lives possessed.

. . . .

They know the magic fruit of Paradise,
Which ripens not on this world's boughs at rest.
All this in their dear circles they impart,
At feasts, to the clear spirits of the blest.
They have against the idle host of cares
Declared a war by open manifest.

. . . .

These lute-cup strains and streams of tone and taste
Make of the poorest inn a heaven confessed.
The pious saint who drinks their breath and blood
Shall sit, bliss-drunk, upon creation's crest,
He shall through dazzling skies of pleasure soar,
With godhead filled, and in delirium dressed.[25]

But this lover of the earth and its fleshly sensations had moments when he saw clearly into things spiritual—saw clearly that the home of the soul is out beyond, and that the body bestowed in this fleeting world is merely a type of prison hampering the true expression of this soul. There is a little poem of his which reveals that, after all, this Hafiz was at heart a trusting believer in God:

[25] William Jones' version, *Literature of All Nations*, New York, E. R. Du Mont, 1900, Vol. V.

My soul is as a sacred bird, the highest heaven its rest,
Fretting within its body-bars, it finds on earth its nest;
When rising from its dusty heap this bird of mine shall soar;
'Twill find upon the lofty gate the nest it had before.
The Sidrah shall receive my bird, when it has winged its way,
And on Empyrean's top my falcon's foot shall stay.

.   .   .   .

No spot in the two worlds it owns, above the sphere its goal;
Its body from the quarry is, from "No Place" is its soul.
'Tis only in the glorious world my bird its splendor shows,
The rosy bowers of Paradise its daily food bestows.[26]

Hafiz—magic singer of Iran—how he vibrated to every tone of Nature! And with what fearing pleasure he has been read by generations of the faithful! For he cries aloud the joys of this earthly existence— and to many that is sacrilege. He spurns dull care, shows solemn remorse the door, and bids the world be happy.

> The lute, then, twang! the goblet clink and kiss!—
> 'Tis dying, drunken Hafiz' farewell hest.

ASSAR

During all these centuries, while the Persian poets were singing of pleasure or piety, revel or religion, the common folk, who could not read verse or anything else, were entertaining themselves with long, long prose romances. Not only peasant but prince delighted in these tales of heroism or love. Many a reciter of stories indeed obtained fame and fortune, many a woman gained the favor of her lord through ability to relate an entrancing romance; professional declaim-

[26] Hermann Bicknell's version, Dole and Walker: *Flowers from Persian Poets,* Crowell, Vol. II.

ers even claimed to be able to induce sleep and cure disease through the magic of the narrative. All Iran, it seems, echoed with song and story. Every bazaar, every street apparently had its romance-weaver; every Persian could tell a good tale.

As we have seen, it was the genius of Persia that took the ancient fables of India and transformed them into the enchanting *Thousand and One Nights*—commonly known as the *Arabian Nights* because of their use by the Arabs. The Iranian admired a narrative containing an intricate and prolonged interweaving of love and treachery, suffering and recompense. Many a story of this kind he possessed, and probably a typical one, and perhaps the most widely known among all classes of Persians was the romance of the two foster brothers, Meher and Mushteri.

We know simply that its author was Assar. That is all. Who Assar was, exactly where he lived, what else he composed no man can say. But this one tale will long keep his name alive in the East, and perhaps in the Western World also.

In the ancient city of Persepolis lived a king who had a son named Meher. Now, another boy, Mushteri, the son of the Grand Vizier, was so beloved by Meher that the two lads were inseparable. They had the same teacher, the same studies, the same pastimes. But another official, with a son named Behram, looked upon all this with jealousy; for he had hoped that his own boy should some day succeed to the position as Grand Vizier. This officer therefore so influenced the old teacher that this kindly but infirm pedagogue reported to the monarch that Mushteri was not a fit companion for Meher, but that Behram was. So enraged was the king by the report of the evil doings of his son and Mushteri that he ordered them to instant execution. And the sentence would certainly have been carried out had not the ruler's nephew, at the risk of his own life, pleaded so passionately for the boys that the king withdrew his command. But he decreed that his son should be placed into close confinement in prison and that Mushteri and the lad who had carried messages for the two companions should be banished.

After long imprisonment the young Prince was released, but the old Vizier, broken-hearted over the loss of his child, sickened and died. Meher, thus set free, immediately sought his mother sitting disconsolate in her luxurious apartment, and great was their joy at being reunited. But neither could trust the temper of the king, and, bringing Meher a casket of precious jewels, she bade him fly. And that very night the boy and his companion fled to the coast and sailed away for a far land. This appeared to Behram to be the opportunity of his life. He sought out the sorrowing father and requested money, gems, and a caravan that he might go forth to seek the boy Meher. Laden with wealth he went forth, with the secret intention, probably, of never returning.

Meanwhile Mushteri and his messenger, Bader, had been despoiled by robbers and left to die in the desert. At length, however, a passing caravan rescued them, and, by means of a small sum given them by their rescuers, they reached the Caspian Sea and sailed forth. But a mighty storm wrecked their ship, and only by chance were they seen by a King, who saved them from a watery grave. Into a magnificent palace they were ushered, where the music, the glittering

gems, and the dancers filled them with bewilderment
and wonder. This King, greatly pleased with the two
boys, promised them everything within his power if
they would remain. But Mushteri had heard of the
flight of Meher, and he was determined to find him
or perish in the attempt.

And what of Meher all this time? After long
wandering he came at last to the realm of the mighty
King Keiwan. When the lad entered the royal court
his graceful and dignified bearing delighted the
monarch, and when Meher presented him with a ruby
more valuable than any in the King's caskets his admiration and wonder were unlimited. But he knew
not whether to believe this young man a genuine Prince
or merely an accomplished robber. When, however,
the sovereign put him through tests of culture and
saw him beat in six moves the most skillful chess player
in the kingdom the ruler knew him indeed for a nobleman.

Now, the king's beautiful daughter, Princess Nahid,
had witnessed all these tests and feats from behind the
screen; she fell in love with the young stranger. And
so delighted was the monarch that he declared she
should wed Meher and him only. And fortune made
the match more certain by the descent upon the city of
King Kara Khan, a rejected suitor, whose hordes of
ruffians were captured by the doughty Prince. Only
through the earnest intercession of Meher was Kara
Khan himself spared for execution.

But love is often sorely tempted. The Princess
Nahid, roaming with her attendants one day through
the palace park, saw Meher asleep, and, in spite of
the protests of her companions, she approached him

and knelt over him without her veil—a deadly sin for a Moslem maid. And he awoke, and, seeing the famous Princess for the first time, he impulsively kissed her—another deadly sin for the unmarried.

Then was Meher summoned before the King—to receive the sentence of death, he supposed. But, instead, the monarch offered him Nahid as a wife. Filled with gratitude and contrition, the Prince fell on his knees, told the true story of his life, and revealed the sin of the kiss. The King listened and forgave, but when Meher declared that before love for Nahid and before marriage came the duty to find his friend, Mushteri, the ruler dismissed him with no little displeasure.

At this very time, however, the evil Behram's caravan, with Mushteri and Bader captives, was approaching this very city. Meher recognized Behram, and sent word to King Keiwan to arrest the young traitor. Then, when Behram was brought before the royal court, Meher, hidden behind the screen, heard the culprit maintain that the captives were merely two servants who had attempted robbery and were now being punished. Nor could Meher feel able to deny this statement; for poor Mushteri had been so beaten and starved that he was unrecognizable by his looks. But when he spoke, then Meher knew the beloved voice, and, rushing from behind the screen, he clasped his long-lost friend.

The King, in his justice, ordered Behram sent forth for execution, but Meher looked upon the trembling wretch with compassion, and so entreated Keiwan that at length the sovereign permitted the rascal to be done with as Meher should decree. And the kindly Prince gave him back his camels and his goods and sent him forth in safety. But Behram, overcome with shame and remorse, soon afterwards took his own life.

Then was Meher married to the beautiful Princess, and they and Mushteri and the faithful messenger returned to their homeland. Great was the joy of the father of Meher, the old King, who soon thereafter resigned the throne and gave the crown to the happy and just and magnanimous Meher.[27]

Such a story breathes a spirit of forgiveness and liberality that many Christians doubtless think limited to their own religion. Strangely enough, Moslem literature is rich in just such stories of a charity that "suffereth long," "is not puffed up," "doth not vaunt itself." Out of the ancient raw tribes of the East the Koran, crude as it may seem to the Western World, has created oftentimes philosophers and idealists not easily surpassed.

JAMI

At last the time came in Persia, as in any other nation, for the national splendor in art and literature to wane and pass away. For Iran the hour of death for the things of the spirit seems to have come at the close of the fifteenth century. The day of joyous song was ended. There might still be historians, lexicographers, grammarians, scholars. Indeed under the Great Moguls, the descendants of Tamerlane, who reigned over both India and Persia, such scholarly activities were lavishly encouraged. But the creative impulse was spent; genuine literature has not come

---

[27] For excellent translations of Persian fiction, see D. L. R. Lorimer: *Persian Tales*, New York, Macmillan, 1919.

forth from the Persian soul in more than four hundred years.

It was the lone poet, Jami, who rang down the curtain on the picturesque pageant of Iranian song and story. Born in the town of Jam in 1414, he was given the thoroughly unpoetic name of Nuruddin Abdurrahman, but early and wisely chose to call himself simply Jami, in honor of his birthplace.

Having studied at Herat and Samarkand, he became so famous for his knowledge, insight, and piety, and especially for his learning in the doctrines of the Sufis that he was commonly spoken of as the Master. At length he was chosen as Head of the Order of Sufi, and, when invited to dwell at the court of the Sultan Abu Said, he became the leader of the most learned group of men Persia had ever known. Monarchs came from afar to seek his counsel; he was looked upon by his day as the greatest product of Eastern culture.

Ninety-nine books were his—volumes of poetry, treatises in theology, essays on grammar and philology —books that cultivated Persians still read with admiration and reverence. And reverence is indeed due; for Iran is still a land of mysticism in religion, and Jami was probably the most thorough-going mystic that this nation ever produced. After a quiet, industrious, and genuinely contented life spent in study and writing, Jami died in the year that Columbus first sighted the New World.

Seven lengthy mystical poems, often spoken of as the "Seven Thrones," are commonly agreed upon as Jami's greatest literary creations. The last of these, *Salaman and Absal,* gained considerable attention among European readers during the earlier nineteenth century through the translation by Edward Fitzgerald; but the poem that Persia justly looks upon as the very highest accomplishment of Jami is *Yusuf and Zulaikha,* the story of the Biblical Joseph and Potiphar's wife.

In this eight thousand line poem we discover a strange revision of the old legend—a recasting under the influence of the Moslem sacred writings. Zulaikha is indeed the wife of Potiphar, but her love for the handsome, young Joseph—all that is ideal in manhood and integrity—is something foreordained, something not her fault, an inevitable passion not to be considered as a sin. Inspired from Heaven, it is a predestined union of two kindred souls, and a union it does indeed become after Potiphar's death. To the Westerner it may be simply a strongly emotional romance, but to the religious Persian, and perhaps to Jami himself, it has symbolized the soul's longing for the highest good and the noblest beauty.

> A nest is Beauty, Love the brooding linnet:
> A mine is Beauty, Love the diamond in it.
> From God's two sides they came, twin emanation,
> To chase and woo each other through creation.
> But in each atom's point, both, clasping, enter,
> And constitute all being's blissful center.[28]

Zulaikha, the daughter of a mighty King, was "passing fair."

> Her stature was iike to a palm-tree grown
> In the garden of grace where no sin is known.
> Bedewed by the love of her father the king,
> She mocked the cypress that rose by the spring.

[28] R. T. G. Griffith's version in *Specimens of Old Indian Poetry,* London, Hall, Virtue & Co., 1852. See also Dole and Walker's *Flowers from Persian Poets,* Crowell, Vol. II.

Sweet with the odor of musk, a snare
For the heart of the wise was the maiden's hair.
Tangled at night, in the morning through
Her long thick tresses a comb she drew,
And cleft the heart of the musk-deer in twain
As for that rare odor he sighed in vain.
A dark shade fell from her loose hair sweet
As jasmine over the rose of her feet.
A broad silver tablet her forehead displayed
For the heaven-set lessons of beauty made.
Her face was the garden of Iran, where
Roses of every hue are fair.
The dusky moles that enhanced the red
Were like Moorish boys playing in each rose-bed.

.   .   .   .

And the rose hung her head at the gleam of the skin
Of shoulders fairer than jessamine.
Her breasts were orbs of a light more pure,
Twin bubbles new risen from fount Kafur:
Two young pomegranates grown on one spray,
Where bold hope never a finger might lay.

.   .   .   .

Two columns fashioned of silver upheld
That beauty which never was paralleled,
And to make the tale of her charms complete,
They were matched by the shape of her exquisite feet.
Feet so light and elastic no maid might show,
So perfectly fashioned from heel to toe.

This was the maiden who at length was wedded to the Grand Vizier of Egypt, Potiphar. But her heart did not go with her hand. In her sleep she had had a vision of a wondrous youth, and, although she had not seen that vision in the flesh, her heart dwelt in love upon it. And then came the day when Yusuf, sold by his brethren, was led into the Egyptian slave market.

The moment that Zulaikha saw him in that market she recognized with joy that this was the lover of her dreams, and she bought him and brought him to her palace. The days passed in contemplation of him, and then her passion burst into expression.

> She told her love, and her sorrow woke
> With a pang renewed at each word she spoke.
> But Yusuf looked not upon her: in dread
> He lowered his eyes and he bent his head.
> As he looked on the ground in a whirl of thought
> He saw his own form on the carpet wrought,
> Where a bed was figured of silk and brocade,
> And himself by the side of Zulaikha laid.
> From the pictured carpet he looked in quest
> Of a spot where his eyes might, untroubled, rest.
> He looked on the wall, on the door; the pair
> Of rose-lipped lovers was painted there.
> He lifted his glance to the Lord of the skies:
> That pair from the ceiling still met his eyes.
> Then the heart of Yusuf would fain relent,
> And a tender look on Zulaikha he bent,
> While a thrill of hope through her bosom passed
> That the blessed sun would shine forth at last.
> The hot tears welled from her heart to her eyes,
> And she poured out her voice in a storm of sighs. . . .

But Yusuf held fast to his ideals of honor and integrity. He sought delay; the passionate spirit of Zulaikha, however, would brook no delay.

> My spirit has rushed to my lips, and how
> Can I wait for the joy that I long for now?
> My heart has no power to watch and wait
> For the tender bliss that will come so late.

Thy pleading is weak, and no cause I see
Why thou shouldst not this moment be happy with me.

Her desire was his also, but the faith of his fathers
was in every fiber of him, and through that strength
he restrained himself. Suddenly he awoke from the
dream of rapture, struggled from the arms of
Zulaikha, and fled the palace. But Zulaikha, wild with
love and desire, pursued him and clutched his garment
as he fled, and the coat, torn in twain, was left in her
hands as her only gift from him. Then

> She rent her robe in her anguish; low
> On the earth, like a shadow, she lay in her woe.

Days lengthened into weeks and weeks into years,
and Zulaikha existed in a mere living death. Then
fortune turned a smiling face. Her husband, the Grand
Vizier, was laid in the tomb, and, free at length, she
and Yusuf entered into that union for which both had
so ardently longed and toward which all destiny had
moved. Exceedingly great was their joy; it was a
mating of two souls that Heaven had meant for each
other. For, as she had declared so confidently in the
days of her sorrow,

> For my love is the sun, and the lotus am I.
> As my love is the lord of the east and the west,
> The place of the lotus for me is the best.

This, then, is the story of poet, sage, and romancer
in Iran, land of roses, wine, and passionate love. To-
day many of its once famous cities lie in ruins; there
remain but mere skeletons of ancient palaces where
song once echoed through the lofty halls; the very
tombs of some of the most noted of the nation's

philosophers and singers are lost beneath the sand. But what poet and philosopher and weaver of romance have created lives on, and though "their mouths are stopped with dust" their fame has not perished from the memory of man. Persia may have been stripped of her ancient earthly glories; the monuments of her former grandeur may now be but crumbling fragments scattered over the desert; the high inspiration with which she once fascinated the Orient may now be almost smothered. But, thanks to her poetic souls of centuries long gone, she still wields her enchantment over the spirits of men.

> Iram indeed is gone with all its Rose,
> And Jamshyd's Sev'n-ringed Cup where no one knows;
>   But still the Vine her ancient Ruby yields,
> And still a Garden by the Water blows.

V

THE DAWN IN CHINA

THE Chinese, like the Hindus, have ascribed to their nation an origin of incredible antiquity —according to some of their historians an age of eighty thousand years. Even the more moderate annalists do not hesitate to place the birth of their realm as far back as 10000 B.C. But research would seem to indicate that the earliest foundations of the former Empire were laid about 3000 B.C., in the days of a ruler named Fohi. There may, of course, have been many monarchs preceding this one, and there is some possibility that the Chinese civilization is as old as that of ancient Egypt.

The documents of the Shu King or Shu dynasty begin with the reign of a ruler named Yao, who evidently governed about 2450 B.C. Curiously enough, this date also marks for several other Asiatic nations —notably the Hindus, the Babylonians, and the Persians—a period of rather sudden increase in racial consciousness and in the advance of orderly government.

The Chinese for many a long century have not been blessed with a rich imagination, but possibly their early forebears possessed more of this valuable quality. For there are accounts enough of an impossible nature, of deeds occurring five or ten thousand years ago in the Celestial Kingdom. But hard-headed, and perhaps hard-hearted, research workers of our day maintain that there is little in the Chinese annals that may be accepted with any assurance previous to the comparatively modern date, 600 B.C. Indeed, one of the most trustworthy of Chinese historians, Se-ma-tsien, presents this as the first date in his works. It is practically certain that the famous reformer-philosopher of China, Confucius, was born in 550 B.C., and from his time on the Chinese writers were so prosaically accurate that the history of the nation from the middle of the sixth century may be considered as reasonably acceptable.

If indeed the Chinese have had a nation and a government for five thousand years, as some of the authors would claim, or for only twenty-five centuries, as many Western historians would maintain, this yellow race has had, in any event, a vast experience. Twenty-two consecutive dynasties are recorded; rebellions, civil wars, invasions, all the mighty convulsions that a government may know, all the joys and sorrows, all the aspirations and defeats—these the ancient realm has experienced.

Three other religions or philosophies besides that of Confucius have contested or mingled with the original faith of the people, and until recently have existed side by side or have even been accepted *in toto* by individuals. The original religion, a kind of monotheism, with the Heaven as a vague, all-embracing God, had linked with it the most devout and zealous ancestor worship, and this later element held the family, the clan, and the nation staunch century after century. Then came Confucius with his emphasis upon a practical philosophy of life, a strict observance of customs that had been beneficial in the past, and a stolid resistance to any trends toward radicalism.

A little later came Lao-tse with his possibly more human and emotional religion, Taoism, which in a few centuries was to degenerate into a species of witchcraft and sorcery for the curing of the sick. Buddhism, driven from its own home, India, entered China shortly before 70 A.D. and swept through the nation with astounding speed. Thus a Chinese might—and often did—take part in the ancient worship of the ancestors, turn to Taoism in time of illness, and at the same time follow the teachings of Buddha in the daily relationships of life. And with the coming of Christianity there is reason to believe that many a native of China, while retaining his faith in the three older religions and in the philosophy of Confucius, added, at least in its social implications, the teachings of Christianity.

With such a variety of religious influences the Chinese, we might suppose, should have created a great deal of the literature of religious and philosophical speculation. But such is not the case. So long has this yellow race struggled with famine, drought, flood, and war, so long has it felt the heavy pressure of the blunt, earthy precepts of Confucius, that not the study of the highly spiritual, but the strict observance of ceremonies and customs of ages has been the chief subject of discussion.

Again, the very nature of the Chinese language is hostile to the expression of the subtleties of philosophy, ethics and religion. Composed entirely of mono-syllables, almost without grammar, and entirely inno-cent of inflections, this unique tongue transforms any one of these monosyllables into any part of speech simply by the manner in which the single unit is used in the sentence. As a spoken language it is one of the most poverty-stricken in existence. Bound by the rigid monosyllabic roots and by the fact that any change in the order of these roots in a sentence means a decided change in the meaning, the Chinese long ago devised the expedient of varying the intonation of a word to give it some difference of meaning. But even this does not grant the language the power to express the finer distinctions of emotion and thought; all statements are necessarily the briefest possible declarations; while throughout it all, at least to foreign ears, there is a sing-song monotony that soon becomes tiresome.

Restricted as is the language, the Chinese system of writing that language reveals even greater limitations. For, first using a picture method of written expression, the nation eventually evolved what is known as an ideographic script, in which each symbol represents not a sound but an idea. In the course of centuries combinations of the original pictures or symbols were made to set forth new ideas, and the result is a language encumbered with at least 40,000 of such symbols. Of course, only the most scholarly would use such a vast alphabet of pictures, but even for quite ordinary printed material some 10,000 symbols may be needed.

In spite of such linguistic fetters and bonds the Chinese have been able to express if not eloquently, at least plainly, a certain definite philosophy of life, a huge amount of poetry, some interesting narratives, and even considerable vigorous drama. The human soul, like a skilled musician, can bring forth appealing expression with even the poorest of instruments.

The Five Classics

That the accumulated writings of China are vast, may be taken for granted; a civilized nation with twenty or thirty centuries of existence would be dull indeed if it had not in so long a period gained such a literary accumulation. Of all the Chinese books and records now extant, undoubtedly the oldest are the so-called *Five Classics,* formerly credited by China itself to Confucius, but now known to have been simply edited by him in the sixth century B.C. How ancient are these works we cannot, of course, know; but the oldest, the *Classic of Changes,* or *Yi King,* is ascribed to the scholar-executive, Wan Wang, who devised about 1140 B.C. a series of sixty-four hexagrams, and with each of these figures placed a bit of poetry explaining its value in foretelling. To the common folk these geometrical combinations represent sure and powerful divination, but until recently the cultured Chinese found in the figures a practical and indeed profound philosophy. To the editor, Confucius, they symbolized so much that when he was an aged man he declared: "If I could add many years to my life I would give fifty to the study of Yi King; for thus might I escape many a grievous error."

The second of the ancient *Classics* is the important *Book of Ceremonies,* or *Li Ki.* Compiled, so tradition says, by the Lord or Duke of Chow about 1150 B.C., this unique volume is without doubt the most voluminous and painstaking work on etiquette ever written. Scarcely a relationship in life, scarcely an event in ordinary daily existence is left unnoticed by the metriculous aristocrat-author and his later editor, Confucius. Whether a Chinese were emperor or coolie, parent or child, eating or drinking, dying or burying his dead, here he could discover the proper ceremony for the occasion. The effect of this book upon Chinese history, character, and viewpoint of life has been beyond calculation; so intricate and far-spread was its influence that for many centuries a government department existed for the one purpose of clarifying and enforcing its rules.

Just as the *Li Ki* set the standards for the social life of the nation, so the *Shu King* or *Classic of Historical Documents* formulated the political ideals that formerly prevailed in China. Including various ancient proclamations, this book is composed mainly of discussions between emperors and their ministers on the subject of government. Portions of it seemingly deal with matters of the twenty-fifth century B.C., and without doubt other sections speak of affairs in the eighth century B.C.; but since so many centuries in the long period furnished no documents for the volume, the earlier Chinese historians, using this work as a basis, invented for the edification of their readers innumerable dynasties and a multitude of fabulous deeds.

What does the book declare about the fundamentals of efficient government? To obtain the views of all, to give up one's own opinion and follow the better opinion of others, to remember the poor and the oppressed—these make for good rulership. "Place good men in office and let none come between them and you, O Emperor!" Do not do what is wrong in order to gain the praise of the populace, and do not oppose the righteous wishes of the people to gain your own desires. Shun idleness and excess, and live in the light of reason. The use of fire, water, metal, wood, earth, and grain must be regulated by the government if the nation is to survive. Three other matters will never be neglected by an efficient government—the tools that add to the conveniences of life, the procuring at all times of abundance of sustenance, and the uprightness of the people's conduct. These, declares the *Shu King,* are the nine great objects of governmental care.

And the wise ruler will never neglect to arouse the enthusiasm of the folk for these nine subjects by means of song. Thus resulted the fourth of the *Five Classics* —the *Shi King,* or *Classic of Poetry.* During many centuries, whenever the ministers of the Emperor met with him for conference, the music-masters, whose duty it was to supervise the songs of the people, met with such officials and recited the best of the lyrics and chants. A great mass of such verse and music had accumulated by the time of Confucius, and he it was who selected and edited three hundred and eleven of the best.

Simple, born of the heart, they deal mainly with agriculture and the plain activities of the home. Hear this bit of lyrical monologue of centuries ago:

> "Get up, husband, here's the day!"
> "Not yet, wife, the dawn's still gray."
> "Get up, sir, and on the right
> See the morning star shines bright!
> Shake off slumber, and prepare
> Ducks and geese to shoot and snare.

"All your darts and line may kill
I will dress for you with skill.
Thus a blithesome hour we'll pass,
Brightened by a cheerful glass;
While your lute its aid imparts
To gratify and soothe our hearts.

"On all whom you may wish to know
I will girdle-ornaments bestow;
And girdle-ornaments I'll send
To any one who calls you friend;
With him whose love for you's abiding
My girdle-ornaments dividing." [1]

Again, is there not a homely sincerity in this ancient
lament of a wife for her absent husband?

Away the startled pheasant flies
With lazy movement of his wings.
Borne was my heart's Lord from my eyes;—
What pain the separation brings!

The pheasant, though no more in view,
His cry, below, above, forth sends.
Alas! my princely Lord, 'tis you—
Your absence, that my bosom rends!

At sun and moon I sit and gaze,
In converse with my troubled heart.
Far, far from me my husband stays.
When will he come to heal its smart?

Ye princely men who with him mate,
Say, mark ye not his virtuous way?
His rule is—covet not, none hate;—
How can his steps from goodness stray? [2]

[1] Versions from *Shi King* and other Confucian books are by James
Legge, Hongkong. Privately printed, 1861; Oxford, Clarendon, 1882.
[2] For other examples see also Herbert Giles: *Gems of Chinese
Literature*, London, B. Quaritch, 1883.

Chun-tsu, often translated as *Spring and Autumn*—this is the last of the *Five Classics,* and the only one written by Confucius. Why such a title? Well, the admirers of the great sage declare that its praises were as stimulating as spring, while its censures were as withering as autumn. To us of to-day, however, the book is nothing more than a rather bald account of the history of Confucius' native province, Lu, from 721 B.C. to 520 B.C. Not only is it almost devoid of philosophical teaching, but later historians, especially the disciple of Confucius, Tso, have dared to find it seriously in error as to historical facts.

It is passing strange that five such works, rather dull at times and often painfully precise and stilted, could have so profoundly influenced hundreds of millions of people throughout the last twenty-four centuries. To the Chinese the *Five Classics* have been indeed life-giving; generation after generation of scholars have spent their days in contemplation and discussion of the volumes; the vast realm with divers races and tongues was long held together by the mere force of this common literary heritage.

CONFUCIUS

Cotton Mather once declared that he desired his life to be simply "a trembling walk with God." A beautiful and tender expression, worthy of the highest spirituality. Such a phrase would have been utterly foreign to the attitude of Confucius, whose words and deeds have not yet ceased to influence almost one-fourth of the human race.

If religion means one's personal relationship with a supernatural power commonly known as God, then

Confucianism is not at all a religion, but merely a code of human conduct. The ancient religion of China has no mythology, no organized priesthood, no thrilling spiritual appeal. It recognizes a few Nature spirits, a spirit of each province or State, ancestral spirits, and a vague god or gods composed of a fusion of all the ancestral spirits of the ruling families. Heaven, or this fusion, does not speak directly to the individual, but reveals itself through the regular, unchangeable order of Nature and through the constant order of the State. There is, maintained the disciples of Confucius, an exact correspondence between Nature and the State. A flood, therefore, is evidence of a mistake by the State; Nature has been jarred out of an exact correspondence.

For many a long century the Chinese Empire was considered to be in just such relationship with Nature, and therefore no man should venture to disturb the unchanging order that had existed from time immemorial. The State was the religion, and the religion was the State. Such a faith, of course, offered no consolation—unless it be a consolation to believe that in some distant day you may be an ancestral god or spirit.

So utterly practical, hard-headed, materialistic was the Chinese race that even this rather unemotional religion had fallen into neglect by the sixth century B.C. Then arose a noble thinker, the royal officer, Lao-tsze, whose *Book of Tao* taught of "faith from within"— the "inner light" of the modern Friends or Quakers. This was, however, too idealistic for the ancient nation, and Taoism soon degenerated into mere magic and witchcraft.

But during practically the same years Confucius came to the people with a type of teaching that they could indeed appreciate—concise, precise rules for living here and now. "The foundation of all good is the virtue of individual men. With this everything begins, and for this every good institution works." "What is benevolence? It is to love all men." This is Confucianism at its best. It is a pity that so much of the code of the famous sage is on a far lower level.

Confucius (Kung-Fu-tze) was born of a noble family in 551 B.C. His father, an old man when the child was born, soon afterward passed away, and the boy was firmly, even severely, trained by his mother. He married early, but at the age of twenty-two, when he became a wandering teacher, he made an amicable arrangement with his wife that they should live apart. Slowly he gathered a group of zealous disciples, held various offices, and was so just in his decisions that in his own province he rapidly reduced crime to practically nothing. But his superiors in authority were not his equal in virtue, and he at length was driven into long exile. Recalled at last, he refused all offices, spent his days in editing the *Five Classics* and in instructing his followers, and died in 478 B.C. Not a prophet, never visionary, he was religiously cold. He found little reason for prayer and no use in investigating gods or other heavenly matters.

His chief object was to transmit, unchanged, the pure traditions of the ancient day—unchangeable because they originated in Heaven. An intense student, he fostered among the Chinese an undying reverence for learning. At twenty-nine he began the study of music, mastered all then known about it, and is be-

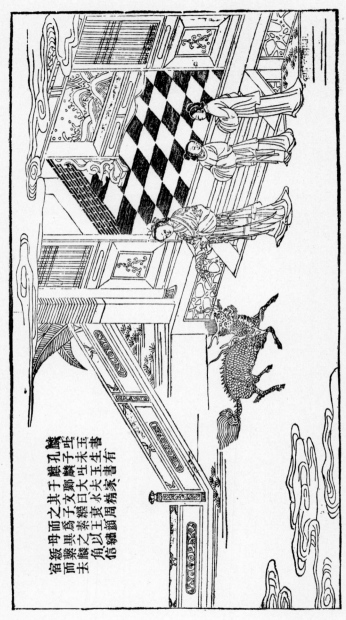

Illustration from "Holy Foot-prints." The Unicorn visits the mother of Confucius to announce the approaching birth of her great son.

lieved to have written several books on the subject. In the midst of his rising fame he went into absolute seclusion for two years and three months because of the death of his mother, and through such an act of self-renunciation impressed so keenly upon the Chinese the belief in honoring the memory of the dead that the nation has not yet departed from it.

When he came forth from retirement he became Assistant-Superintendant of Public Works and so improved agriculture that he became known to millions. Later as Minister of Justice he was so efficient that, according to ancient tradition, he destroyed the usefulness and the necessity of the office. But fame breeds envious rivals, and one of these, to ensnare the Governor, sent that executive eighty beautiful girls and one hundred and twenty fine horses. The ruler's morale weakened, and Confucius went into exile.

Nothing of bitterness was heard from him in all those thirteen years of wandering. When once a man sent to know what kind of being Confucius was, he replied: "He is simply a man who in the eager pursuit of knowledge forgets his food; who in the joy of his attainments forgets his sorrow; and who does not perceive that old age is coming on." Returning to his own section of China in 485, he spent the last seven years as he would have desired to spend them— in learning and teaching. But yet he died with the belief that his mission had been a failure.

His very death, however, made his code a philosophy triumphant. For his zealous followers began to grant him certain attributes of a god and gave his teachings the sanctity of the divine. He himself would certainly have objected to such an attitude.

Concerning spirits he declared: "Honor them with a sense of piety, but hold yourself aloof from them." "Honor the spirits of thy ancestors and act as though they are ever-present witnesses of thine actions, but seek to know nothing further about them."

John Lord has declared: "Take away belief in future existence and future rewards and punishments and there is not much religion left. There may be philosophy and morality, but not religion, which is based on the fear and love of God and the destiny of the soul after death." Judged by this standard Confucius did not create a religion, but simply a rather utilitarian philosophy. His doctrines are ethical, social, political. He offered no solution of or for the Hereafter. "As long as you know not life, how can you know anything about death?" Indeed, he seemed to have little or no regard for religious speculations. Among subjects absolutely taboo in his presence were marvels, feats of strength, rebellions, and spiritual beings.

How to act here and now—that was, in his opinion, the paramount subject. A man of much ceremony, always particular as to customs and dress, he would not even sit upon a mat unless it was in exactly the correct position. Always moderate, temperate, charitable, hospitable, he had that placidness born of faith in the ultimate goodness of Providence. Like Socrates and Jesus and Mohammed, he evidently was not interested in prolific authorship; more than three thousand of his disciples have attended to that particular lack. As a man of the world his constant question was, "What will the world think of this?" He declared the most important word in life to be "reciprocity," and he presented the essence of this idea in his famous rule: "What you would not others should do unto you, do not unto them." To him the true application of religion was to be found in the observance of humanity, uprightness, decorum, truth, and wisdom.

His maxims may possess a dry, business-like tone, but they served to bring religion down from the nebulous state of mere visionary speculation, and revealed that the rules prescribed in the better creeds of the world are practicable for conducting all daily affairs. While his precepts may not encourage originality and individual brilliancy, they have undoubtedly promoted the national solidarity of one of the oldest and most extensive governments man has yet known.

Many of his statements might well be taken to heart in our own day. How, for instance, may we attain success in popular government? "Advance the upright and set aside the crooked; then the people will gladly submit." "Good government exists when those who are near are made happy and when those who are far off are attracted."

As to the training of the individual Confucius presents in terse and often blunt terms just what is needed. "The man of wisdom makes the difficulty to be overcome his first business, and success only a secondary consideration." "A man should say, I am not concerned that I have no position; I am concerned how I may fit myself for one." "What the superior man seeks is in himself; what the small man seeks is in others." "Above all hold faithfulness and sincerity as first principles." And what man has not felt the truth of this advice? "Faithfully admonish your friend and kindly try to lead him. If you find him impractical, stop. Do not disgrace yourself."

And what teacher would fail to agree with these statements? "Learning without thought is labor lost; thought without learning is death of the mind." "Rotten wood cannot be carved." What, after all, is humanity's chief weakness? "The disease of men is this: that they neglect their own fields and go to weed in the fields of others; and what they require from others is great, while what they lay upon themselves is light."

Here, then, was a man of such solid judgment and extreme common sense that he maintained a civilization intact and almost unchanged for more than two thousand years. Unchanged because his philosophy of life and conduct suspected all idealistic innovations. Intact because his philosophy called for the exercise of prolonged caution and deep consideration of the tried and tested rather than a venturesome snatching up of Utopian theories. Confucius—he it was who for an astoundingly lengthy period saved China from disintegration.

Followers of Confucius

Just as the ancient Hebrews built up in their *Talmud* a vast commentary of legends and stories and sayings illustrating the teachings of the Old Testament, so the followers of Confucius developed a great mass of tales and historical sketches to impress the principles of their master. Again, Confucius, in writing a history of his own province, set the example for scores of his disciples, and numerous indeed were the treatises on state chronology, agriculture, and legal subjects prepared by the successors of the industrious sage.

So great became the zeal of the research workers that at length, in 221 B.C., Che-Hwang Ti, believed to have been the first Emperor of all China, and certainly the builder of the famous Chinese Wall, became fearful lest this study of antiquity should counteract all his efforts to strengthen the monarchy, and therefore ordered the destruction of all books except those dealing with medicine, magic, and farming. Severe indeed was his ruling; any person found possessing any volume on forbidden subjects was compelled to labor for four years upon the Wall. More than four hundred scholars who dared to disobey were executed, and the land was ablaze with fires made of the bamboo tablets then used in lieu of books.

Not only was this radical effort futile, but it actually proved to be a blessing. For the people now began to use silk and rag-paper instead of bamboo, the brush pencil was introduced, and those experiments in printing from wood-blocks began which by 593 A.D. had reached such perfection that the rulers of the nation could decree that books should be thus printed.

Of the huge number of writings by the followers of Confucius many are exceedingly dull to the Western reader. Chuang-Tzu, a philosopher of the fourth century B.C., gained high renown among his countrymen for his so-called mysticism, but to us of to-day his speculations on the life beyond seem commonplace. A disciple of slightly earlier date, Tso-Chiu Ming, so improved upon Confucius' *Annals of the State of Lu* that his method of recording history was long the accepted standard. Tau Kung of the last years of the fourth century B.C. wrote a great deal to emphasize the rulings found in the *Book of Ceremonies,* or *Li Ki,* edited by Confucius, and thus gave to the Chinese numerous rather logical reasons for acting thus and so at a funeral or a wedding or other function.

Much more interesting to the modern reader are some of the writings of Lieh Tzu, a fourth century disciple of Lao Tze, the founder of Taoism. One of his brief sketches dealing with a judge's decision, has sometimes been cited as a specimen of Oriental mental sleight-of-hand. A poor man, so the story goes, once chanced upon a deer, which he killed and hid in a ditch until darkness should come. Thanking Providence for such a piece of luck, he went on with his usual task of gathering wood, but in the course of the day he forgot the location of the hiding place. At length he concluded that he had simply dreamed the whole incident, and went on home.

But another peasant had actually seen the affair, and secretly obtained the game. When he reached home he declared to his wife, "A man dreamed that he got a deer, but did not know where to find it. Now I have the deer, and his dream was, therefore, a reality." "No," replied his wife, "it is you who dreamed you saw such a man. Did he really get the deer, and does such a man actually exist? Since you yourself have got the deer, how can his dream be a reality?" "Well," retorted the husband, "since I have the deer, it is of no consequence whether the man dreamed the deer or I dreamed the man."

That night the man who had killed the animal dreamed where the deer then was and who had obtained it. Sure enough, the next morning he located the carcass, and he at once went to court to regain it. But the wise judge announced the following decision: "The plaintiff began with a real deer and an alleged dream. Now he enters court with a real dream and an alleged deer. However, the defendant really got the deer which the plaintiff says he dreamed, and is now trying to keep it. But, according to the defendant's wife, both the woodman and the deer are mere figments of a dream, and hence no one at all got the deer. However, here before us is a real deer, and it is best that you divide it equally between you."

When the Emperor heard of the case he declared that the judge himself must have dreamed the case, but as only Confucius could have distinguished between dream and reality, the ruler's minister advised that the judge's decision be confirmed. Such was subtlety in fourth century China.[3]

MENCIUS

Probably the most famous follower of Confucius was Meng Tzu, known among Western readers as Mencius. Born in 372 B.C., he became an intense student of Political Science, and was looked upon as the greatest Chinese writer, editor, and thinker after Confucius. True to the nature of his race, his whole bent was toward practical applications of rules for the betterment of the people and their government. In spite of the fact that he did not hesitate to make scathing criticisms of whatever oppressive methods he observed, he was highly respected and even obeyed by governors and emperors. Refusing to accept any

[3] For excellent versions of Chinese short stories see Brian Brown's *Chinese Nights Entertainments,* New York, Brentano, 1922.

office whatever, he wandered with his small group of disciples from one province to another until his death at the age of eighty-four.

So useful was his philosophy, so powerful his influence, so deep his imprint upon the character of the nation that for centuries after his passing a tablet or a statue in his honor stood in every temple dedicated to the service of Confucianism. Truly, as a molder of public opinion, he deserved to stand side by side with the elder philosopher and sage.

There is a deal of common sense in the thoughts of Mencius. "The great man is he who does not lose his child-heart." Is it not very much the same idea as that of Jesus, "Except ye become as little children, ye shall not enter the kingdom of heaven"? Again, might not this declaration by Mencius alleviate a great deal of the discontent of our day? "There is nothing more strengthening to the heart than to keep your desires few. Note the man who has few desires. In some matters he may not be able to keep his heart, but they will be very few. Note the man whose desires are many. In some things he may be able to keep his heart, but they will be very few." And would it not be well for all administrative officers to remember this? "Is there any difference between killing a man with a sword and killing him by misrule?"

Mencius accepts something of the old Puritan view of the necessity of hardships and suffering in this world. "When Providence," says he, "is about to grant a position of great responsibility to a man it first strengthens his mind with suffering and his body with toil. It tries him with hunger and poverty, and opposes all his endeavors. Thus it arouses his mind, fortifies his soul, and supplies his deficiencies." Only by innate power may a human being really control a people. "When one subdues men by force they do not submit in their hearts. When he subdues them by virtue or character they are pleased in their hearts and really do submit."

He often expressed the view that men gain the approving smile of Heaven in their undertakings, not because Heaven chose them for the undertaking, but because their conduct of the matter is worthy of Heaven's choice. "Heaven," says Mencius, "sees according as my people see; Heaven hears according as my people hear." And, thought this sage, men are largely judged in this world by their own estimate of their worth. He noticed that the successful are generally found in the company of the successful. Like seeks like. "If Confucius had lodged with a quack doctor or with a slave, how could he, then, have been Confucius?" A certain high self-respect is eminently befitting every man. Be not too familiar with any man. "Friendship should be maintained without any presumption on the grounds of one's age or station or the standing of one's relations. Friendship with a man is friendship with his virtue or character, and does not admit of assumptions of superiority." The genuinely wise man will hold his distance, and will be "affectionate to his parents, lovingly disposed to people in general, and kind to all creatures."

There is something Emersonian at times in this early sage of the yellow race. With a more supple and subtle language in which to express himself he might have equaled Emerson in theories as to the conduct of life. As it is, Mencius, compelled to deal with the more concrete, materialistic aspects of existence, distinguished rather sharply between the roots and causes of happiness and unhappiness among individuals, nations, and governments.[4]

LITERATURE IN THE HAN DYNASTY

In 202 B.C. Kao-ti, founder of the Han Dynasty, became the ruler of China, and so enthusiastic was he in the cause of letters that during his reign the Imperial Library grew from almost nothing to more than 11,000 manuscripts. The zealous Emperor encouraged every type of writing, and fruitful indeed were his efforts. Then it was that Ssuma Ch'ien, "the Herodotus of China," composed his famous *Historical Annals* (*Shichi*), covering the many centuries between 2697 B.C. and 140 B.C. Later came the tremendous history of this Han Dynasty by Pan Ku, a work filling one hundred and twenty volumes! And it should be remembered that Pan Ku and his many imitators, when they wrote a history, made a thorough job of it; history to them meant not only the account of political changes and war, but accounts of nearby nations, essays on music, treatises on law, lengthy explanations of the sciences, descriptions of religions, customs, and rites, even commentaries on and collections of poems and other literary productions.

In this same Han Dynasty vast masses of verse also were created. The poetry is not strong; it does not vibrate with passion; but it does have a romantic melancholy about it that is not without tenderness and attractiveness. Here is the effect of a beautiful flower

[4] See James Legge: *Life and Works of Mencius,* London, 1875, Trübner & Co.

惟十有五年三月既朝
丁亥王在大室
家王巳乃
召大雁命
馬拜稽首
大用作朕
顯休列考
大其子己伯
孫萬年
永寶用

戰王呼善夫
學宮大
巳乃錫
山召大馬
天子所巫
二賜鼎
對揚不
揚顯

upon a sensitive soul; here is the sorrow of absence
from home; here is the longing for the coming of
spring and the sunshine. Such was the earlier poetry
in the centuries between 200 B.C. and 600 A.D. After
the latter date the brief four or five syllabled line was
superseded by the seven syllabled verse, and with this
change came a new subject—the praise of wine. So
popular did this theme become that one is reminded
of the wine-loving poets of Persia in the days of Omar
Khayyam. Thus the lines of one of these bibulous
singers, Li T'aipai, ask repeatedly the question: If
life is but a dream, why not drink deep of the cup, and
sleep under the power of wine? When I wake, am I
not right in simply inquiring what season of the year
it is, and, having found that it is spring, turn once more
to my wine and pass again into sweet oblivion?

In this period also there was created a good deal of
what might be termed "Home, Sweet Home" verse—
poems dealing with the peaceful delights of the cottage
nestled among the trees, far from the turbulent life of
the city. For example, note the long-time favorite,
My Humble Home, by Liu Yu-Hsi of the eighth
century:

Hills are not famous for height alone: 'tis the Genius Loci
that invests them with their charm. Lakes are not famous for
mere depth: 'tis the residing Dragon that imparts to them a
spell not their own. And so, too, my hut may be mean; but
the fragrance of Virtue is diffused around.

The green lichen creeps up the steps; emerald leaflets peep
beneath the bamboo blind. Within, the laugh of cultured wit,
where no gross soul intrudes; the notes of the light lute, the
words of the Diamond Book, marred by no scraping fiddle, no
scrannel pipe, no hateful archives of official life.

K'ung-ming had his cottage in the South; Yang Hsiung his cabin in the West. And the Master said, "What foulness can be where virtue is?" [5]

THE COMING OF BUDDHISM

With the coming of Buddhism to China in the first century A.D. we might reasonably expect an outburst of new and more powerful literature. Not so, however. True, many Chinese scholars now made the arduous journey to India and wrote accounts of the wonders that they saw there. True, also, a great deal of writing was produced dealing with the new theological or philosophical ideas introduced by Buddhist missionaries. But there was no apparent increase in imaginative power, no outburst of fervent poetry, little evidence of ability to tell a tale in a more vivid manner. Perhaps once more the deplorably restricted language of the nation hampered authors; possibly the innate matter-of-fact nature of the Chinese would not admit of the display of fervor or enthusiasm or passion that we of the West expect to find in a renaissance.

Indeed, the only prominent change that took place may have been a change for the worse. There began to develop that sure sign of sterility in scholarship— the making of countless anthologies or collections. Sometimes the collections were groups of ancient poems; sometimes they were vast compilations of facts. For century after century this tendency increased until it seemed that the only work expected of a scholar was the editing of examples of the works of the distant past or collections of data of dim antiquity. In truth, no nation has ever equaled the Chinese in the

[5] H. A. Giles in *Gems of Chinese Literature*, London, B. Quaritch, 1883.

making of encyclopædias. So huge became some of
such collections that no one man in the course of a
long life could have read even one of them through.
One at least, a work of the early fifteenth century,
was of such stupendous dimensions that all thought of
printing it was given up; it contained nearly 23,000
manuscript volumes. For centuries its tens of thousands of pages lay untouched in the library of the
Emperors, and even after five hundred years of neglect
portions of the original manuscripts still exist.

But this failure to publish the largest encyclopædia
yet attempted by man did not destroy the zeal of the
uninspired scholars. A hundred years later Ma Twan
Lin succeeded in editing a great collection of information that became so popular that four centuries of use
have not dimmed the high esteem which Chinese students have so persistently held for it. It had, however,
a dangerous rival—if length counts for anything—
within the last one hundred and fifty years; for in
the days of the Emperor K'anghi a group of scholars,
after forty years of toil, produced an encyclopædia of
5,020 volumes! And it was actually printed—though
limited to one hundred copies.

Certainly there seems to have been during the last
fifteen centuries a curious limitation in Chinese
scholarly and literary endeavors. The writers apparently have learned readily enough what foreign sources
have given them in science and other informative subjects, and this they have passed on easily enough. But
there they have stopped; they have seemed utterly
unable to add to the knowledge, to produce new
theories, to discover hidden principles. Perhaps it is
the lack of imagination; perhaps it is the age-old

aversion to making a venture; perhaps it is the innate reverence of the past that looks with disfavor on innovations.

A CHINESE MARCO POLO

As has been indicated earlier, the coming of the Buddhist missionaries, of course, caused many a convert to long to make the pilgrimage to Buddha's native land, India. And naturally, like Americans visiting Europe, a large number of such travelers from China felt the urge to write a book on what they had seen.

Of the innumerable volumes of this type, perhaps the *Travels in India* of Fa-hien of the fifth century is the best and the most famous. Fa-hien became a Buddhist priest, made the long and dangerous trip to India, translated great amounts from the Hindu writings, and wrote one of the most remarkable books of travel in existence.

Marco Polo finds here indeed a rival. Fa-hien not only presents vivid descriptions of mountains, deserts, cities, and rivers, but retells ancient tales, especially those dealing with Buddhistic miracles, that would make Baron Munchausen positively jealous. Evidently Fa-hien was a thorough convert; he doubted not. Hear, for instance, this bit from his *Travels:*

At this place the monks and nuns may be a thousand, who all receive their food from the common store, and pursue their studies, some of the mahayana and some of the hinayana. Where they live, there is a white-eared dragon, which acts the part of danapati to the community of these monks, causing abundant harvests in the country, and the enriching rains to come in season, without the occurrence of any calamities, so that the monks enjoy their repose and ease. In gratitude for its kindness they have made for it a dragon-house, with a carpet for it to sit on, and appointed for it a diet of blessing, which they present for its nourishment. Every day they set apart three of their number to go to its house and eat there. Whenever the summer retreat is ended, the dragon straightway changes its form and appears as a small snake, with white spots at the side of its ears. As soon as the monks recognize it they fill a copper vessel with cream, into which they put the creature, and then carry it round from the one who has the highest seat at their tables to him who has the lowest, when it appears as if saluting them. When it has been taken around immediately it disappears; and every year it thus comes forth once. The country is very productive, and the people are prosperous and happy beyond comparison.[6]

Again, note Fa-hien's faith or gullibility, as you choose:

Going on from this to the southeast for three yojanas, they came to the great kingdom of Sha-che. As you go out of the city of Sha-che by the southern gate, on the east of the road is the place where Buddha, after he had chewed his willow branch, stuck it in the ground, when it forthwith grew up seven cubits, at which height it remained, neither increasing nor diminishing. The Brahmans, with their contrary doctrines, became angry and jealous. Sometimes they cut the tree down, sometimes they plucked it up and cast it to a distance, but it grew again on the same spot as at first.[7]

Truly, those were the days of miracles. Is it any wonder that Fa-hien's book was devoured by young and old for centuries, and added much to the strength of Chinese Buddhism?

[6] Version with some changes, by James Legge, *Hongkong,* 1861; *Chinese Literature,* N. Y. Colonial Press, 1900; Herbert Giles' version, Cambridge Univ. Press, 1923.

[7] *Ibid.* See also Herbert Giles: *Travels of Fa-hien,* Cambridge University Press, 1923.

Su Tang Po

It seems that every nation has its one period of literary splendor that outshines all the other eras in its history. Greece had its Age of Pericles, Rome its Augustan Era, England its Elizabethan Period, and China had its Sung Epoch. This Sung period of the eleventh century A.D. is not infrequently compared by cultivated Chinese to our own English days of Shakespeare and Ben Jonson.

Such it may be to the oriental scholar; but to the Westerner there seems still to be lacking in the productions of the Sung era that fervor which is found in the literature of Athens or the writings of England at her best. True, it was in this eleventh century that Sze Ma Kwang wrote his overwhelming *History of China* in three hundred and fifty-four volumes. True, also, the greater part of Chinese mythology and poetry, aside from the works of Confucius and his disciples, must be credited to this time of Sung. But the fire of an awakened nation is not apparent, unless it be evidenced in the long and turbulent "novels" and dramas that now began to appear.

Of the poetry of this Sung Age it may be said that the elements of pathos, melancholy, longing, and similar sentiments make the verse interesting reading, but the reflections of a Wordsworth, the emotions of a Tennyson, and the dramatic tone of a Browning are simply not there, and no amount of "reading between the lines" can put such qualities there. The milder ability of our minor poets, however, is present in most agreeable form.

Of all the poets of the Sung Period probably the

most popular, perhaps the most famous, is Su Tang Po or Su Tung P'o. Chinese scholars point out that he brought the language to such a state of conciseness and finish as it had never known before. Like most of the verse writers of his times, he is to-day scarcely more than a name; practically nothing is to be found concerning his life. But every Chinaman of the cultivated classes during the last eight centuries has memorized and recited with deep admiration the numerous poems that have been handed down by him. And one at least has long been known among English-speaking scholars—the Song of the Cranes:

> Away! away! My birds fly westward now,
> To wheel on high and gaze on all below;
> To swoop together, pinions closed, to earth;
> To soar aloft once more among the clouds;
> To wander all day long in sedgy vale,
> To gather duckweed in the stony marsh.
> Come back! Come back! Beneath the lengthening shades,
> Your serge-clad master stands, guitar in hand.
> 'Tis he that feeds you from his slender store.
> Come back! Come back! Nor linger in the West! [8]

This Su Tang Po, called by Giles "an almost universal genius," had the unusual ability to make the Chinese language express the subtleties of philosophy; but it is rather for his more "human" bits of verse and short prose sketches that he is remembered to-day. It is such a note of applied philosophy as the following that has made Su Tang Po charming to his countrymen:

[8] Herbert Giles' version in "Chalet of Cranes," *Gems of Chinese Literature,* London, B. Quaritch, 1883.

In Ssuch'uan there lived a retired scholar named Tu. He was very fond of painting and possessed a large and valuable collection. Among the rest was a painting of oxen by Tai Sung, which he regarded as exceptionally precious, and kept in an embroidered case on a jade-mounted roller. One day he put his treasures out to sun, and it chanced that a herd boy saw them. Clapping his hands and laughing loudly, the herd boy shouted out, "Look at the bulls fighting! Bulls trust to their horns and keep their tails between their legs, but here they are fighting with their tails cocked up in the air! That's wrong." Mr. Tu smiled and acknowledged the justice of the criticism. So truly does the old saying run: For plowing, go to a plowman; for weaving, to a servant-maid.[9]

CHINESE NOVELS

Whatever Chinese novels or romances may lack in quality they certainly make up in quantity. The older ones evidently were intended for readers or listeners with all the patience in the world; but even now a group of coolies, after working like horses all day long, will sit up the entire night listening intently to the sing-song recital of one of these interminable tales.

What do these narratives deal with? Well, there is the love theme—we have that with us always—and while romantic courtship was almost unknown in the former China and is not too plentiful even to-day, it flourishes in vivid colors in the old-time stories. And with it, of course, goes intrigue. Then, too, there are tales of bandits—sometimes of the Robin Hood type, who rob the rich to help the poor. There are innumerable stories in which a poor, but brilliant scholar passes the State examination wonderfully and thus ob-

[9] Translated by Herbert Giles in *Gems of Chinese Literature,* London, B. Quaritch, 1883.

tains office and wealth. For many a century indeed the scholar was a far greater and far more admirable character to the Chinese than any general could possibly be, and the student's rise has been the source of gratification to untold generations of novel readers. But the soldier is not neglected in fiction. Many are the stories dealing with how a military leader by a ruse or trick fooled the enemy and saved the nation. And there are narratives of usurpation and plotting, and, of course, stories based on superstition.

In all probability the tale that has been most admired throughout the long era of China's existence is *The Story of the Three Kingdoms,* written during the Yuan Dynasty. It is huge; the old-fashioned family Bible could scarcely equal it in bulk. Dealing with the period of romantic chivalry in the third century A.D., it, is, in a sense, the national epic of China, known to mandarin and to coolie alike. It is a vast series or conglomeration of wild adventures, love stories, descriptions of battles, pictures of famine, rise of scholars, deceptions by generals and governors, illustrations of wifely devotion and filial conduct, humorous sketches, what not. There is fiction enough in it to make a hundred novels; the Chinese who buys *The Story of the Three Kingdoms* assuredly gets his money's worth.

Of a somewhat later date is another ancient favorite —a rather close rival of the *Three Kingdoms.* This is *The Dream of the Red Chamber.* To the Westerner it may not seem to be much of a masterpiece; but when the cultivated gentleman of the Celestial Empire reads its tale of a young man's love affairs with his two pretty cousins and notes the gradual decay of the old and famous family portrayed in it, there are likely to be words of sincere praise.

Filling four thousand pages, it introduces more than four hundred characters. It possesses a tremendous plot and is rather remarkable in the amount of its details and in characterization. Giles rightly calls it "a panorama of Chinese social life, in which almost every imaginable feature is submitted in turn to the reader." It is written in an easy style, and the plot is frequently interrupted by the introduction of poems of rather high merit.

It opens with chapters linking the world of the supernatural with our own. In repairing Heaven, the Goddess of Works cast aside one large stone. So long had this stone been in Heaven that it had become spiritualized, could even suffer, and had a genuine ambition to do some useful work. Here on earth it long sheltered with its shade a flower, which at length grew into a beautiful girl. Long afterwards a priest saw the stone, and read its story on it—a tale, not of statesmen and warriors, but of earthly lovers. There is something of genuine tragedy in it, as the boy and the girl are driven to insanity and death by the selfishness and perversity of spiritually blind relatives. And one feels that there is something of a just and artistic ending when one finds the family in ruin, the beloved girl in her grave, and the boy, born with a bit of the precious stone in his mouth, retiring from the world and its vexations to become a Buddhist priest.

Still another of these old-time favorites in fiction is *Travels in the West* (*Hsi Yu Chi*). Much of this story deals with a stone monkey born of a stone egg. This creature, chosen king of the monkeys, at length defies, not only the hosts of Heaven, but God Himself! In fact, he declares that he should take God's place. Then God, in His wisdom, sends down Buddha to humiliate and convert him. The monkey in his conversations with Buddha declares that one of the chief reasons why he should be the God lies in the fact that he can jump six thousand miles. Buddha, however, stoutly maintains that the creature cannot even jump off of Buddha's hand. The contest is on. The monkey jumps a tremendous distance and writes a sentence on the spot where he alights. When a little later, however, he discovers his sentence is written merely on the second finger of Buddha he is duly humiliated and converted.

The animal now attempts to lead a Buddhist traveler to the Far West. After long journeying they finally come to a very slender bridge across a vast river. The traveler cannot be induced to attempt the crossing, and then Buddha himself appears poling a boat. But strangely enough, the boat has no bottom! Ah, declares Buddha, "steady though the storm may rage and the seas may roll, there is no fear as long as the passenger is light. Free from the dust of mortality the passage is easy enough." They enter the craft. Just as they shove off, a dead body floats away. The traveler shivers with alarm and fear. "Fear not," says the monkey cheerfully, "that dead body, my friend, is your old self!" "Accept my congratulations!" smilingly says the boatman.

The seventeenth century story writer, Pu Sung-Ling, often called "the Last of the Immortals," wrote a huge number of brief bits of fiction in what many have declared the most beautiful Chinese style.

Whether or not the style is "beautifully Chinese" matters not so much to us who must read in translation, but the contents, with their ever-present applications of practical philosophy, are, we feel, just what would please a Chinese audience. Pu Sung-Ling's *Strange Stories,* although written about 1650, were not published until 1740; for his family was too poor to pay for the printing. But since the first appearance of the work there has been many an edition.

The narratives are indeed practical—intensely didactic at times. The student Liu falls in love. "If you want something belonging to me," says his sweetheart, "take this mirror. It will show me to you so long as you attend to your books." At length Liu became neglectful of his studies, and her image faded from the mirror. Then, at length, he buckled down to his volumes, and, having become a successful scholar, he looked in the mirror, suddenly heard a voice—her voice—crying, "A pretty pair we make, I must declare!" and turning he saw her there, standing by his side.

Again, is not the moral lesson plain enough in this tale by Pu?

A man named Sun Pi-Chen was crossing the Yung-tze when a great thunder-storm broke upon the boat and caused her to toss about fearfully, to the great terror of all the passengers. Just then an angel in golden armor appeared, standing upon the clouds above them, holding in his hand a scroll inscribed with certain words, also written in gold, which the people in the boat easily made out to be three in number, namely, Sun Pi-chen. So turning at once to their fellow-traveler, they said to him, "You have evidently incurred the displeasure of God. Get into a boat by yourself and do not involve us in your

punishment." And without giving him time to reply whether
he would do so or not, they hurried him over the side into a
small boat and set him adrift. But when Sun Pi-chen looked
back, lo! the vessel itself had disappeared.[10]

So popular have been such stories as the *Red
Chamber* and the *Three Nations* that for generation
after generation Chinese dramatists, sure of gaining
an appreciative hearing, have drawn repeatedly upon
them for plots for successful plays.[11]

CHINESE DRAMA

Chinese drama, if rightly understood by occidental
readers and audiences, would prove to be, by all odds,
the most interesting and entertaining phase of the literature of this ancient nation. For more than two thousand years this people has had dramatic performances.
The earliest ones evidently dealt almost exclusively
with religious subjects, with, of course, something of
reverence for government in them; for to the Chinese,
religion and the national government were long closely
akin. For untold generations only two actors were
supposed to speak on the stage; any others that might
be there were not only silent but supposedly invisible.
The plots have always been simple and rather effective,
while the language has at all times been the vernacular
of the people—a fact that for many a long day caused
the scholarly classes to look down with contempt upon
drama and refuse to produce this type of literature.

But the national government very early recognized

[10] Translated by Herbert Giles in *Gems of Chinese Literature,*
London, B. Quaritch, 1883.

[11] For interesting accounts of Chinese fiction see Herbert Giles:
History of Chinese Literature, New York, D. Appleton, 1901. Excellent specimens in J. F. Davis' *Chinese Novels,* London, J. Murray,
1822.

the power of the stage, and until recently not only controlled it, but supported it. Indeed, as long ago as 713 A.D. one of the emperors had established an Imperial Dramatic School, where budding actors, known as the Young Folk of the Pear Garden, were carefully trained.

No matter what happened to China itself the theater seemed ever to grow stronger and more influential. The Mongolian Invasion in the twelfth century might have been supposed to spell the doom of the drama; for the Mongol cared nothing for literature and at the time had not even an alphabet. But scarcely had a Mongolian chief ascended the Chinese throne when dramatic performances suddenly increased in both quantity and quality. Strolling players in great numbers wandered over the land with their plays, and so interested were the audiences that a drama sometimes lasted three days. Again, when in 1368, a native dynasty, the Ming, succeeded the Mongol, a still greater impetus was given to the theater. Finally, with the coming of the Manchu Dynasty in 1644, many of the finest dramatic productions in Chinese Literature were produced.

Melodrama, comedy, the less pessimistic type of tragedy—all have been found for ages on the Chinese stage. It should be remembered, however, that the sense of poetic justice is exceedingly strong in the theater audience of the ancient nation, and the evil inevitably is paid for in full. We shall not find, therefore, that deeper tragedy frequently presented by European dramatists, in which no answer, no recompense for the bitterness of life is offered.

Your Chinese maintain that drama consists of three

elements: action, speech, and singing, and consequently some of the plots, meager in themselves, are "pieced out" by a great deal of chanting by one or another of the principal actors. But only a minor portion of the plays offer any such starvation rations; performances with thirty acts are not unusual, and several generously present the audience with forty-eight acts.

Of the more ancient dramatic productions one exceedingly famous collection has come down to our times—the *Hundred Plays of the Yuan Dynasty.* The great majority of the authors found here belong to the years 1235-1280, and centered their activities about Peking. The remainder are mainly from Hangchow in the South, and worked between 1280 and 1335. Possibly the best known of all these *Hundred Plays* to English-speaking readers is the *Sorrows of Han,* translated by John Francis Davis as long ago as 1826.

An historical tragedy, it deals with the encroachments of the Tartars, who were encouraged by the weakness of the courtiers and generals in the Chinese Emperor's court. "Too much love, too seldom a council, never a war"—these are what caused the downfall of the ancient kingdom. The drama is brief in its unpadded plot, is admirably unified, and possesses deep seriousness and considerable grandeur in both treatment and language. Its five acts—for the Prologue may justly be considered as a full act—close with the usual idea of poetic justice; for the evil-doer does not receive the prize for his unethical efforts.

The Tartars are hammering at the great Northern Wall; but the young Han Emperor is dallying with his harem. Dissatisfied with the ladies he possesses, he sends forth his minister, Mao, to gather fresh beauties for the collection. But Mao, a dishonest fox, demands a great bribe for every portrait of a girl to be submitted to the ruler. The parents of the most beautiful young woman are unable to pay the fee; Mao therefore has her picture disfigured. The Emperor, offended that the family should submit the likeness of an ugly woman, has her placed in seclusion. But the chance hearing of her playing the lute brings him to her, and he deserts all others for this lovely one.

Mao flees to the Tartars, shows a true portrait of the girl to their chief, and thus causes that ruler to demand her as his wife. Knowing that the kingdom will be lost unless she sacrifices herself, the young woman endures the agony of departing from her sorrowing Emperor, and accompanies the messenger of the Tartars. On the way, however, she suddenly casts herself into a swift mountain river, and, despite all efforts of the Tartars, is drowned. The Tartar chief, filled with admiration for her nobility, delivers up the treacherous Mao to be executed by the Chinese, and vows eternal peace with the Han Dynasty. Thus justice is gained—but at what a price! Though there shall be peace in the Empire, nevermore shall the Emperor know the meaning of peace in his own soul.

Still others of the *Hundred Plays* have become fairly well known to the Western world—especially the *Heir of Old Age,* also translated by John Francis Davis, and the *Orphan of Chaou,* translated into French by Père Premare. But to many a cultivated Chinese, probably the most highly regarded of these early plays is the thoroughly natural drama, *The Sufferings of Tou-E,* by Kuan Han-Ching. Strangely enough, after hundreds of years it still is a favorite under the title, *Snow in June*. It would be impossible to estimate the millions of Chinamen who have seen this drama in the centuries that have passed since it was composed.

Sold as a child, Tou-E at length becomes the wife of the son in the family and is the overworked drudge of her talkative mother-in-law. For thirteen long years she bears with meekness the mistreatment, and then her husband dies. As the dutiful daughter-in-law, she remains, however, with the older woman. At length two bandits force their way into the house, demand that the two women marry them, and offer the mother-in-law and the young widow all they possess.

Upon the refusal of the women, the younger man puts poison into the rice bowl of the older woman, but the other man takes it by mistake and is dead within a few moments. The young bandit now threatens Tou-E that if she will not marry him he will accuse her of the crime. Taken before a judge, she is tortured so cruelly that she makes a false confession. As she is kneeling to be beheaded she declares that three things will prove her innocence: her blood, instead of falling, will rise to a banner ten feet above her; snow will fall, although the season is summer; there will be three years of drought.

All comes true as she predicted. The matter is noised throughout the province. At last a good judge (once the poor scholar, her father, who had sold her) investigates the case, is guided by the ghost of his daughter, and discovers the real murderer, the young bandit, who is punished by being cut into one hundred and twenty pieces. Thus justice prevails ultimately, as in all Chinese tragedies.

As one reads such productions one is compelled to realize that a great advance in dramatic skill and effectiveness must have occurred in the ancient Yuan period. Dialogue takes the place of mere description or narrative; plot frequently becomes far more plausible; the tale unfolded sometimes becomes genuinely enticing— even to a reader in this Western world.

Thus in *The Intrigue of a Lady's Mind* (*Chao Mei Hsiang*) we find that two generals shortly before their death arrange that the son of the one shall marry the daughter of the other. The son, on his way to take the State examination, visits the home of the other general's widow and falls desperately in love with the daughter—so desperately, in fact, that he becomes dangerously ill. A maid, overriding all conventionalities —for the family is still mourning the death of the general—arranges a meeting for the young couple one moonlit night; but the mother surprises them and sends the young man away in disgrace. He passes his examinations most brilliantly, and is so admired by the Emperor that this official decrees the marriage of the loving couple. And thus the lovers unwittingly comply with the wishes and plans of their fathers.

Another evident fact of the Yuan era is that there was a very notable increase in the use of humor on the stage. For instance, a miser in one of the plays declares:

One day, when I was hungry for roast duck, I went to that shop in the market—you know the one. They were just then roasting a fat duck, and the juice was running down into the pan. Well, as I pretended to haggle over the price I handled the duck and soused my hands deeply in the pan of juice. Then, hurrying home, I got a bowl of boiled rice, and after each spoonful of rice I sucked a finger. By the time I had swallowed the fourth big spoonful I fell asleep. And then, while I dozed, a mean cur came and licked my remaining fingers. When I awoke and discovered that theft I became so disgusted that I have been sick ever since.[12]

Even as death approaches, the miser thinks of saving. He orders his son not to waste money buying a coffin, but to use instead the old watering trough in the back yard. When the boy declares it to be too short the old fellow directs him to chop his body in two to make it fit. "And," says he, "attend to this now: don't use my good ax to do this, but borrow one from a neighbor; for if you use my good cutting edge you'll have to spend some coppers having it re-sharpened."

Even in the moment of death, unable to speak, he persistently holds up two fingers, until one of the mourners catches the idea that two candles are burning. When one light is blown out the old man's soul departs in peace. Thus long ago the Chinese audience learned to expect very much the same broad humor that the Shakespearean theater-goer enjoyed in a far-distant land in a far later period.

Interesting as are those older plays of the Yuan Dynasty, their main defect is their poor motivation. Chance enters entirely too often, and too easily. Again, plots are too frequently twisted absurdly to bring about the "moral ending," the poetic justice expected by the audience. With all the advance made during the era and with all the increase in varieties of types of characters on the stage, they are generally in-

[12] Author's version.

deed mere *types* and not individuals with their own particular or peculiar individualities.

The Mongol reign, while tolerant, was never popular. At length a Buddhist monk, Chu Yuan-Chang, drove out the invaders, and, becoming the Emperor Hung-Wu, he founded the Ming Dynasty in 1368. And then began another flourishing era of Chinese drama. Even the scholars had now become interested in this type of literature, and condescended to write plays in the language of the people. In so doing, they improved that language and gave it standing as a literary medium. A great number of skilled troupes performed all over the empire. Even after nearly six centuries more than six hundred plays of the period are extant.

It was during this era that the drama increased vastly in length. No longer contented with five acts (or the prologue and four acts), authors dared now to expand their plays to six or seven times that size. Characterization certainly improved, and a deeper sense of the problems of life was revealed on the stage.

Possibly the best specimen of dramatic production under the Ming Dynasty is the still popular *Pi Pa Chi,* written by Kao Tsi-Ch'ing in 1404. A young scholar, Tsai-yung, prefers to stay in his native village with his old parents and his lately acquired wife. But his father demands that he go to the capital to try for fame and wealth by taking the State examination.

The scene now transfers to the palace of the imperial minister. Two matrimonial agents are thrown out by the minister, who declares that his daughter, Niu-hsi, shall marry only the scholar that wins in the national examinations. Meanwhile the scholar's wife,

Sculpture of second century of our era, in Shantung. Top register—a
man apparently wounded, shielded from attack of enemies. Middle register—Ching K'o, 227 B.C., attempting to kill the King of Ch'in. His javelin
struck a pillar and the King escaped. Third register—Two legendary
sovereigns, assigned by tradition to the 29th century B.C. Fuhsi with
square and Nükua with compasses. They have dragon bodies, indicative
probably of semi-divine character.

Wu-niang, has started for the capital; for she feels
that she must save her husband's starving parents.
Even then the imperial minister is ordering that Tsai-
yung and Niu-hsi shall marry. Wu-niang unexpectedly
obtains some rice and is returning with it to the aged
parents when she is waylaid and robbed of the grain.
She is upbraided by the old couple at home, and is even
accused by her mother-in-law of having secreted better
food for herself. When, at length the old lady, already greatly weakened by privation, discovers that
the girl is living on bark and roots, she dies of the
shock! An old friend comes to the rescue and gives
money for a proper burial.

The new wife of Tsai-yung, the prime-minister's
daughter, Niu-hsi, has become acutely aware that she
is not the "dear one" of her husband's heart; all the
songs he plays on his lute turn to laments for those
at home. At this point a "fake" messenger enters
with a counterfeit letter declaring that the old parents
are happy and very prosperous. The rich Tsai-yung
is so pleased that he bestows upon the messenger exceedingly costly gifts. But meanwhile the young
scholar's aged father also has died, his final words to
his friend, Chang, being, "I leave you my cane. When
this ungrateful son of mine returns, thrash him for me
with this and drive him out of the house."

To pay for the old gentleman's funeral Wu-niang
cuts off her hair and attempts to sell it. Chang again
comes to the rescue and foots the bill. Now that her
hair is gone, he advises her to dress as a nun and go to
the capital. With Tsai-yung's lute among her scanty
possessions, she fares forth. And the new wife of
Tsai-yung, having discovered the cause of his sorrow,

gains her father's consent to send a servant to bring the first wife.

There, in a Buddhist temple in the capital city, Wu-niang unrolls pictures of her parents-in-law to worship before them, and then, forgetting the portraits, leaves them where Tsai-yung soon afterward finds them. Then as a nun she enters the prime minister's palace, and meets Niu-hsi. Through the unnaturally generous aid of this second wife, she is reunited with her husband. And the play closes with Tsai-yung and his two wives setting forth on the journey to the ancestral tomb to mourn and worship for several years. Thus, after nineteen hundred years Confucius' ideal of filial devotion was still pervading the drama.

And now a word as to Chinese drama under the Manchus and the Republic. The last of the Ming rulers committed suicide in 1644. A Manchu leader, who had been asked to help put down a rebellion, became Emperor—the one who forced all China to adopt the queue. This early Manchu period was possibly the strongest in Chinese history. A time of firm, strong administration, it was also a time of encouragement of authorship, and thousands of dramas resulted between 1644 and 1800.

Two plays are generally accepted by Chinese scholarship as the outstanding masterpieces of the era —two historical tragedies: *The Blood-Stained Fan,* by Kung Shang-jen, and *The Palace of Eternal Life,* by Hung Sen, both written shortly before 1700. The first deals mainly with the attempts of the heroine to kill herself because of the condition of the country and because her lover has been forced into political exile. Her blood stains a fan that he had given her. An artist paints the bloodstains into pictures of peach blossoms. After years of war, the lovers meet, but they renounce personal love for that higher love known as patriotism.

The Palace of Eternal Life tells the romantic tale of Yang Kuei-fei, the beautiful, capricious concubine of Ming Huang, who, tradition declares, founded the Chinese theater. The Palace of Eternal Life is the name they bestowed upon the great house and grounds where they amused themselves so voluptuously. Many indeed are the romances related of this fascinating woman, who brought such toil and sorrow to the people through her egoism and self-centered character that the populace at length demanded her death. Like Cleopatra in life, she was like her in death; for Yang-Kuei-fei chose to kill herself rather than have others butcher her dainty body.

Very different is another highly popular "historical" play, *Ch'un Yin Hui,* or *Meeting of Many Heroes,* derived from that vast storehouse of narrative, *The Three Kingdoms.* In this drama the general, Chu Ko-liang, is required by his ruler to obtain one hundred thousand arrows within five days, to be used in destroying the enemy's great fleet. Chu spends two and a half days under a tree in calm meditation. A companion, finding him there and considering the task impossible, suggests that he commit suicide. Instead the general places some straw men in the prows of his boats and sails toward the enemy's navy. The foe, because of the dense fog, cannot ascertain the size of the attacking force, but orders the archers to shoot as fast and as long as possible. The arrows strike the straw men until the canny Chu has the necessary hundred thousand. The Chinese long deemed this *Meeting of Many Heroes* a genuinely great play, and in the old days never failed to leave "standing room only." [13]

Of the vast masses of Chinese writings but a minute portion has been translated into any Western language. Europe and America know the work of Confucius and, to some extent, the philosophy of Mencius. The verses of *Shi-King* and of a few later volumes of poems are now in English, but apparently a good deal more has been turned into French. We of the occidental world are at least beginning to gain some inkling of the meaning of Chinese dramas—such as *Snow in June.*

But what multitudes of tales and novels of the ancient Celestial Empire are absolutely unknown to the white race! What huge numbers of folk-songs and lyrics and ballads in general are utterly lost so far as we Westerners are concerned! What dramas of intrigue and tragedies of love await the skillful translator! We have but peeped into the tremendous library of Chinese Literature.

[13] For detailed information about Chinese drama see Herbert Giles: *History of Chinese Literature*, New York, D. Appleton, 1901, and A. E. Zucker: *Chinese Theater*, Boston, Little, Brown, 1925.

CHAPTER VI

THE DAWN IN PALESTINE

ONE of the outstanding miracles in the spiritual history of mankind is that out of a bit of territory so small that it would hardly serve as a county in one of the Western States of America, and from a people insignificant in number, there should have come a literature which has literally conquered the world. That is exactly what occurred in the tiny piece of earth commonly called the Holy Land.

No matter what the creed or religion of any later commonwealth, that government has been directly and powerfully influenced by two waves of religious thought originating in the homeland of the Jew. First in point of time came the ethical and philosophical teachings of the Hebrew Old Testament; and second, the vibrant, personal message of brotherhood and universal love as proclaimed by Jesus, found in the New Testament.

It is very fitting that from this narrow strip of land about the Dead Sea should come two of the world's main religions. Whatsoever a man or a nation soweth, that shall the man or nation also reap. And the folk of the Holy Land for innumerable centuries sowed religion, religious contemplation, religious teaching; and the harvest was inevitably religious genius, and that abundantly. Never did a nation study more constantly, more intensely the theory of God and God's relationships toward man. It was as natural for a Jesus to be created in Israel, as for an Edison or a Ford to be created in America.

Indeed, the Hebrew Literature is the richest contribution of the East to the world in general. All the world's genuine religions have come out of the Orient; for the birth and growth of a religion require time, leisure, contemplation, intense thought—things which the young West cannot or will not grant as yet. Of all these oriental spiritual contributions the Hebrew religion and literature are unmatched in purity of thought, profound understanding of the problems of life, depth of spiritual insight. In poetic imagery, in clear, powerful narrative, in artistic condensation, the writings of this small ancient Hebrew people have never been excelled. Nation after nation has been founded upon the Bible.

And yet the life story of the Jewish nation is so insignificant in a physical and political way, that the mighty empires of antiquity scarcely condescended to speak of it in their records. Semitic in origin, these Hebrews may have taken their name from the word *Ibrim,* meaning "the people of the other side"—that is, on the other side of the Euphrates. Probably led out of Mesopotamia by an early chieftain named Abraham, they settled in the hills of Palestine, waged prolonged war against the Canaanites, who held the valleys, gradually gained these rich lowlands, were at length driven through failure of crops into Egypt, and there became Egyptian slaves for some centuries. At length they were led forth by an astute, strong-willed pioneer named Moses, and reëntered their beloved Palestine under a leader named Joshua.

There followed another period of conquest by these

Hebrews, and once more they ruled over the Holy Land. A strong monarchy was finally perfected under their second king, David, who ruled about 1000 B.C. But the despotism and sloth of later monarchs led to a division of the country into a Northern section, known as Israel, and, a Southern, known as Judah. Naturally a nation thus divided against itself fell an easy victim to invaders, and the Assyrians and Babylonians overcame Israel in 722 B.C. and Judah in 586 B.C. Thus occurred a second captivity, this time in Babylon, where the Hebrews remained until the Edict of Cyrus set them free in 538 B.C.

Back they flocked to Palestine, where they rebuilt their cities and their temple to the One God. But their very success and prosperity were their undoing; for envious nations looked with covetous eyes upon the small but exceedingly wealthy nation, and conqueror after conqueror ravaged the land. Persian, Greek, Roman successively sucked away the life blood of the government, and Jerusalem, as the center of Jewish power and religion, was finally destroyed by the Roman, Titus, in 70 A.D. Then in later centuries came the Turk, who long possessed the sacred land of Hebrew and Christian, despite the romantic struggle of the Crusaders to recapture the birthplace of Jesus. At last came the World War of our own day, and the British marched into Jerusalem, set the land free from its ancient masters, and made it once more an independent commonwealth. An active movement is now in progress to "rebuild Palestine," and modern engineers and architects are at work transforming the topography of this ancient land.

The very geography of the Holy Land long made

it one of the strategic spots of the East. Commerce
seemed inevitably to traverse it. There was rich and
mighty Egypt to the South; there was the non-Semitic,
highly cultured Philistia near at hand, Syria was to the
North, with its brilliant capital, Damascus; to the
East was powerful Assyria, with Babylon, noted for
arts, sciences, commerce, and sin. The caravan roads
from Assyria to Egypt wound through Palestine, and
wealth, ideas, and culture came with those caravans.

In spite of the efforts of the Jewish nation these
ideas, this culture from abroad, invaded the country.
For these ancient Hebrews were a self-isolated folk.
Clannish, proud, stubborn, they wanted to be left
alone; they welcomed no change in their customs and
institutions. For the Hebrew race has been, and is,
an individualistic race. Its separatist tendency has not
been forced upon it; that tendency was deliberately
chosen at least twenty-five centuries ago. Its sepa-
ratism has been a cause of much friction, suffering, and
cruel persecution; but with its deep racial pride, its
astounding endurance, its acquisitive faculty, the race
has survived every ordeal and has flourished under
conditions that would have annihilated a weaker
people.

No matter what any individual or any nation may
think of the Jew as individual or nation, all the world
owes to the Hebrew an everlasting debt of gratitude
for one trait—his genius for religion. No other race in
the history of mankind has evolved religions of such
high ethical import, such vitality, such tremendous
influence as this ancient group of people of Israel.

Their language, in spite of its few inflections, its
bald syntax, its lack of elaborate sentence structure, is

full of strength and forceful sounds, and in ancient times lent itself well to the eloquent and sublime imagery needed in the expression of the idea and the ideal of the Deity. The Hebrews in their earliest days in Mesopotamia doubtless used the ordinary Chaldaic of the district, but after the settlement in Palestine the mingling of Chaldaic and Phœnician evolved into the primitive Hebrew language used in the Mosaic books. It was not, however, until that splendid national period between the tenth and the eighth centuries, B.C., that the language of the ancient Jew reached its Golden Age of expressiveness. Then followed invasion, ravage, conquest, and the consequent mingling of foreign elements with the speech of Israel. Fighting against overwhelming odds, Hebrew practically ceased to be a spoken language about 300 B.C. The debased Aramaic succeeded the pure tongue of the founders of the Holy Land, and only in religious ceremonies and now and then in sacred writings was Hebrew to be found. Aramaic itself, while useful enough for commercial and other everyday activities of life, was not the literary medium for the expression of the higher thoughts of man, and there came a time when Jewish writers—as in the case of the New Testament authors—turned to the universally known Greek as the instrument of communication. Far later, probably in the twelfth or thirteenth century, the strange mixture of Hebrew, Teutonic, and Slavic tongues called Yiddish became practically an international medium of expression for the Jew.

But in whatever language the Hebrew has found himself forced to write, he has expressed himself with singular vividness and outstanding personality.

Whether it has been David, Heine, or Disraeli, there is generally to be discerned clearly that indefinable attitude which marks the writings as Jewish.

Types of Hebrew Literature

We might examine Hebrew literature from many standpoints—according to its historical development, according to its types, according to its messages or philosophies. Perhaps the first two methods should be followed here.

The first period of Jewish literary history might be limited to 1500-1050 B.C., or the period before the days of David. What things did men think and talk and write about in those far distant times? Oral traditions, naturally; then tales of suffering and bondage under the haughty Egyptians, and stories of the ultimate rescue from the hands of the tyrant and the conquest once more of the homeland. There were laws to be made and written down—laws to keep the folk in the paths of righteousness and national security. And above all else, there was this theme of the mysterious One God and His attitude toward all mankind.

Much that was conceived and written is, of course, forever lost. In fact, there may have been an earlier Old Testament, sometimes called the *Wars of Jehovah,* now totally vanished except for some portions imbedded in the first chapters of *Genesis.* In this earlier literature, too, these oppressed Hebrew tribes probably accepted from other Semitic peoples, especially the Assyrians or Babylonians, the Epic of the Creation and the Epic of the Flood. Certainly in those harsh times before David made Jerusalem "glorious among nations," there came into existence such war-songs as

the so-called *Song of Moses,* found in *Exodus* xv, and
the *Song of Deborah,* found in *Judges* v.

And, as the folk sat about the campfires at night,
they must have originated, as all other primitive nations have done, many a fable and riddle. There are,
for instance, those ancient "nuts to crack," commonly
designated as Samson's Riddles, long afterwards
placed into the Scriptures known as *Judges* xiv and
xv. And there is Jotham's Fable, as another example, in *Judges* ix. Such were the natural attempts at
literary expression among the wandering Hebrew before 1050 b.c.

Then comes the genuinely great creative period between 1050 and 750 b.c. This was the period, according to many Biblical authorities, when the History
and Prophecy writings from *Genesis* to *Kings*—books
that have literally swayed the world—were created.
What so natural, also, now that the nation was established, that the history of its feverish past should be
stressed and that tales of dim heroes and narratives
of half-forgotten battles should be revived to inspire
the patriotism of the people?

Long, bitter experience had granted wisdom also,
and many a popular proverb—we may see them in
I Samuel x and xxiv—was handed down from father
to son, and put into written form for posterity. Ba-
laam's oracles, the Blessing of Jacob, David's pathetic
Lament for Saul, such a pæan of trust as Psalm xlvi
—"God is our Refuge"—possibly such patriotic outbursts as Isaiah's Doom of Babylon, found in *Isaiah*
xiv, and the same sage's confident prophecy of the
Future Glory of Israel, as found in *Isaiah* lx—these

are but a few of the treasured literary heritages given
to the nation in this vigorous second period.

Then there came a day of humiliation, when all the
race cowered in spiritual sackcloth and ashes. The
record of this is found in the third period, from 750 to
400 B.C. Here we find the Literature of the Babylonian Exiles—the stifled moan of a captive people, interspersed with the clear-voiced prophecies of such stern,
undaunted seers as Hosea, Isaiah, Micah, Jeremiah,
and Ezekiel. Under such bondage and sorrow there
must inevitably be memories of "the good old days";
hence the *Memoirs* of Nehemiah. How often the soul
of the stricken race must have burst forth in songs of
sorrow! Hear the words of despair still echoing down
through the centuries in the poems known to us of to-
day as *Lamentations*. But, on the other hand, hear
the note of staunch faith, mingled as it may be with
tones of regret and desperation, in the *Psalms* of the
Babylonian period.

It was indeed the days that tried men's souls. And,
in order that the corrupting influence of the masters
might not invade the camps of the enslaved Hebrews,
these strong, far-seeing leaders literally "laid down
the law." There must be no departure from the strict-
ness of the national rules and customs of the past; indeed those rules and customs must, if anything, be
made more strict. Hence arose the Codes in *Deuteronomy* and *Ezekiel*.

Release from bondage at last came, and the
Jewish people returned to their homeland. But, perhaps, it was not the same people; possibly the corrupting influences of Babylonia had entered, in spite of
their prophets and priests. True, a kingdom of some

SILOAM INSCRIPTION

SILOAM INSCRIPTION FOUND IN THE ROCK-CUT AQUEDUCT OF
JERUSALEM. HAILS THE COMPLETION OF THE WATERWORKS OF
HEZEKIAH

splendor was reëstablished in Israel and Judah, but was the old-time spirituality ever to return? It is in the literature of the fourth period, from 400 to 100 B.C., that we may find the answer.

The writings now seem to possess the characteristics of retrospection and imitation. The last of the prophets speak—often in gloomy and sarcastic language. What has become of the solid, four-square virtues of the nation? they repeatedly ask. And yet in their pessimism over their perverse and stiff-necked generation they seem to perceive far off the coming of a Messiah—a Teacher of Righteousness and Love.

Like all periods interested more in the form than in the spirit it was a great day for collecting and codifying. There were the final collections of the prophetic sayings and priestly narratives. There were collections—undoubtedly well done—of the *Psalms* that had expressed so fervently the faith of the fathers. There was the creation of such books of doubtful sacred character—practically non-canonical or apocryphal volumes—as *Esther, Ruth,* the *Proverbs,* the cynical *Ecclesiastes,* the powerful drama *Job,* and that collection of fervent love songs which only the imagination of a theologian could transform into a religious symbolism—the *Song of Songs* or the *Song of Solomon.*

Previous to the Babylonian captivity, even, some of the kings and great hordes of the common folk had been prone to turn aside into the pleasant byways of idolatry. It was so often "the easiest way." Now, however, with the nation free and back once more in the Holy Land, many of the leaders were filled with an intense desire to make the Hebrew people realize that they must be a witness to the true God and an example of what the phrase "Children of God" means. But this required, so the leaders thought, absolute certainty as to the true ritual, the true laws, the true customs, the true Scriptures. Conference after conference of rabbis and scholars met to settle for all time this or that item of racial religion or creed. At such a conference the Old Testament Canon was fixed; henceforth this collection was sacred; all else was secular.

Sternly monotheistic, highly spiritual in a somewhat narrow way, these leaders of the Hebrew nation were firmly established in their belief that Jerusalem would now triumph over all persecution. The tiny nation had seen the mighty Egyptian, Assyrian, and Babylonian Empires crumble into dust. It had beheld the triumphal march of Alexander and the humiliation of the Persian monarchy. It had seen Greek civilization sweep across Asia to India. The successors of Alexander had founded new kingdoms in Syria and Egypt —and Israel had not been a mere spectator of all this; she had been subject to first one and then another of these conquering nations. Now an alien tongue was creeping in. Despite the exhortations of prophet and priest, the kingdom around the River Jordan was feeling the spirit of Greek culture. Significant indeed is it that a Greek translation of the Old Testament (the Septuagint), made, not at Jerusalem, but at the Greek city of Alexandria, by command of a Greek ruler, Ptolemy Philadelphus, was so much better than any native Scriptures that the Rabbis in the very Temple at Jerusalem had to turn to it for correct readings of their own sacred writings.

It was a sure sign of a waning nation—a nation

whose day of intellectual and spiritual glory was passed. Other books might be written in Israel— *Ecclesiasticus* with its famous passage in praise of famous men, the volumes known as the *Maccabees* with their stirring battles and tales of martyrdom, *Esdras, Judith,* and others. But the great era of the ancient Jewish realm was ended.

Then came the Roman subjugation again, and after a time the destruction of the very heart of the nation— the Temple at Jerusalem. The symbol of the soul of a people vanished on that sorrowful day. There was no longer a nation, a united people; the Jewish race became wanderers, dispersed among all the kingdoms and governments of the civilized world.

But in the days of this final Roman dominance there had come forward one plain man of the people, simple, dignified, sure of his ground. His name was Jesus, and he came from the little settlement of Nazareth. He had a new message for His people—the message of love, brotherhood, justice toward all. He spoke his message, and went his way—through the most humiliating form of death then known, crucifixion. But what a difference to all civilization meant that message of a young philosopher from an obscure village in a conquered kingdom!

It is with him mainly, then, that the fifth and last period of Hebrew literature (100 B.C.-300 A.D.) deals. True, there is that vast wilderness of Jewish traditions, legends, essays, stories, what not, called the *Talmud,* coming to fruition largely in this period. True, there were in these centuries many noble rabbinical volumes. There were indeed such interesting authors as Flavius Josephus. But the writings that have swept the world and changed the whole course of man's march are the teachings of this Jew, Jesus, as recorded by his followers. Believe what mankind may about this young Hebrew's deity or divinity, the historical fact remains that his doctrines have gradually transformed civilization.

Out of a nation that devoted its intellectual powers to the one theme of religion there thus came the most profound and influential religious teacher in the history of the world. It is no miracle; rather, it is the natural result of one nation's united thought and endeavor. And, as Coleridge has said, "In every generation and wherever the light of revelation has shone men of all ranks, conditions, and states of mind have found in the Bible a correspondent for every movement toward the better felt in their own hearts."

THE LAW

What are the main books produced during the long and troubled history of the Hebrew race? They are the collection known as the Bible, consisting of sixty-six books divided into the Old Testament of thirty-nine books, and the New Testament of twenty-seven books; the vast collection commonly called the *Talmud,* the Rabbinical Writings, consisting mainly of commentaries on the Old Testament; and that semi-secret, traditional material, long oral, and even yet written down in only brief excerpts—the *Kabbala.*

The original Jewish sacred or semi-sacred works are easily separated into three divisions: the *Law,* the *Prophets,* and the *Writings.* The last mentioned group is composed of material considered so doubtful as to inspiration that the ancient Hebrews could not

include it among the rolls of genuinely authoritative
writings to be read aloud in the synagogues, and yet
it was so full of spiritual meaning and was so dear to
the people that the rabbis gladly encouraged its reading in private.

Five books composed the Law—*Genesis, Exodus,
Leviticus, Numbers* and *Deuteronomy*—all having
the collective name of the *Pentateuch*. To those early
Hebrews it seemed beyond doubt that these rolls containing the history and customs and ordinances of the
scribes were by Moses, and indeed Biblical scholars
until comparatively modern days have held to the same
view. Now, however, it is commonly believed that
the *Pentateuch* was put into its final form after the
Exile of the Jews into the Babylonian realm and before the return of the prophet-leader, Ezra; that is,
between 600 and 450 B.C. Undoubtedly it was this
same virile Ezra who soon after he came back from
the Holy Land made these volumes or rolls authoritative. It is fairly clear, indeed, to present-day scholars
that very little of the *Pentateuch* goes back to Moses
and his era, but that much of the collection may have
been the work of the rabbis among the captive tribes
in Babylonia. If there is any section really from the
hand of Moses, it is the set of rules in Chapters 20-23
in *Exodus*.

Much of the Book of *Genesis* is now thought to be
by two authors—the one from the North of the Holy
Land, the other from the South. If so, the Northern
writer composed the simple but majestic story of
Eden and the romantic narrative of the wooing of
Rebekah. From the pen of the Southerner probably
came the vivid history of Joseph in Egypt, while from

a rather inartistic combination of sketches by both men there resulted that portion dealing with the Selling of Joseph. As for the Flood story—we have already found it in the Assyrian and Babylonian writings, and doubtless a number of Hebrew scribes during the second activity transcribed it. As for that magnificent exhortation, *Deuteronomy,* far from being a production of Moses, it was, in all probability, written as late as 650 B.C. by some Hebrew having no connection with the authors of *Genesis* or any other book of the *Law.*

Be all this as it may, the fact remains that in this ancient *Pentateuch* is some of the most majestic literature yet created by man. Admirable in simplicity and compression, and oftentimes infused with genuine dramatic power, it has inspired for more than twenty-five centuries, not only the Hebrew race, but all the Christian nations of the world. These ancient traditions and legends and mandates, told at night about the campfires during dismal captivity and around thousands of thresholds after the return to Israel, have lost none of their effectiveness in the march of civilization.

Read, for instance, that concise, comprehensive, dignified story of the Creation. Its accuracy may, of course, he doubted; but its directness and clearness are beyond dispute. "In the beginning God created the heaven and the earth. And the earth was without form and void; and darkness was upon the face of the deep. And the Spirit of God moved upon the face of the waters. . . . And the Lord God formed man of the dust of the ground, and breathed into his nostrils the breath of life; and man became a living soul."

And note the simple grandeur of the narrative of

the Deluge.   Direct, grim, unsparing, it has the highest qualities of genuine folk-lore.   And is there in all religious literature a more tragic conflict between earthly love and devotion to God than the brief narrative of Abraham and Isaac?   And what a story of determination to possess the Divine Guidance and Blessing is found in the little tale of Jacob and the ladder and the struggle with the Angel of the Most High! It is such traditions, such legends, that knitted together the Hebrew race so strongly that all the woes of exile and all the sufferings of long wandering could not destroy the spirit, the confidence of the people.

The Prophets

Even more majestic, even more thrilling, infinitely more filled with inspiration for mankind, are the volumes of the Biblical collection called the *Prophets*. Eight books or rolls come under this title—*Joshua, Judges, Samuel* 1 and 2, *Kings* 1 and 2, *Jeremiah, Ezekiel, Isaiah,* and the *Twelve Minor Prophets*. Thus the early Hebrews distributed the prophetic writers of their race—eight scrolls deposited in their synagogues—but we of to-day find it easier to consider them as twenty-one different volumes.

It was not without long consideration, discussion, and even struggle that these compositions of the prophetic spirits of the Hebrew nation became sacred or accepted Scripture.   The *Law* was long sufficient for the primitive folk.   But then there came a time when students of these Prophets began to find in such writings history to substantiate the ancient *Pentateuch*. These Prophets not only foretold the national destiny, but had proved beyond cavil or doubt that the success of this destiny depended upon strict obedience to the Law. Thus gradually the immense value of the Prophetic Books as supports of the validity of the *Pentateuch* and as object lessons of the workings of the *Law* dawned upon the Rabbis and the scholars. And the result was that at length these declarations of Samuel, Joshua, Ezekiel, and their kindred spirits almost superseded the *Law* in importance. Certainly by the third century B.C., in the reading ceremony in temple and synagogue, some portion from the *Prophets* was commonly read after a section from the *Law*.

There can be little doubt that many a manuscript was lost during the Babylonian Exile. After the joyful Return, fragments of the old prophetic writings were probably gathered from far and wide, and patched together as well as possible. But perfection and absolute accuracy were impossible in such a task, and the narrative of the days of the Israelites from Exodus to Exile and afterwards, as found in *Joshua, Judges, Samuel,* and *Kings,* contains many a doubtful passage.

What is, however, of genuine importance to both Hebrew and Christian civilization is that portion of the narrative of the Prophets beginning with Elijah's epoch-making struggle in the ninth century against the worship of Baal as upheld by the Canaanites. With his triumph over this false worship begins the faith of the civilized world in monotheism and a religion based solidly upon righteousness. Then, too, it is in the high story of these Prophets that we find another important theory of religion. It is when Amos, about 760, in the North of the Holy Land demanded morality and obedience to law lest God should use the Assyrians as a scourge of punishment against the Hebrews. Just there was impressed upon civilized man the thought—right or wrong, as you choose—that the Divine Power *does* take an active interest in the affairs of this world, and *does* visit His retribution upon the unrighteous.

What those confused Hebrews needed was not so much constant haranguing, nagging, scolding, as something definite in the way of comprehensible rules to follow. It was Ezekiel who supplied this national want. It was Ezekiel who had suffered as a captive in Babylon, the powerful church-statesman, the writer of vivid, straightforward words, who compiled the Code that the humblest peasant of the nation could understand and follow. He was of a decidedly ecclesiastical turn of mind—this stanch man Ezekiel. He believed in rituals; they impressed upon the folk the power and the majesty of the Church. He even took over the ancient Canaanite rite of sacrifice of animals in religious ceremony, and he so spiritualized the procedure that the nation accepted it without quibble.

Those Prophets were a grim, unsparing set of teachers and preachers. To most of them the first and most important task seemed to be to put "the fear of God" into the people, and with fiery threats and terrifying prophecies they went about the business. But this policy of fear can easily be overdone. The Hebrew, like any other human being, longed now and then for a little of the sweet tenderness of sympathy.

Therefore there arose out of Bablyon the voice of one who was as honey to the soul of the Israelites. We probably shall never know who he was—this Prophet, sometimes called a Second Isaiah, who in the fortieth chapter of the Book by that name, cries to his fellow countrymen, "Comfort ye, comfort ye, my people, saith your God!" It was the very message that the bewildered, discouraged race needed. Here is majestic consolation. Here is the convincing vision of a patient, loving, even though firm and just Ruler. It was this Second Isaiah who revealed to the Hebrews and to millions since those ancient days that the Almighty may indeed permit the innocent to suffer in order that mankind may be redeemed. It is a message that in a way might have served as a Prologue for the ghastly tragedy of the Messiah to be enacted a few centuries later.

There is another bit of the writings of the Prophets that served the nation well. It is that ethical rehearsal of what was probably an old folk-tale, rewritten about 300 B.C.—the *Story of Jonah.* Through that legend the most clannish nation of antiquity was presented with a bitter lesson on national egotism and intolerance. Bitter indeed it must have been; for was not Jonah sent to save Nineveh, the very enemy of Israel? That story must have gone down the early Hebrew throat with many a painful gulp!

These Prophets are strong medicine for a strong people. To this day there is iron in them for every reader. Their hatred of oppression, their zeal for holiness and justice, their enduring hope and faith have not lost their antique power. Hear the strong words of Amos to the children of Israel:

For three transgressions of Israel, and for four, I will not turn away the punishment thereof; because they sold the righteous for silver, and the poor for a pair of shoes. . . . Prepare to meet thy God, O Israel. For, lo, he that formeth the mountains, and createth the wind, and declareth unto man what is his thought, that maketh the morning darkness, and treadeth upon the high places of the earth, The Lord, The God of hosts, is his name.[1]

And what expressions of love and forbearance and patience came forth from the pathetic domestic experiences of Hosea! And Micah—what noble pronouncements are his!

Will the Lord be pleased with thousands of rams, or with ten thousands of rivers of oil? Shall I give my firstborn for my transgression, the fruit of my body for the sin of my soul? He hath showed thee, O man, what is good; and what doth the Lord require of thee but to do justly, and to love mercy, and to walk humbly with thy God?

What exalted visions of the future glories of their homeland! These Prophets knew in all its rich fullness the meaning of patriotism.

I will take you out of all countries and will bring you into your own land. . . . And ye shall dwell in the land that I gave to your fathers; and ye shall be my people, and I will be your God. Break forth into joy, sing together, ye waste places of Jerusalem; for the Lord hath comforted his people, he hath redeemed Jerusalem!

Comfort ye, comfort ye my people, saith your God! Speak ye comfortably to Jerusalem, and cry unto her, that her warfare is accomplished, that her iniquity is pardoned; for she hath received of the Lord's hand double for her sins. The voice of him that crieth in the wilderness, Prepare ye the way of the Lord, make straight in the desert a highway for our God! Every valley shall be exalted, and every mountain shall be made low; and the crooked shall be made straight, and the rough places plain. And the glory of the Lord shall be re-

[1] Excerpts from the Old Testament are from the King James Version, 1611.

vealed, and all flesh shall see it together: for the mouth of the
Lord hath spoken it.

And what vengeance these Prophets foresaw for the
oppressors of their nation! Hear Isaiah pronounce
the Doom of Babylon:

Hell from beneath is moved for thee to meet thee at thy
coming; it stirreth up the dead for thee, even all the chief ones
on the earth; it hath raised up from their thrones all the kings
of the nations. All they shall speak, and say unto thee, Art
thou become like unto us? Thy pomp is brought down to the
grave, and the noise of thy viols; the worm is spread under
thee, and the worms cover thee. . . . They that see thee shall
narrowly look upon thee, and consider thee, saying, Is this
the man that made the earth to tremble, that did shake kingdoms; that made the world as a wilderness, and destroyed the
cities thereof; that opened not the house of his prisoners?

Prepare slaughter for his children for the iniquity of their
fathers; that they do not rise, nor possess the land, nor fill the
face of the world with cities. For I will rise up against them,
saith the Lord of hosts, and cut off from Babylon the name,
and remnant, and son, and nephew, saith the Lord. I will
also make it a possession for the bittern, and pools of water:
and I will sweep it with the besom of destruction, said the
Lord of hosts.

Lastly, with what confidence, what tender affection
those later Prophets nurtured their visions of a De-
liverer, a Messiah, to come in the days beyond:

Surely he hath borne our griefs, and carried our sorrows:
yet we did esteem him stricken, smitten of God, and afflicted.
But he was wounded for our transgressions, he was bruised for
our iniquities: the chastisement of our peace was upon him;
and with his stripes we are healed. All we like sheep have
gone astray; we have turned every one to his own way; and
the Lord hath laid on him the iniquity of us all.

THE WRITINGS

Free at length, a small but recognized nation, the Hebrews naturally longed to gather up their finer legends, narratives, essays, and poems, not as specimens of inspired or sacred writings, but as literary productions satisfying their national pride. The result of such collecting was the so-called *Writings*.

These the rabbis and the scholars could not conscientiously consider as worthy of a place with the *Law* and the *Prophets* in the synagogue and its service; but to the people these creations of other days seemed at length almost as authentic, almost as authoritative as the highly reverenced rolls of scrolls in the Temple. In fact, so influential, so much a part of the educative process of the race had these *Writings* become that finally at a conference of rabbis at Jamnia, about 100 A.D., portions of these works not hitherto coming under the title of "inspired" now passed into the Canon, or sacred readings. Thus may popular opinion influence the evolution of theology.

Undoubtedly the finest of the *Writings* are in poetry —the *Psalms*. Long attributed to David, it is now believed that he personally composed few of them, although he may have caused the creation of some of them by poets of his reign. Rather, they belong to a much later era, and some may have been written as late as 300 B.C. Whatever the period of their composition, however, these *Psalms* comprise the noblest hymn-book in the history of religious literature—a hymn-book intended for use in the Great Temple at Jerusalem, but one that has brought comfort and consolation and æsthetic pleasure to tens of millions since that Temple crumbled into dust.

These songs were loved by the Hebrew folk. Jesus quoted frequently from them, and doubtless realized the powerful impression they had made upon the memory of the people. Exquisite not only in contents but in style, they satisfy every requirement, of genuine poetry. Theirs is not strictly the teaching of an orthodox creed; in fact, in many a Christian church to-day they are recited willingly by congregations who could not vouch for the theological tenets of the lines. But they contain a sustaining philosophy, a tenderness, a personal relationship to God, a humanness that must be admitted by even the skeptic to be most consoling to the human soul. In short, their appeal is not to the brain but to the heart. Their faith, trust, and utter confidence have given spiritual strength, not only to the ancient Hebrew nation, but to many a nation since Jerusalem fell.

God is our refuge and strength, a very present help in trouble.

Therefore will not we fear, though the earth be removed and though the mountains be carried into the midst of the sea.

Though the waters thereof roar and be troubled, though the mountains shake with the swelling thereof.

There is a river the streams whereof shall make glad the city of God, the holy place of the tabernacles of the most High.

God is in the midst of her; she shall not be moved: God shall help her, and that right early.

Simple searching, eloquent—these church songs of old Israel. Unhampered by the modern device of rhyme—a device largely coming to us through the Spanish, and not at all a necessity of good poetry— they have that highly natural rhythm commonly called parallelism. In such a form of verse idea balances with idea, phrase with phrase, even sentence with sentence. Hear it in these two lines:

The Lord is my shepherd; I shall not want.
He maketh me to lie down in green pastures: he leadeth me beside the still waters.

There is something so logical in this weighing of one thought with another, something so symmetrical, that many nations have early discovered its effectiveness. The early Anglo-Saxons made it the basis of their poetical construction, and the primitive Germans and French did likewise. But as the Hebrew race progressed in musical and literary appreciation— largely, by the way, through the magnificent service in the Temple—their ear became trained for something more intricate than the simple balancing of phrase against phrase, and the result was elaborate acrostics and combinations of balancing expressions almost beyond the power of the translator to interpret into another language. Surely many a devout Jewish soul must have thrilled there in the vast cathedral at Jerusalem as chorus responded to chorus, and all the genius of the language was exploited in the marvelous combinations of literary and musical affects.

Many are the appeals to the heart in these Psalms! Every human emotion, except humor, is present in all fullness. Those ancient worshipers were impressed by the wonders of Nature—the mighty ocean, the burning deserts, the everlasting mountains. And to them Nature was God expressing Himself; hence every description in these songs that touches upon the handiwork of Jehovah is tremendously effective.

He shall be like a tree planted by the rivers of water, that bringeth forth his fruit in his season; his leaf also shall not wither; and whatsoever he doeth shall prosper.

He made darkness pavilions round about him, dark waters, and thick clouds of the skies.

As the hart panteth after the water brooks, so panteth my soul after thee, O God.

Here, then, in the songs of their Church, the Hebrews could find not only the majesty of God, but His sympathy with mankind, His understanding of human weakness, His loving kindness and forgiveness.

Though your sins be as scarlet, they shall be as white as snow. Though they be red like crimson, they shall be as wool.

These Psalms, the outpouring of several hundred years of Jewish spiritual life, were a sustaining force in the national existence of Israel. They have not proved less efficacious in soothing the troubled heart of man in all the centuries that have passed since then.

There is still another lengthy section of the *Writings* of genuine value—those dirge-like expressions entitled *Lamentations*. With all their tone of sorrow, they are of very conscious style and formation. The man who wrote them was not in too lamentable a state to be neglectful of artistic effects; he at least laments beautifully. In spite of this impression of self-consciousness, the dirges must have expressed rather effectively the deep humiliation that had repeatedly come upon the Hebrew race. Dealing with the catastrophes which had overwhelmed Jerusalem and the Jews, this unknown poet chants with true Eastern vehemence and extravagance the utter hopelessness— for the time being, at least—of the outlook. But to the matter-of-fact reader of the Western World this supposedly deep agony of sorrow is proclaimed in entirely too artificial a manner to be convincing.

Far beyond *Lamentations* in the matter of abandonment to extravagant emotionalism is that "Song of Songs," called the *Song of Solomon*. In this ecstatic composition, with its luxury of expression, we may hear indeed the passionate soul of the Orient speaking. That it has anything to do with sacred or religious inspiration was long disputed by the Hebrews themselves, and to many a student of to-day the statement that it is a book of high religious significance seems utterly unfounded. All the efforts throughout the ages to infuse into this genuinely beautiful poem a symbolism representing the love of God for man, or *vice versa,* have not been particularly successful. Would it not be just as useful, just as sensible, for us to look upon this recitative or series of lyrics as simply a marvelous outpouring of human love—that love between man and woman which often glorifies life? In all probability Solomon had little or nothing to do with the authorship. Far more credible is the conclusion that the composition is made up of numerous love songs which, during the centuries of Jewish national history, had been sung at wedding feasts. Possibly this very condensation of ages of love-making is one of the causes of its being one of the most passionate expressions yet written by man.

Of the eleven books commonly considered as the *Writings* there are two that are anything but ecstatic. They are those worldly-wise and even cynical volumes called *Proverbs* and *Ecclesiastes*. It is indeed true that the *Book of Proverbs* has some idealism in it, but on the whole it smacks too much of the Ben Franklin ethics—it pays to be honest. The rather merciless wit and scorn of these sayings have long been characteristic of the Hebrew race—a sarcasm based on bitter experience and disillusionment.

He that blesseth his friend with a loud voice, rising early in the morning, it shall be counted a curse to him. A continual dropping on a very rainy day and a contentious woman are alike. Whoso diggeth a pit shall fall therein, and he that rolleth a stone, it will return upon him. Seest thou a man wise in his own conceit? There is more hope of a fool than of him. He that hath no rule over his own spirit is like a city that is broken down and without walls. A fool's mouth is his destruction, and his lips are the snare of his soul. Even a fool, when he holdeth his peace, is counted wise, and he that shutteth his lips is esteemed a man of understanding. Better is a dry morsel and quietness than an house full of sacrifices with strife. A soft answer turneth away wrath, but grievous words stir up anger. Better is a dinner of herbs where love is, than a stalled ox and hatred therewith. As a jewel in a swine's snout, so is a fair woman who is without discretion. As vinegar to the teeth and as smoke to the eyes, so is the sluggard to them that send him. Go to the ant, thou sluggard; consider her ways, and be wise.

And *Ecclesiastes*—what an essay in skepticism! Is there any good under the sun? queries its unknown author. Is there such a thing as happiness? This pursuit of riches, fame, and the pleasures they are supposed to bring—vanity, vanity, saith the preacher, all is vanity! And then comes that remarkable twelfth chapter, which in the King James Version, has a melody seldom if ever surpassed in the English language:

Remember now thy Creator in the days of thy youth, while the evil days come not, nor the years draw nigh when thou

MOABITE STONE, PALESTINE, BEARS THE INSCRIPTION OF MESHA,
KING OF MOAB, CONTEMPORARY OF KING AHAB

shalt say, I have no pleasure in them; while the sun, or the light, or the moon, or the stars be not darkened, nor the clouds return after the rain. . . . Or ever the silver cord be loosed, or the golden bowl be broken, or the pitcher be broken at the fountain, or the wheel broken at the cistern. Then shall the dust return to the earth as it was, and the spirit shall return to God who gave it.

It is such passages that have made the Scriptures a consolation, an æsthetical as well as an ethical gem, a source of racial memories which have profoundly affected European and American civilization.

As for the narratives in the *Writings,* they too are, in some instances, gems of literature. The story of Daniel—a late production, probably of the second century, B.C.—the legend of Belshazzar's Feast, the romantic tale of Esther, that perfect idyll of Ruth and Naomi—these and many others reveal why the legends and traditions of those early Hebrews sank deeply into the soul of the nation and gave the people that pride of race which carried them safely through such terrific ordeals.

There remains one great book of the *Writings* that has compelled the admiration of all students of literature. It is that remarkable narrative-drama, *Job.* It has been conjectured, with considerable probability, that here is to be found the influence of the Greek theater upon a nation that otherwise revealed little or no endeavor to create for the stage.

"It is a noble Book—all men's Book," declares Carlyle. "It is our first, oldest statement of the never-ending Problem—man's destiny and God's way with him here in this earth." It is indeed a deep poem. In its noble sincerity and simplicity it reveals the later chastened philosophy of the Jewish people, who had gone through so many experiences for the sake of their God. Its epic broadness is at once apparent; it is *our* questioning and doubts, every man's questioning and doubts. And yet in the end it has that "repose of conciliation" which is noticeable in so many great works of art.

There is no more tragic figure in literature than Job —and yet how many Jobs man's indifference and cruelty have created! A victim of circumstance, he sits there on the ash heap of humiliation, scourged by physical torture and mental doubts, advised unto distraction by his all-wise friends. To whom may he turn for guidance and comfort? His own wife, weary of his sufferings and lamentations, at length exclaims, "Why do you not curse God and die?" And yet, with the consciousness of righteousness, he maintains his integrity. But God the Mysterious speaks out of the cloud and thunder and with a few words bursts the bubble of even this man's egotism of integrity. "Who can say that he is pure? Who can say that he is good?" Such questions from the Most High humble even the stubborn, though well-meaning Job, and he bows himself before God.

The book is indeed a drama, a five-act play. As Professor Genung has pointed out in his *Guidebook to the Biblical Literature,* the plot easily falls into the following divisions:

Act I. To Job's blessing and curse, i-iii. (The stroke devised and executed; the silent friends; Job's access of bewilderment.)

Act II. To Job's ultimatum of doubt, iv-x. (Wisdom misfit and insipid; the world-order a hardness and chaos; Job's plea for mutuality and mediation.)

Act III. To Job's ultimatum of faith, xi-xix. (The friends' false attitude; Job's life resolve of integrity; conviction that his Redeemer—next of kin—liveth.)

Act IV. To Job's verdict on things as they are, xx-xxxi. (No outward terms of profit and loss; yet wisdom still supreme; Job's life record ready for presentation.)

Act V. To the vindicating denouement, xxxii-xlii. (The self-constituted umpire fails; the whirlwind words display wisdom and power of creation; Job emerges to vindication and mediation.) [2]

Of course, the ever-present question that Job asks, and that Isaiah and many another have asked, is not answered: Why do the wicked prosper, and the innocent so often suffer? It is one of the great enigmas—unanswerable by man. But in this long Platonic dialogue between Job and his "comforters" and God, the problem is brought before us with vividness, keenness and majesty.

THE NEW TESTAMENT

The collection of books known among Christians as the New Testament, though written mainly in Greek, is nevertheless Hebraic to the very core. The chief character, Jesus, whose philosophy inspires the whole, was a Jew; practically every writer of the narratives, essays, and letters in the collection was a Hebrew; all the authors had come under Hebrew influence and were steeped in the lore and wisdom of the Old Testament.

This New Testament is the story of a Movement—

[2] J. F. Genung: *Guidebook to Biblical Literature*, Ginn & Co., Boston, 1916.

the most effective piece of propaganda yet devised by man. Its ideals and theories have literally revolutionized civilization and re-created the world.

Probably four and one-half centuries intervened between the last compositions of the Old Testament and the writing of this New Gospel. Expressed mainly in a corrupted, but universal Greek which was not the happiest medium for the highest type of literary creation, this later Testament can scarcely compare with the Old merely as a specimen of writing; but from the standpoint of effectiveness this collection of the teachings of Jesus and the commentaries on these teachings is far more influential than the Hebrew Scriptures.

We have seen how easily the older book may be divided into the *Law,* the *Prophets,* and the *Writings.* Into no such divisions can the New Testament fit. This collection consists of four stories dealing with the life, deeds, and sayings of Jesus, a group of writings called the *Acts,* dealing with the founding of the Christian Church, various *Letters* or *Epistles* by leaders in this founding of the organization, and a vision known as the *Revelation* or *Apocalypse.* Some of these productions, such as portions of the *Acts* and some of the *Epistles,* fail to measure up to the standards of the highest literature; but others, such as the Gospels or stories by Mark and John, and several of the Epistles by John and Paul, are remarkable for their vividness, energy, philosophy, and elevated tone.

Naturally there has been a world of conjecture and controversy concerning the real authors of these various books comprising the New Testament. By some of the older authorities it was held that the Gospels by Matthew and John were written by actual companions of Jesus, and that Mark was a disciple of Peter, who had been a close friend of the Nazarene. Later authorities hold that the story bearing Matthew's name was composed about 80 A.D. by some unknown Christian who had access to a record written by Matthew of the days of Jesus and also the record written by Mark. Luke's Gospel also may not have been written by Luke at all, but may have been compiled from Luke's diary by some unknown editor.

Because of the fact that Matthew's story is so well told, it became highly popular for reading in Church services, and thus attained first place in the series of the four Gospels. But to-day Mark's account is looked upon as much more reliable and valuable, because it is probably older than any of the others, and was copied down directly from the statements of old men who had seen, heard, and known Jesus. Indeed Mark must have been a remarkably good journalist. With the true sense of news values, he at the same time must have had the perseverance that the genuine reporter must possess. But all these writers of the first three Gospels, with their almost identical stories, tell with many a realistic touch the strange narrative of the physical life, the death, and the teachings of the most effective Ethical Guide this world has yet known.

The Gospel of John, however, stands alone. Different in style, more elevated in tone, more philosophical than the other stories, it is more nearly the *spiritual* biography of Jesus. Its author, who also may have written the *Epistles* of John, was a deeper scholar, a more mature thinker than his fellow narrators. The influence of Greek speculation, the thoughts of Paul are in his works. In it we find, not so much what the

Man of Galilee did, as why he did it. Composed possibly as late as 100 A.D., is a portrayal of the *soul* of Jesus.

Be all this mooted subject of authorship as it may, the fact remains that in the four Gospels we discover one of the most dramatic, most tragic stories ever written. Its deeds are thrilling, its parables of tremendous significance, its speeches searching and eloquent. Here is the narrative of a man in an obscure corner of the world who at the age of thirty began to preach a seemingly new philosophy of life, performed miraculous deeds (many of these probably through applied psychology), inspired a little band of followers to go forth and teach to the known world this new type of ethics, and then, after some two and a half years of service, suffered the most shameful death that the Romans could devise.

His death was the inevitable outcome of His teachings. Were he to appear in America or Europe to-day with the same philosophy spoken publicly with the same vigor and directness, He would undoubtedly receive imprisonment if not actual death. For He was and is a dangerous man to those believing in vested rights. His theories, if actually carried into practice, would revolutionize the world, and most of us do not want the world revolutionized. His doctrine of Universal Brotherhood, His Golden Rule, and His advice as to a calm non-resistance would bring world peace so quickly that most of us would be immensely uncomfortable. His insistence upon the unimportance of rites is an open menace to the influence of half the churches over the simple-minded folk. His reiterated belief that wealth and rulership—the will to dominate

—are relics of barbarism is a plain insult to the powerful financial and political interests of every nation on
the globe. His demand for applied democracy—the
sharing of all with the less fortunate—would simply
make impossible the accumulation of riches in the
hands of individuals.

And so the crowd killed Him—just as, in all probability, they would do to-day. His absolute faith in the
goodness and justness of God, and His urgent call for
a return to the simplicities and the genuine essentials
of the "good life" were affronts to a sophisticated and
cynical world. And what made Him still more dangerous and obnoxious was the unanswerable logic, the
felicity, the driving, dynamic eloquence of His expression. The Sermon on the Mount is the most positive declaration of the way of righteousness ever
spoken to mankind; the scorching rebukes to the
Scribes and Pharisees of His day, and of all days, are
the most withering expressions ever applied to hypo-
crites.

And yet this man whose tongue seemed to the
wicked of his day a flame of fire, could speak with all
the tenderness of a mother:

Come unto me, all ye that labor and are heavy laden, and I
will give you rest. Take my yoke upon you, and learn of me;
for I am meek and lowly in heart: and ye shall find rest unto
your souls. For my yoke is easy and my burden is light.

Let not your heart be troubled: ye believe in God, believe
also in me. In my Father's house are many mansions; if it
were not so, I would have told you. I go to prepare a place
for you. And if I go and prepare a place for you, I will come
again, and receive you unto myself; that where I am, there ye
may be also.

As a teller of stories of vast ethical import His equal is yet to be discovered. Compression, vividness, impressiveness, applicability—these are traits that have made His parables household tales throughout the Christian world. The thumb-nail sketches of the Good Samaritan who believed that every man was his brother, the Prodigal Son whose father is a symbol of the patient love of the Almighty, the Sower who, like many a teacher, wasted much of his energy upon stony soil—such sketches and many others reveal the genuine power of fiction in capturing and imprinting the wisdom of experience.

The more one reads these four Gospels the more one is impressed with the idea that this man Jesus was the Master Teacher of all times. But, like most teachers, he was driven to the death by the mob's incredible capacity for resisting instruction.

To the student with a liking for history the *Acts* are interesting as showing the rise and growth of a movement destined to be world-wide, and also the intense zeal of these early believers in the Christian doctrines. To the mystically minded the *Book of Revelation* may offer the thrill of a sublime vision, a partly obscure, but mainly vivid and eloquent prophecy of things yet to come in the spiritual evolution of the race. But to the average reader some of the *Epistles* will undoubtedly make a most human appeal. For these letters are so intimate, so practical at times, so idealistic at other times.

Frequently they are but the common-sense advice or instructions of leaders to the pioneer congregations scattered through Greece and Asia, but now and then the *Epistles* rise to an eloquence and a height of philosophy truly impressive. Thus Paul, writing in grammatically correct, but decidedly bald Greek, suddenly bursts forth with a gem-like essay that has captivated all its readers:

If I speak with the tongues of men and of angels, but have not love I am become as sounding brass or a clanging cymbal. And if I have the gift of prophecy, and know all mysteries and all knowledge, and if I have all faith, so as to remove mountains, but have not love, I am nothing. And if I bestow all my goods to feed the poor, and if I give my body to be burned, but have not love, it profiteth me nothing. Love suffereth long, and is kind; love envieth not; love vaunteth not itself, is not puffed up, doth not behave itself unseemly, seeketh not its own, is not provoked, taketh not account of evil; rejoiceth not in unrighteousness, but rejoiceth with the truth; beareth all things, believeth all things, hopeth all things, endureth all things. Love never faileth: but whether there are prophecies, they shall be done away; whether there are tongues, they shall cease; whether there is knowledge, it shall be done away. For we know in part, and we prophesy in part; but when that which is perfect is come, that which is in part shall be done away. When I was a child, I spake as a child, I felt as a child, I thought as a child: now that I am become a man, I have put away childish things. For now we see in a mirror, darkly, but then face to face: now I know in part, but then shall I know even as also I have been known. But now abideth faith, hope, love, these three; and the greatest of these is love.[3]

THE APOCRYPHA

Such, then, are the writings comprising the undisputed Scriptures of the Christian world. There are, however, some fourteen other compositions variously

[3] Revised Edition.

accepted or rejected by the early Hebrews and the later Catholics. Thus the Alexandrian Jews readily accepted as inspired certain books utterly rejected by the Palestine Jews; while of these fourteen writings embraced by the Hebrews of Alexandria, eleven are declared as true Scripture by the Roman Catholic Church, although regarded as totally unscriptural by the Protestant Church. Whether inspired or not, these narratives, essays, and preachments found in the so-called Apocrypha are genuinely interesting reading, and in certian sections rise to true nobility.

There is, for instance, the *Book of Judith,* a story of a woman's conquest over her nation's enemy, a narrative that swept over Europe during the first seven centuries of Christianity, and inspired numerous poetical translations or adaptations. Then, there is the *Book of Tobet,* a romance of characteristic Oriental richness—one that likewise fired the imagination of early Europe. There is also that highly imaginative piece of history known as the *Second Book of Maccabees*—a "red-blooded" story, as the modern magazine editor would say, filled with startling pictures of martyrdom for the faith, the clang of armor, the clash of battle, the staunch words of staunch men.

Best of all, perhaps, is that remarkable medley, *Ecclesiasticus,* a volume of shrewd philosophy of behavior. Keen, cutting, beautiful sometimes, cleverly wise always, it may indeed bring additional wisdom to the wise reader and shame to the foolish. It is notable for its epigrams; thoroughly sane, it is an epitome of what the American loves to call "horse-sense." And yet the book is not earthy. There is a simple, saving majesty throughout. Every British schoolboy, and

many an American one also, has heard on some dignified occasion those high, solemn words:

Let us now praise famous men,
And our fathers that begat us.
　The Lord manifested in them great glory,
Even His mighty power from the beginning.
　Such as did bear rule in their kingdoms,
And were men renowned for their power,
Giving counsel by their understanding,
Such as have brought tidings in prophecies:
　Leaders of the people by their counsels,
And by their understanding men of learning for the people;
Wise were their words in their instruction:
　Such as sought out musical tunes,
And set forth verses in writing:
　Rich men furnished with ability,
Living peaceably in their habitations:
　All these were honored in their generations,
And were a glory in their days.
　There be of them, that have left a name behind them,
To declare their praises.
　And some there be, which have no memorial;
Who are perished as though they had not been,
And are become as though they had not been born;
　And their children after them.
　But these were men of mercy,
Whose righteous deeds have not been forgotten.
　With their seed shall remain continually a good inheritance;
Their children are within the covenants.
　Their seed standeth fast,
And their children for their sakes.
　Their seed shall remain for ever,
And their glory shall not be blotted out.
　Their bodies were buried in peace,
And their name liveth to all generations.

Peoples will declare their wisdom,
And the congregation telleth out their praise.[4]

Finally, there is that volume almost as worthy, the *Wisdom of Solomon.* Doubtless a collection of maxims and statements based on nearly two thousand years of a nation's varied experiences among friends and foes, it is decidedly worth while as a guide to those who would be wary in their journey through this life. There is many a noble expression in the book—noble especially in the faith that upholds its author or authors.

The souls of the righteous are in the hand of God, and there shall no torment touch them. In the sight of the unwise they seemed to die, and their departure is taken for misery, and their going from us to be utter destruction; but they are in peace. . . . For God created man to be immortal and made him to be the image of His own eternity.[5]

This, in brief, is the story of the sacred or semi-sacred writings of the ancient Jewish race. In its unity of impression, its high dignity of expression, its incomparably elevated ethical content, we can see the secret of its far-reaching influence.

THE TALMUD

There remains, lastly, that volume of Hebrew writings representing the traditions, the reflections, and the folk-lore which have arisen from and centered about the ancient Scripture. It is the oft-mentioned, but little

[4] Ecclesiasticus XLIV, 1-19. See also M. R. James: *Apocrypha Anecdotes,* Cambridge University, 1897.
[5] For interesting examples of the ethics and philosophy of the Apocrypha see C. E. Lawrence: *Wisdom of the Apocrypha,* London, J. Murray, 1920.

understood *Talmud*. An entire library in itself, it is the product of long thinking, reflecting, and feeling on the part of generations of religious-minded people.

There was a great religious awakening among the Hebrews after the return from Babylon. There was a genuine consciousness among the leaders and among a large number of the laymen of a mission, a God-given mission, to preserve the vital truth of monotheism. To accomplish this it seemed necessary to the Jew that there should be a more marked and deeper distinction between the Israelites and the Gentiles. And the best way to emphasize this distinction—in their eyes—was to insist upon the observance of the Hebrew Law—the *Torah*.

Ezra and Nehemiah were undoubtedly among the originators of this new national movement and attitude, but after their death the idea or ideal progressed with intense zeal. One of the chief purposes in the founding of the "Great Synagogue" at Jerusalem—really a university in both teaching and research—was to preserve and interpret for the people this all-sufficient *Torah* and to translate the *Pentateuch* into the popular Aramaic so that the folk might know thoroughly and comprehend the ancient *Law*. Scribes and rabbis toiled with almost fanatical zeal in the triple task of translating, copying, and instructing.

A most radical result of this national movement was the founding of religious schools in practically every town and village of the Holy Land—in reality, a sort of public school system. Then came forward that energetic organizer and profound scholar, Hillel I, President of the University or Great Synagogue at Jerusalem. He looked upon the vast bulk of tradition heaped in the archives of the institution, and heard on every hand the even greater hoard of oral legends, and he resolved that it all should be reduced to some system. It was a task too tremendous for any one man or any one generation, and Hillel passed on with the work unfinished.

Then came the destruction of the Temple at Jerusalem—and even greater veneration for the *Torah*. Manuscripts may have been lost or burnt, but the sayings, the rules, the stories were deep in the hearts of scholars, priests, and people. By 200 A.D. there existed what might be called a codified oral *Talmud*—a literary accumulation handed down from generation to generation through astounding feats of memory. Naturally, however, divergences would appear, and when at length the Jerusalem *Talmud* was finished and at least partly written in the fourth century, and the Babylonian *Talmud* was completed in the sixth century, there were distinct differences both in size and in contents.

But in both is a revelation of the social life of the Jews in their home circle or as exiles among other nations. There have been attempts to classify and name the various strata of the huge accumulation; there is, for instance, the *Mishnah,* containing the collection of rabbinical rules and precepts, the *Gemara* or commentaries on difficult questions in theology and law, the *Haluchak,* or collection of petty regulations, rites, and ceremonies that led to a genuine slavery in religious details among the orthodox Hebrews. Of far more importance from the literary viewpoint is the division called the *Haggadah*—the tales, parables, legends, jests that many centuries of Jewish national experience

had contributed. The effect of this particular section
of the *Talmud* upon European fiction is beyond all
calculation; from Greece and Italy to Scotland and
Scandinavia those ancient bits of narrative have become the common possession of peasant, scholar,
romancer, and poet.

Indeed, there can be little doubt that this same
Talmud gave form, and to some extent, content to another famous religious book, the *Koran*. Much that
Mohammed wrote into this rival of the Bible was
straight from or colored by the *Talmud,* and long
after the founder of Moslemism was in his grave the
influence of the Jewish book was still powerful among
the Moors, Arabs, and Turks.

What are the qualities of this famous, but little-read
volume of Hebrew lore? It is, first of all, supremely
wise—alive with that wisdom which both the joys and
the sorrows of long, long earthly existence at length
grant some of us. Second, it is shrewd—keenly
shrewd, sardonically shrewd, if you will, at times. And,
third, it is genuinely witty, often with a wit that is
frequently kindly, but perhaps as frequently painfully
sharp. But there are also portions that rise to an
idealism, a magnanimity, a sense of brotherhood and
love truly impressive and affecting. For example, hear
how wisely those rabbis and scholars and philosophers
of the Israel of long ago spoke:

Even when the gates of Heaven are shut to prayer, they are
open to tears. Four shall not enter Paradise: the scoffer, the
liar, the hypocrite, and the slanderer. To slander is to murder.
If a word spoken in its time is worth one piece of money,
silence in its time is worth two. Bless God for the evil as well

as the good. When you hear of a death say, "Blessed is the righteous Judge."

He who has no wife lives without comfort, without help, without joy, and without blessing. Man and wife well matched have Heaven's glory as their companion; man and wife ill matched are encircled by a devouring fire. The loss of a first wife is like the loss of a man's sanctuary. If a man divorce his wife the altar itself sheds tears over him.[6]

And hear this little parable of the fortitude of a mother and resignation to the will of God:

Rabbi Meir was sitting on the Sabbath day and instructing the people in the synagogue. In the meantime his two sons died; they were both of fine growth and enlightened in the law. His wife carried the dead bodies into the upper room, laid them upon the bed, and spread the white cloth over them.

In the evening Rabbi Meir came home. "Where are my sons?" he inquired, "that I may give them my blessing?" "They went to the synagogue," was the reply. "I looked around," said he, "and did not see them."

She reached him a cup; he praised God at the close of the Sabbath, drank, and asked again, "Where are my sons, that they also may drink of the wine of blessing?" "They cannot be far off," said she, and set before him something to eat. When he had given thanks for the food, and had eaten, she said, "Rabbi, grant me a request." "Speak, my love," he answered.

"A few days ago a person gave me some jewels to take care of, and now he asks for them again. Shall I give them back to him?" "This my wife should not need to ask," said Rabbi Meir. "Wouldst thou hesitate to return every one his own?" "Oh, no," replied she, "but I would not return them without thy knowledge."

[6] Probably the best English version of the *Talmud* is by M. L. Rodkinson, Boston, New Talmud Pub. Co., 1896.

Soon after she led him to the upper room, approached, and took the cloth off the dead bodies. "Oh, my sons!" exclaimed the father sorrowfully, "my sons!" She turned away and wept. At length she took his hand, and said, "Rabbi, hast thou not taught me that we must not refuse to return that which hath been entrusted to our care? Behold, the Lord gave, and the Lord hath taken away; blessed be the name of the Lord."

"The name of the Lord be praised!" rejoined Rabbi Meir. "It is well said, 'He who hath a virtuous wife hath a greater treasure than costly pearls. She openeth her mouth with wisdom, and on her tongue is the law of kindness.'" [7]

What a world of thought, reflection, vision, religious ecstasy among this people of ancient Israel! Egypt with its manifold gods and magnificent temples, India with its two mystic religions, the Mohammedan world with its fanatical zeal for the faith of Mecca seem but infantile, religiously speaking, as compared to this little nation of Hebrews who clung so tenaciously to the Ideal of the One God that their belief became the belief of practically all civilization. Religions may arise, flourish, and fall, but those astounding records of religious reflection, those monuments of ethics and philosophy, the Old Testament of the Jews, the New Testament of the Christians, and the *Talmud* of those unnumbered generations of Hebrew seekers for truth, seem destined to be among the permanent treasured possessions of mankind.

[7] Excellent selections are to be found in William MacIntosh's *Gleanings from the Talmud,* New York, Dutton, 1905.

BIBLIOGRAPHY

Aiken, C. F.: *Ghamma of Gotama,* Boston, 1900. Marlier & Co.

Anesaki, Masaharn: *Buddhist Ethics and Morality,* Yokohama, 1912. Asiatic Society of Japan.

Arnold, Edwin: *Gulistan of Sadi,* New York, 1899. Harper.

Arnold, Edwin: *Book of Good Counsels,* Edinburgh, 1893. John Grant.

Arnold, Edwin: *Indian Idylls,* Boston, 1883. Roberts Brothers. *Ibid.* London, 1883. Trübner.

Arnold, Edwin: *Poetical Works,* Boston, 1883. Roberts Brothers.

Atkinson, James: *Laili and Majnum,* London, 1836. A. J. Valpy.

Atkinson, James: *Shahnameh,* London, 1836. A. J. Valpy.

Babylonian and Assyrian Literature, New York, 1900. Colonial Press.

Baikie, James: *Amarna Age,* New York, 1926. Macmillan.

Baikie, James: *Life of the Ancient East,* New York, 1923. Macmillan.

Balls, William L.: *Egypt of the Egyptians,* London, 1915. Pitman.

Barnett, L. D.: *Path of Light,* London, 1920. Murray.

Baynes, Herbert: *Way of Buddha,* London, 1914. Murray.

Beal, Samuel: *Dhammapada,* London, 1878. Trübner.

Beck, Lily: *Story of Oriental Philosophy,* New York, 1928. Cosmopolitan Book Corporation.

Bell, Gertrude: *Poems from the Divan of Hafiz,* London, 1928. Heinemann.

Benjamin, S. G. W.: *Persia and the Persians,* Boston, 1887. Ticknor.

Bible (American Revised), New York, 1887. American Bible Society.

Bigelow, W. S.: *Buddhism and Immortality,* Boston, 1908. Houghton.

Binyon, L.: *Poems of Nizami,* London, 1928. The Studio.

Botta, Anna: *Handbook of Universal Literature,* Boston, 1876. Houghton.

Breasted, J. H.: *Ancient Times,* New York, 1916. Ginn.

Breasted, J. H.: *Development of Religion and Thought in Ancient Egypt,* New York, 1912. Scribner.

Breasted, J. H.: *History of the Egyptians,* New York, 1905. Scribner.

Brewster, Earl: *Life of Gotama,* New York, 1926. Dutton.

Brinkley, Frank: *China,* Boston, 1902. Millet.

Brown, Brian: *Chinese Nights Entertainments,* New York, 1922. Brentano.

Brown, Brian: *Wisdom of the Egyptians,* New York, 1923. Brentano.

Browne, E. G.: *Literary History of Persia,* New York, 1906. Scribner. *Ibid.* London, 1902. T. F. Unwin. *Ibid.* (four volumes), Cambridge, 1929. Cambridge University Press.

Browne, E. G.: *Persian Anthology,* London, 1897. Macmillan. *Ibid.* London, 1927. Methuen.

Browne, E. G.: *Poems from the Persian,* London, N. D. Benn.

Brugsch, H. K.: *History of Egypt,* London, 1881. Murray.

Budge, E. A. Wallis: *Book of the Dead,* London, 1899. Longmans. *Ibid.* Chicago, 1901. Open Court Pub. Co. *Ibid.* in *Egyptian Literature,* New York, 1901. Colonial Press.

Budge, E. A. Wallis: *Literature of Ancient Egyptians,* London, 1914. Dent.

Bunsen, C. C. J.: *Egypt's Place in Universal History,* London, 1848. Longmans.

Burton, R. L.: *Arabian Nights,* London, 1885. Published by the author.

Buss, Kate: *Studies in Chinese Drama,* Boston, 1922. Four Seas.

Bynner, Witter: *The Jade Mountain; a Chinese Anthology,* New York, 1929. Knopf.

Campbell, Killis: *Seven Sages of Rome,* New York, 1907. Ginn.

Carus, Paul: *Gospel of Buddha,* Chicago, 1897. Open Court Pub. Co.

Chen, Ivan: *Book of Filial Duty* (Haiao Ching), London, 1920. Murray.

Clouston, W. A.: *Some Persian Tales,* Glasgow, 1892. Bryce.

Collins, Edward: *Wisdom of Israel,* London, 1906. Murray.

Coomaraswany, Ananda: *Buddha and the Gospel of Buddhism,* London, 1916. Harrap.

Costello, Louisa: *Rose Garden of Persia,* London, 1911. Gibbings.

Cranmer-Byng, L.: *Classics of Confucius,* London, 1920. Murray.

Cranmer-Byng, L.: *Rose Garden of Sadi,* London, 1920. Murray.

Cranmer-Byng, L.: *Rubaiyat of Hafiz,* London, 1920. Murray.

Cranmer-Byng, L. (Editor): *Wisdom of the East Series,* London, 1920. Murray.

Dahlke, Paul: *Buddhist Essays,* London, 1908. Macmillan.

Davids, Caroline: *Buddhism,* London, 1912. Williams & Norgate.

Davids, Caroline: *Gotama, the Man,* London, 1928. Williams & Norgate.

Davids, Caroline: *Psalms of the Early Buddhists,* London, 1909. Frowde.

Davids, T. W. Rhys: *Buddhism,* London, 1903. Society for Promoting Christian Knowledge.

Davids, T. W. Rhys: *Buddhism, Its History and Literature,* New York, 1896. Putnam.

Davids, T. W. Rhys: *Dialogues of the Buddha,* Oxford, 1910. Oxford University Press.

Davids, T. W. Rhys: *Early Buddhism,* London, 1908. Constable.

Davies, Norman: *Mastaba of Ptahhetep,* London, 1900. Egypt Exploration Fund.

Davies, Norman: *Tomb of Antefoker,* London, 1920. Allen & Unwin.

Davis, F. H.: *Persian Mystics,* London, 1907. Murray.

Davis, J. F.: *Chinese Novels,* London, 1870. Murray.

Dole and Walker: *Flowers from Persian Poets,* New York, 1901. Crowell.

Douglas, R. K.: *China,* London, 1887. Society for Promoting Christian Knowledge.

Drinkwater, John: *Outline of Literature,* New York, 1923. Putnam.

Driver, S. R.: *Introduction to Literature of the Old Testament,* New York, 1892. Scribner.

Dunlop, J. C.: *History of Fiction,* London, 1845.

Dutt, Romesh: *Ramayana and Mahabharata,* New York, 1910. Dutton.

Dwight, H. G.: *Persian Miniatures,* New York, 1917. Doubleday.

Edwards, A. H.: *Bustan of Sadi,* New York, 1911. Dutton. *Ibid.,* London, 1920. Murray.

Egyptian Literature, New York, 1901. Colonial Press.

Eliot, Charles: *Hinduism and Buddhism,* London, 1921. Arnold.

Eliot, C. W. (Editor): *Harvard Classics,* Vol. 45, New York, 1917. Collier.

Erman, Adolf: *Handbook of Egyptian Religion,* London, 1907. Constable.

Erman, Adolf: *Life in Ancient Egypt,* London, 1894. Macmillan.

Erman, Adolf: *Literature of Ancient Egyptians,* New York, 1927. Dutton.

Fitzgerald, Edward: *Variorum Edition of Writings,* New York, 1902. Doubleday.

Forke, Anton: *Yang Chu's Garden of Pleasure,* London, 1920. Murray.

Fowler, H. T.: *History of the Literature of Ancient Israel,* London, 1912. Macmillan.

Frazer, R. W.: *Literary History of India,* New York, 1898. Scribner. *Ibid.,* London, 1907. Unwin.

Gardiner, J. H.: *The Bible as English Literature,* New York, 1906. Scribner.

Genung, J. F.: *Guidebook to Biblical Literature,* Boston, 1919. Ginn.

Gibb, E. J. W.: *History of Ottoman Poetry,* London, 1900. Luzac & Co.

Gibb, E. J. W.: *Ottoman Poems,* London, 1882. Trübner.

Giles, H. A.: *China and the Chinese,* New York, 1902. Columbia University Press.

Giles, H. A.: *Gems of Chinese Literature,* London, 1883. Quaritch.

Giles, H. A.: *History of Chinese Literature,* New York, 1901. Appleton.

Giles, H. A.: *Strange Stories from a Chinese Studio,* London, 1880. Laurie.

Giles, H. A.: *Travels of Fa-hsien,* Cambridge, 1923. Cambridge University Press.

Giles, Lionel: *Musings of a Chinese Mystic* (Chunag Tzu), London, 1920. Murray.

Giles, Lionel: *Sayings of Confucius,* London, 1920. Murray.

Giles, Lionel: *Sayings of Lao Tzu,* London, 1920. Murray.

Giles, Lionel: *Taoist Teachings,* London, 1920. Murray.

Griffis, W. E.: *China's Story,* Boston, 1911. Houghton.

Griffith, F. L.: *Stories of the High Priests of Memphis,* Oxford, 1900. Clarendon Press.

Griffith, R. T. H.: *Ramayana*, Benares, 1870. E. J. Lazarus & Co. *Ibid.*, London, 1870. Trübner.

Griffith, R. T. H. *Yusuf and Zulaikha*, in *Specimens of Old Indian Poetry*, London, 1852. A. Hall, Virtue.

Gunn, B. P.: *Instruction of Ptah-hotep*, London, 1908. Murray.

Hammond, Eric: *Splendor of God* (Bahaism), London, 1920. Murray.

Harper, R. F.: *Assyrian and Babylonian Literature*, New York, 1901. Appleton.

Hebrew Literature, New York, 1901. Colonial Press.

Hilprecht, H. V.: *Old Babylonian Inscriptions*, Philadelphia, 1893. University of Pennsylvania Press.

Hindu Literature, New York, 1901. Colonial Press.

Hopkins, E. W.: *Great Epic of India*, New York, 1901. Scribner.

Horne, C. F. (Editor): *Sacred Books and Early Literature of the East*, New York, 1917. Park, Austin & Lipscomb.

Howell, E. B.: *Inconstancy of Madame Chuang and Other Stories from the Chinese*, New York, 1924. Stokes.

Jackson, A. V. W.: *Early Persian Poetry*, New York, 1920. Macmillan.

Jackson, A. V. W.: *Persia Present and Past*, New York, 1906. Macmillan.

Jackson, A. V. W.: *Zoroaster*, New York, 1899. Macmillan.

Jackson, A. V. W.: *Zoroastrian Studies*, New York, 1928. Columbia University Press.

James, M. R.: *Apocrypha Anecdotes*, Cambridge, 1897. Cambridge University Press.

Jennings, William: *Analects of Confucius*, London, 1895. Routledge.

Johns, C. H. W.: *Ancient Babylonia*, New York, 1913. Putnam.

Johnston, R. F.: *Chinese Drama*, Shanghai, 1921. Kelly and Walsh.

Jones, William: *Complete Works,* London, 1807. John Stock-dale.

Jones, William: *Poems,* London, 1777. N. Conant.

Kapadia, S. A.: *Teachings of Zoroaster,* London, 1920. Murray.

Keith-Falconer, I. G.: *Kalilah and Dimnah,* Cambridge, 1885. Cambridge University Press.

Kenrick, John: *Ancient Egypt,* New York, 1885. John B. Alden.

King, L. W.: *Babylonian Religion,* London, 1901. Trübner.

Kinkaid, C. A.: *Tales from Indian* Epics, Oxford, 1918. Oxford University Press.

Knatchbull, Wyndham: *Kalila and Dimna,* Oxford, 1819. Baxter.

Ku Hung Ming: *Conduct of Life* (Confucius), London, 1920. Murray.

Lal, Magen: *Diwan of Zeb-Un-Nissa,* London, 1920. Murray.

Langdon, Stephen: *Lectures on Babylonia and Palestine,* New York, 1906. Steckert.

Lanoye, F. T.: *Rameses the Great,* New York, 1885. Scribner.

Lawrence, C. E.: *Wisdom of the Apocrypha,* London, 1920. Murray.

Leaf, Walter: *Versions from Hafiz,* London, 1898. Richards.

Lederer, Florence: *Secret Rose Garden of Sa'd,* London, 1920. Murray.

Legge, James: *Chinese Classics,* Hongkong, 1861. *Ibid.* (Second Edition), Oxford, 1895. Clarendon Press. *Ibid.,* New York, 1875. Hurd & Houghton.

Legge, James: *Life and Teachings of Confucius,* London, 1875. Trübner.

Legge, James: *Shi King,* Oxford, 1879. Clarendon Press.

Lillie, Arthur: *Buddha and Early Buddhism,* New York, 1900. Scribner.

Literature of the World (E. Gosse, Editor), New York, 1898. Appleton.

Loomis, A. W.: *Confucius and Chinese Classics,* San Francisco, 1867. A. Ronan & Co.

Lorimer, D. L. R.: *Persian Tales,* London, 1919. Macmillan.

Macdonald, Frederika: *Iliad of the East* (Ramayana), New York, 1908. John Lane.

MacIntosh, William: *Gleanings from the Talmud,* New York, 1905. Dutton.

Macy, John: *Story of the World's Literature,* New York, 1925. Boni & Liveright.

Maspero, Gaston: *Art in Egypt,* New York, 1912. Scribner.

Maspero, Gaston: *Dawn of Civilization: Egypt and Chaldea,* London, 1910. Society for Promoting Christian Knowledge.

Maspero, Gaston: *History of Egypt, Chaldea, Syria, Babylonia, and Assyria,* London, 1903. Grolier Society.

Maspero, Gaston: *Life in Ancient Egypt and Assyria,* New York, 1914. Appleton.

Maspero, Gaston: *Manual of Egyptian Archæology,* New York, 1914. Putnam.

Maspero, Gaston: *New Light on Ancient Egypt,* New York, 1909. Appleton.

Maspero, Gaston: *Popular Stories of Ancient Egypt,* New York, 1915. Putnam.

Max Müller, F. (Editor): *Sacred Books of the East,* Oxford, 1880. Clarendon.

Max Müller, F.: *Asvaghoska: Extracts from the Life of Buddha,* New York, 1900. Theosophical Publishing Co.

Mills, L. H.: *The Gathas,* Oxford, 1906. Oxford University Press.

Monier-Williams, M.: *Brahmanism and Hinduism,* London, 1891. Murray.

Monier-Williams, M.: *Buddhism,* London, 1899. Murray.

Monier-Williams, M.: *Hinduism,* New York, 1879. Pott, Young & Co.

Monier-Williams, M.: *Indian Epic Poetry,* London, 1863. Williams & Norgate.

Monier-Williams, M.: *Indian Wisdom,* London, 1875. Allen.

Monier-Williams, M.: *Story of Nala,* Oxford, 1879. Clarendon.

Monier-Williams, M.: *Sakoontala,* Hartford, 1856. Stephen Austin.

Moulton, R. G.: *Literary Study of the Bible,* Boston, 1899. Heath.

Moulton, R. G.: *Modern Reader's Bible,* New York, 1907. Macmillan.

Muir, John: *Metrical Translations from the Sanskrit Writers,* London, 1863. Williams & Norgate.

Muir, John: *Original Sanskrit Texts,* London, 1863. Williams & Norgate.

Naville, Edouard: *Origin of Egyptian Civilization,* Washington, 1908. Smithsonian Institution.

Nicholson, Reynold: *Mystics of Islam,* London, 1914. Bell.

Nicholson, Reynold: *Translations of Eastern Poetry and Prose,* Cambridge, 1922. Cambridge University Press.

Old, W. G.: *Shu King* (Confucius), London, 1904. Lane.

Oldenberg, Hermann: *Buddha,* London, 1882. Williams & Norgate.

Oriental Collections, London, 1798. Cadill & Davies.

Ouseley, George: *Biographical Notices of Persian Poets,* London, 1846. Oriental Translation Fund.

Parah, K. P.: *Meghaduta,* Bombay, 1902. Published by Author.

Persian Literature, New York, 1904. Colonial Press.

Persian Poets Series, New York, N.D. Stokes.

Petrie, W. M. Flinders: *Arts and Crafts of Ancient Egypt,* Edinburgh, 1909. Foulis.

Petrie, W. M. Flinders: *Egyptian Tales,* London, 1895. Methuen.

Petrie, W. M. Flinders: *History of Egypt,* London, 1905. Methuen.

Petrie, W. M. Flinders: *History of Egypt During the Seventeenth and Eighteenth Dynasties,* London, 1924. Methuen.

Petrie, W. M. Flinders: *Religious Life in Ancient Egypt,* London, 1904. Constable.

Polano, H.: *Selections from the Talmud,* Philadelphia, 1876. Claxton, Ramsen, & Haffelfinger.

Radan, Hugo: *Sumerian Hymns and Prayers,* Philadelphia, 1911. University of Pennsylvania Press.

Radhakumuda, M.: *Men and Thought in Ancient India,* London, 1924. Macmillan.

Rawlinson, George: *Ancient Egypt,* New York, 1900. Putnam.

Rawlinson, George: *Egypt and Babylon,* New York, 1885. Alden.

Rawlinson, George: *Five Great Monarchies of the Ancient Eastern World,* New York, 1870. Dodd.

Rawlinson, George: *History of Ancient Egypt,* New York, 1886. Alden.

Rawlinson, George: *Religions of the Ancient World,* New York, 1884. Fitzgerald.

Rawlinson, George: *Story of Ancient Egypt,* New York, 1887. Putnam.

Records of the Past (Samuel Birch, Editor), London, 1874-1890. S. Bagster.

Records of the Past (F. B. Wright, Editor), Washington, 1902-1913. Records of the Past Exploration Society.

Reed, Elizabeth: *Persian Literature,* Chicago, 1893. Griggs.

Remminner, E. D.: *Story of Rustem,* New York, 1909. Scribner.

Richardson, W. L. and Owen, J. M.: *Literature of the World,* Boston, 1922. Ginn.

Ridpath, J. C. (Editor): *Library of Universal Literature,* New York, 1910. Fifth Ave. Library Soc.

Rodkinson, M. L.: *Talmud,* Boston, 1896. New Talmud
Publishing Co.

Rogers, Alexander: *Book of Joseph and Zuleikha,* London,
1892. Nutt.

Ross, James: *Gulistan,* London, 1890. Scott.

Rostovtsev, Mikhael: *A Large Estate in Egypt in the Third
Century, B.C.,* Appleton, Wisconsin, 1922. University
of Wisconsin.

Roy, P. C.: *Mahabharata,* Calcutta, 1883. Bharata Press.

Ryder, Arthur: *Kalidasa Translations,* New York, N.D.
Putnam.

Ryder, Arthur: *Little Clay Cart,* Cambridge, Mass., 1905.
Harvard University Press.

Ryder, Arthur: *Mahabharata,* Chicago, 1920. University of
Chicago Press.

Ryder, Arthur: *Panchatantra,* Chicago, 1929. University of
Chicago Press.

Ryder, Arthur: *Shakuntala,* New York, N.D. Dutton.

Sacred Books and Early Literature of the East, New York,
1917. Park, Austin & Lipscomb.

Sacred Books of the East, New York, 1900. Colonial Press.

Smith, George: *Assyrian Discoveries,* London, 1875. Low.

Smith, George: *Assyrian Explorations,* New York, 1870.
Scribner.

Smith, George: *Chaldean Account of Genesis,* New York, 1876.
Scribner.

Smith, George: *History of Assurbanipal,* London, 1871. Williams & Norgate.

Steiger, G. N.: *History of the Orient,* Boston, 1926. Ginn.

Stoddard Library (J. L. Stoddard, Editor), Chicago, 1910.
George L. Sherman & Co.

Thomas, E. J.: *Buddhist Scriptures,* London, 1920. Murray.

Thompson, R. C.: *Epic of Gilgamish,* London, 1928. Luzac
& Co.

Ticknor, George: *History of Spanish Literature,* New York, 1849. Harper.
Tracts of the Union of American Hebrew Congregations, Cincinnati, 1925.
Trübner Oriental Series, London, 1901-1910. Trübner.
Turkish Literature, New York, 1901. Colonial Press.

Wagiswara, W. D. C.: *The Buddha's Way of Virtue,* London, 1912. Murray.
Waring, E. S.: *A Tour to Sheerez,* London, 1807. T. Cadell & Co.
Warner, C. D.: *Library of the World's Best Literature,* New York, 1896. R. S. Peale & J. A. Hill.
Weber, A. F.: *History of Indian Literature,* London, 1878. Trübner.
Whinfield, E. H., *Lawa-ib,* London, 1906. Royal Asiatic Association.
Whinfield, E. H.: *Masnavi,* London, 1870. Trübner.
Whitney, Dwight: *Oriental and Linguistic Series,* New York, 1873. Scribner.
Wilkinson, J. G.: *Manners and Customs of the Ancient Egyptians,* Boston, 1883. Cassino.
Wilson, C. E.: *The Haft Paikar,* London, 1924. A. Probsthain.
Wilson, C. E.: *Rumi's Masnavi,* London, 1910. A. Probsthain.
Wilson, H. H.: *Meghaduta,* Calcutta, 1813. P. Perivia.
Wilson, H. H.: *Select Specimens of the Theater of the Hindus,* Calcutta, 1827. Published by the Author.
World's Greatest Books (S. S. McClure, Editor), New York, 1910. McKinley, Stone & Mackenzie.
World's Greatest Literature, New York, 1910. Collier.

Zeitschrift für Agyptische Sprache, Berlin, 1873.
Zucker, A. E.: *Chinese Theater,* Boston, 1925. Little.

INDEX

A

Aaron the Just, 175
Aballah-Ben-Mokaffah, 104
Abidhamma-Pitaka, 95
Abraham, 296, 309
Abul-Kasim Mansur, 186-201
Abu Said, 244
Acts, 324, 328
Adapa, 65, 66
Aditi, 80, 167
Æsop, 95, 97, 111
Æsop's Fables, 111
Agni, 79, 80, 101
Ahura, 37, 38
Ahura-Mazda, 167, 168, 169, 170,
 174
Aiken, C. F., 339
Akhenaten, 40, 41
Akkadians, 50
Alauddin Kaikubed, 208
Alexander, 77, 178, 211, 304
Alexander Book, 211
Alexandria, 304
Ali, 177, 178
Al Mamoun, 176
Alphabet, Babylonian, 51
Amen, 39
Amen Ra, 42
Amenemhat, 45
Amenemhat, Teachings of, 46
Amenti (Amanti), 13, 22, 44
Ammon, 25, 26, 27
Ammon-Ra, 5
Amos, 310, 312
Amshashunds, 167
Anacreon, 234
Analects of Confucius (Jennings),
 344
Ancient Babylonia (Johns), 344
Ancient Egypt (Kenrick), 345
Ancient Egypt (Rawlinson), 348
Ancient Mariner (Coleridge), 219
Ancient Times (Breasted), 340
Anena, 29
Anesaki, M., 339
Angra-Mainya, 168
Animals, Egyptian sacred, 6

Annals of the State of Lu, 265
Anshar, 56, 57
Antef, 15, 43
Antef's Festival Dirge, 15
Anu, 55, 56, 58, 59, 63, 65, 66
Anwari, 207
Any, Maxims of, 47
Apocalypse, 324
Apocrypha, 303, 329-332
Apocrypha Anecdotes (James),
 332, 344
Apsu, 55
Arab, 67, 175, 176, 178, 335
Arabian Culture, 175
Arabian Invasion of Persia, 175,
 176
Arabian Literature, 157
Arabian Nights, 109, 239
Arabic, 4, 104, 109, 111, 178, 340
Aramaic, 299, 333
Architecture, Egyptian, 1
Aristotle, 170, 171
Armarna Age (Baikie), 339
Arnold, Edwin, 101, 129, 131, 132,
 159, 226, 339
Arnold, Matthew, 193, 196
Art, Egyptian, 1
Art in Egypt (Maspero), 346
Arya, 74
Aryan, 74, 75, 82, 83, 112, 122, 163,
 166, 170
Asadi, 182-185, 186
Assar, 238-243
Asshur, 52
Assurbanipal, 53
Assyria, 49-53, 54, 175, 298, 304,
 308
*Assyrian and Babylonian Litera-
ture* (Harper), 71, 344
Assyrian Conquest of Palestine,
 297
Assyrian Discoveries (Smith), 64,
 69, 349
Assyrian Epic, 53-64
Assyrian Explorations (Smith),
 349
Assyrian Literature, 49-73, 86
Assyrians, 52, 297, 300, 310

351

Index 353

354 Index

Index

Index